30 Days a Black Man

ALSO BY BILL STEIGERWALD

Dogging Steinbeck: Discovering America and Exposing the Truth about "Travels with Charley"

30 Days a Black Man

The Forgotten Story That Exposed the Jim Crow South

BILL STEIGERWALD

GUILFORD, CONNECTICUT

An imprint of Globe Pequot

Distributed by NATIONAL BOOK NETWORK

British Library Cataloguing in Publication Information Available

Library of Congress Cataloging-in-Publication Data

Names: Steigerwald, Bill.
Title: 30 days a black man : the forgotten story that exposed the Jim Crow
    South / Bill Steigerwald.
Other titles: Thirty days a black man
Description: Guilford, Connecticut : Lyons Press, [2017] | Includes
    bibliographical references and index.
Identifiers: LCCN 2016056358 (print) | LCCN 2016057727 (ebook) | ISBN
    9781493026180 (hardback) | ISBN 9781493026197 (e-book) | ISBN 9781493038824
    (paperback)
Subjects: LCSH: Sprigle, Ray, 1886-1957. | African
    Americans—Segregation—History. | United States—Race relations—History.
Classification: LCC E185.61 .S796 2017 (print) | LCC E185.61 (ebook) | DDC
    305.800973—dc23
LC record available at https://lccn.loc.gov/2016056358

♾™ The paper used in this publication meets the minimum requirements of American National Standard for Information Sciences—Permanence of Paper for Printed Library Materials, ANSI/ NISO Z39.48-1992.

Printed in the United States of America

To my mother, Kathryn,
who gave me her good journalism genes

Contents

FOREWORD

A white American pretending to be black is sure to make news.

It was front page news and all over television when Rachel Dolezal—an NAACP official from Spokane, Washington, who claimed to be black—was "outed" as a white woman.

And the same kind of sensational coverage was given to a Black Lives Matter activist, Shaun King, supposedly a biracial man, when reporters wrote that he was really a white man. The subjects of those 2015 stories opened the door to mockery and contempt from both black and white Americans. And the gates to confusion were flung wide open.

Did Dolezal and King see some advantage to being black in America? Given the history of slavery, segregation, and the continuing reality of black people facing everything from higher levels of poverty to higher levels of jail time when compared to whites, why would anyone pretend to be black?

During the 1948 journalistic mission of Ray Sprigle and John Wesley Dobbs, to be black meant living in a rigidly segregated America still dealing with the threat of white people lynching "uppity" blacks. Being black or pretending to be black was a high-risk game, especially in the Jim Crow South. Any player better have a good reason.

Ray Sprigle had a good reason. The nationally renowned journalist wanted to expose to the white readers of the *Pittsburgh Post-Gazette* what it was like to be a black man in the South. So he shaved his head, sunburned a heavy tan on his skin, and with black civil rights leader John Wesley Dobbs of Atlanta as his guide took a car ride across the race line in mid-twentieth-century America.

Bill Steigerwald's book—*30 Days a Black Man: The Forgotten Story That Exposed the Jim Crow South*—narrates Sprigle's epic, monthlong journey through black life in the land of Dixie. Steigerwald, like Sprigle, worked as a journalist for the *Pittsburgh Post-Gazette*, and has a unique perspective on his fellow newspaperman.

But Sprigle was more than a star reporter. Steigerwald presents him as a passionate, professional journalist, and an intelligent, principled man.

This is a man who earned a Pulitzer Prize for exposing Supreme Court justice Hugo Black's membership in the Ku Klux Klan in 1937. He had also won acclaim for reporting on the horrors taking place behind locked doors at Pennsylvania's state mental hospitals—while going undercover as a patient and later as a hospital attendant. He was a truth teller committed to unveiling hidden stories of all kinds, even when the truth required him to shave his head, change his name, and darken his skin.

Over thirty days, Sprigle learned of the daily humiliations experienced by blacks in the 1948 Deep South. He learned what it felt like to have to ride behind the white folks in the segregated, all-black "Jim Crow car" on the train. He was told that black women couldn't try on clothes at downtown department stores because no white person wanted to buy any dress worn by a black. He was shocked to find out that a "sales girl will carefully pin a cloth over her black customer's head before she'll let her try on a hat." He heard of a telephone operator who yelled at a black woman who didn't refer to her as "Ma'am."

And then there were the unequal schools and the constant threat of violence. As a white man Sprigle knew about the Jim Crow South's segregated schools, but he was confronted by a another level of inequality when he came face to face with a "leaking old wreck of a shanty" that passed for a school for black children. Interviewing black dentists, prosperous farmers, and indigent sharecroppers, he heard the bitter tale of a black church deacon killed by police officers while being held in prison on trumped up charges. He learned about a black World War II veteran killed for casting a vote in Georgia and how the dead man's family was forced to move out of the county. The reader can sense Sprigle's pain in telling the tale.

Sprigle's newspaper exposé, headlined "I Was a Negro in the South for 30 Days," was a twenty-one-part series in the *Post-Gazette* that was syndicated to papers nationwide. Bill Steigerwald recounts his daring undercover mission as a testament to the world-changing power of journalism. The series—and the impact it had on millions of ordinary white readers, the northern and southern press, and civil rights advocates like Eleanor Roosevelt—helped open mid-century white America to the possibility of a Supreme Court decision ending segregation in public schools; to Dr. Martin Luther King's eloquent call for racial equality; to the urgency of civil rights marches, the sit-in movement, Freedom Rides, and Congress passing a Voting Rights Act.

Yet Sprigle was not the first American writer to use a disguise to expose the horrors of racism. In 1859, a well-known humorist named Mortimer Thomson, then working for the *New York Tribune*, pretended to be a slave buyer to observe a large slave auction in Savannah, Georgia.

Thomson wrote in painful prose about families divided at slave auctions and how "the separation is . . . more hopeless, than that made by the Angel of Death, for in the latter case the loved ones are committed to the care of a merciful Deity, but in the other instance, to the tender mercies of a slave driver."

In her book *Undercover Reporting: The Truth About Deception*, NYU journalism professor and historian Brooke Kroeger calls Thomson's account "one of the most significant anti-slavery narratives in the run-up period to the Civil War." It was reprinted by various US papers and republished in summary form in the *London Times*. One southern paper condemned Thomson for his "misrepresentation and falsehood . . . [trying] to impose on the willing credulity and excite the mawkish sentimentality of the abolition fanatics of the North."

Sprigle is heir to Thomson's work and acts as a journalistic bridge to John Howard Griffin and his 1961 best-selling book, *Black Like Me*. Griffin also darkened his skin so he could spend several weeks in the South as a black man. *Black Like Me* was, according to *New York Times* book reviewer Dan Wakefield, "one of the few books that do more than take us across the familiar arid landscape of generalizations and statistics, but convey the feel, sight, sound, and sweat of what the abstractly titled 'Negro problem' is all about."

Black journalists themselves have marshaled the power of disguise to expose racism's various guises. In August 1992, Lawrence Otis Graham, a black corporate lawyer with a six-figure salary, published a piece in *New York Magazine* entitled "Invisible Man"—a direct nod to black author Ralph Ellison's 1952 novel of the same name—about his experience posing as a black busboy at an all-white country club in Greenwich, Connecticut: "a place so insular that the word *Negro* is still used in conversation."

Among other racist conversations Graham heard between white club members was one about whether to get a "Negro" or "one of these Spanish people" to help out around the house. One member recommends hiring African Americans because, "even though you can't trust either one, at least Negroes speak English."

Today, there are some in politics and the media who say that America focuses too much on race. There are some who argue that "playing the race card" is a cheap way of avoiding responsibility for one's actions. And there are some who say America is "post-racial" and "colorblind."

But nearly seventy years since Sprigle's journey into the segregated South, African Americans and Hispanics are still more than twice as likely as whites to live under the poverty line. African Americans still are a shockingly large portion of the 2.2 million Americans in jail. And median household income for black families is only a little over half that of white families.

With statistics like these, the effort to force Americans to confront ongoing racial differences is still relevant and compelling.

As a story from the Jim Crow past, Bill Steigerwald's recounting of Sprigle's mission and the unjust and unequal world he passionately exposed is surprisingly fresh.

It is a reminder to never offer a blind eye to race, even in twenty-first-century America with our recent black president and historic numbers of immigrants. Steigerwald reminds us of what an honest conversation about race can accomplish as we continue on the path toward a more equitable future.

JUAN WILLIAMS
AWARD-WINNING JOURNALIST FORMERLY AT NPR AND
WASHINGTON POST, CURRENT FOX NEWS CHANNEL
CONTRIBUTOR AND CO-HOST OF "THE FIVE," AND AUTHOR OF
EYES ON THE PRIZE: AMERICA'S CIVIL RIGHTS YEARS, 1954–1965

CHAPTER I

Jim Crow, U.S.A.

The two black men racing past the cotton fields in their 1947 Mercury were up to no good. Because their enormous dark green and chrome sedan attracted unwanted attention, they had to be cautious and alert as they crossed the Delta's vast grid of dirt roads and cotton plantations. No one white knew who they were or why they were in Mississippi, and they had to work extra hard to hide their sophistication and curiosity. The night before they drove into the Delta, friends in Jackson had briefed them on tactics, strategy, and proper behavior, as if they were a pair of elderly saboteurs about to be dropped into Nazi-occupied France.

The men were warned not to stop and speak to sharecroppers working or walking along the roads. They were told never to argue with the "riders" who made up the armed mounted patrols that plantation owners used as field foremen and general overseers. They were also told not to talk too much in front of the white folks who held all the power and owned everything of value in the Delta. Above all, they were warned not to appear too interested in the dismal living conditions and suppressed civil rights of the huge black workforce that served "King Cotton."

The men appeared to be just a couple of accidental travelers, two innocent old gents from the big city of Atlanta. They were nothing of the sort. The sixty-one-year-old in the passenger seat wearing the floppy checkered cap and heavy black-framed glasses was an imposter. He called himself James Rayel Crawford and carried a fake Social Security card in his wallet to prove it. But in actuality he was Ray Sprigle, a nationally famous newspaperman from the *Pittsburgh Post-Gazette*. He wasn't a light-skinned black visiting from the North. He wasn't even a black. He was 100 percent German-American white with a deep Florida tan, a spotless Republican voting record, and a 1938 Pulitzer Prize for proving a US Supreme Court justice was a member of the KKK.

The only genuine black man in the speeding Mercury was the lead-footed sixty-six-year-old driver, John Wesley Dobbs. Arguably the most influential black political and civic figure in Atlanta, he was a celebrated public speaker who had two cars and owned a handsome house in the wealthiest black neighborhood in America. Confident and driven, a flask of whiskey in his inside coat pocket, Dobbs could quote long poems and passages from Shakespeare from memory and often preached his favorite civil rights gospel that the only way for blacks to achieve full freedom and equality was through the three Bs—"Bucks, Ballots and Books."

It was May 27, 1948. Ray Sprigle had come down into the Deep South to see—and feel—for himself how ten million black Americans lived under the system of legal segregation known as Jim Crow. For nearly three weeks he had been eating, sleeping, and living as a black man. Dobbs was his guide to the black world. Because he was the longtime grand master of Georgia's Prince Hall Masons fraternal group, he was known and trusted by middle-class blacks across the South. In Atlanta and in the small towns of rural Georgia, Alabama, and Tennessee, Dobbs was introducing the undercover journalist to black doctors and undertakers, to sharecroppers, and to the families of lynching victims. When he told them Sprigle was gathering information for the NAACP, they believed it.

Dobbs was also Sprigle's driver and protector. He knew how to comfortably and safely travel the South's dirt and clay back roads, where for black motorists the bathrooms were usually in the bushes and an "uppity" black man in a nice car could quickly find himself in serious trouble with white folks or the county sheriff.

Sprigle was a seasoned newsman. He had spent time in the Deep South before. He had covered the Blitz in London in 1940 during World War II, gone undercover into state mental hospitals, and witnessed a dozen death penalty electrocutions. He was not a civil rights crusader or a soft-hearted liberal, but what he was seeing made him ashamed to be an American. Now he and Dobbs were passing through the deepest, meanest, poorest part of the Jim Crow South, where decades of strict racial segregation and white supremacy had achieved a feudal level of oppression nearly a hundred years after the end of slavery. If the wrong people in the Delta found out they were on a secret mission for a Yankee newspaper and were in cahoots with the boss of the National Association for the Advancement of Colored People, it could cost them their lives.

—◆—

By 1948 lynchings in the South had declined, dropping to about three per year in the 1940s, but the sticks could still be a lawless and deadly place for blacks. In 1946, about sixty miles east of Atlanta, two young married couples from the town of Monroe were tied up and shot to death in broad daylight by eighteen white men armed with pistols, rifles, and shotguns. Despite the outrage of both the nation and President Truman, a $12,500 award for information, and a six-month investigation by the FBI, the easily identified murderers were never prosecuted.

Then there was the venerable Ku Klux Klan. No longer the potent political force in the Democratic Party it once was in the South—or in Ohio, Indiana, western Pennsylvania or elsewhere—its membership and influence had shriveled to almost nothing from its 1920s peak. Yet as the 1950s and 1960s would prove, the KKK's theology of hate and intolerance had not gone extinct among the populace. When John Wesley Dobbs answered the NAACP's call to give a white northern journalist an inside look at the lives of southern blacks, he knew firsthand what the risks were. Ray Sprigle could only imagine the dangers he would face pretending to be a black man in the land of Jim Crow, which is why he drew up a new will before leaving Pittsburgh.

Mississippi had more lynchings than any other state since 1882, but the spring of 1948 was quiet. It was the beginning of yet another long, productive, peaceful growing season for the Delta's 100-percent cotton economy. Around the world, however, the second half of mankind's bloodiest century was off to an ominous start. A war between Arabs and the newborn state of Israel had just exploded in the Holy Land. The Cold War was heating up after the Soviets blocked the roads and rail lines to Berlin. Stalin was ready to explode his first atom bomb, and France was losing its grip on Indochina. Earlier that same day in South Africa, the white National Party narrowly won control of parliament, thanks to its campaign promise to immediately implement a nasty new system of racial separation the world would soon know as *apartheid*.

At home the mighty United States was trying to meet pent-up consumer demand, return to a peacetime economy without wage and price controls, and defend the broke and broken countries of Western Europe from the hungry Soviet Union. From Manhattan to Hollywood prices were rising, unions were striking, babies were booming. The population of the country had grown to not quite 147 million, including twenty-six million in the ten states of the South. The unemployment rate was low— less than 4 percent—but the inflation rate for the year was going to be an economically and politically disruptive 18 percent.

The price of everything seemed impossibly cheap compared to today, but that was because the 1948 dollar had ten times the purchasing power of today's dollar. A gallon of gas was twenty-six cents—$2.60 in today's inflated currency. A loaf of white bread cost fourteen cents. A ticket to see John Wayne in *Red River* was sixty cents. A newfangled ten-inch Admiral black-and-white TV was a four-hundred-dollar luxury, yet a year's tuition at Harvard cost 1948 grad Bobby Kennedy a paltry $550. A new Ford could be in your future for fifteen hundred dollars. Meanwhile, the minimum wage was forty cents an hour and the annual median family income was thirty-one hundred dollars.

It was a simpler, harder, more backward, poorer, and more dangerous age. Americans on average were less educated, less healthy, and less free. They also had less stuff. Half of households did not own a car and only 2 percent owned two. Nearly 50 percent of Americans did not have a telephone. TVs were selling like crazy in the spring of 1948 and would reach a million by the end of the year. But so far only 172,000 sets had been sold and the Television Age existed only for those who lived between Manhattan and Philadelphia. Radio and print were the dominant national news media. Movies were the mass entertainment. Every man wore some kind of hat. Baseball was unchallenged as America's pastime. Highways were deadly and cars were deathtraps. Trains and trolleys were the transit of the masses. Bing Crosby, Nat King Cole, and Dinah Shore were pop stars.

Jazz—specifically bebop stars Charlie Parker, Dizzy Gillespie, and Sarah Vaughan—was the hippest music from coast to coast and on campus.

The men who would shape America's politics for the next half-century were unrecognizable or too young to find. Richard Nixon and John Kennedy were twenty-something rookies in the House of Representatives. Representative Lyndon Johnson of Texas was a staunch segregationist who believed his party's civil rights program was "a farce and a shame" and "an effort to set up a police state in the guise of liberty." Ronald Reagan was a liberal New Deal Democrat and a union leader in Hollywood. George W. Bush and Bill Clinton were a year and a half old. Martin Luther King Jr. of Atlanta was a nineteen-year-old college graduate headed for a Baptist theological seminary near Philadelphia.

In Washington President Harry Truman was universally unloved, running for election in the fall and expected by everyone to lose to whomever the Republicans nominated in July. The previous year he had surprised the country and the Democratic Party by mounting a federal crusade against inequality and discrimination in America. Truman, who had been raised by a family of white supremacists in Missouri and didn't bother to hide his racism even as a US senator, was planning to issue an executive order to desegregate the armed forces. In the meantime, he and liberal Democrats in Congress were pushing for civil rights legislation that if passed would outlaw legal segregation in the South. Southern political leaders—all Democrats and all diehard segregationists—were already planning their futile revolt.

~ ~

The multi-troubled region Ray Sprigle would live in for a month had recently been examined in depth by John Gunther, one of America's greatest journalists. In his 1947 bestseller, *Inside U.S.A.*, Gunther called the South "the problem child of the Nation." He had plenty of good reasons. The South had the worst schools, the highest murder rates, the worst health, and the least economic wealth of any region in the country. Hundreds of thousands of white and black Americans in the Cotton Belt lived in extreme poverty. Not one of the country's top universities or symphony orchestras was in the South. Except for a handful of writers like Thomas

Wolfe and William Faulkner, it had about as much culture, sneered its greatest detractor H. L. Mencken, as the Gobi Desert.

Black Americans had it tough everywhere, but for most of them the Deep South was a hard, oppressive, and hopeless place. Millions of blacks had been quietly emancipating themselves by train and bus, leaving in what would someday be branded "the Great Migration." But about ten million still lived from Virginia to Texas. Mississippi and Georgia each had a million black citizens—a half and a third of their populations, respectively. Alabama's three million souls included nearly a million blacks, almost as many as New York, New Jersey, and Pennsylvania combined. From 1910 through the mid-1940s, about 2.7 million blacks had migrated from the South to manufacturing cities like Chicago, Cleveland, Pittsburgh, and Los Angeles. Another three million would leave by 1970. Like poor whites who fled the dead-end rural poverty of Dixie in equal numbers between 1910 and 1948, most blacks migrated for economic reasons. During war or peace, even the lowest-paying factory jobs in northern cities paid three times what could be made working the land in Mississippi or Georgia.

Black Americans had another persuasive reason to join the Great Migration: to free themselves from the chains and humiliations of Jim Crow. The system of legal segregation, named after a nineteenth-century minstrel show character, had controlled and haunted the daily lives of southern blacks since 1890. Under its finely tuned but often fundamentally absurd laws, which were written and enforced in different ways by state and local governments, black sharecroppers in the Delta, black farm owners in Alabama, and black insurance company executives in Atlanta were all mistreated equally.

They were strictly separated from whites in all public spaces—from ocean beaches and libraries to schools, streetcars, courtrooms, elevators, tennis courts, and maternity ward nurseries. They were forbidden to stand in line with whites at banks and train stations and had to form separate lines. Their children were under-educated in separate but criminally unequal schools. Courtrooms had white Bibles and black Bibles. And though blacks were often the majority population in a given town or county, they were prevented from attaining state or local political power by a combination of onerous poll taxes, literacy tests, voter intimidation, and the very real fear of white violence.

Under Jim Crow blacks were also subjected to a dense, unwritten web of petty rules and social "etiquette" that never let them forget they were deemed by authorities to be inherently inferior to anyone with white skin. For instance, black adults were never to call whites by their first names, only "Mister." They had to sit in the backseat if they were in a car driven by a white person and they had to give white motorists the right-of-way at intersections. On some buses or trolleys in some towns, they had to enter by the rear doors and leave by the front. In other places it was the opposite. "Legalized humiliation" is what one black minister called Jim Crow.

Civil rights and desegregation were in the headlines every day. In 1947 Jackie Robinson had broken the modern color barrier in Major League Baseball with much fanfare and some ugliness. The National Football League had quietly integrated itself a year earlier. Between them the two professional leagues could barely field a complete baseball team of black players, but they were decades ahead of the national curve on desegregation. The rest of the United States was effectively a segregated country, either by law in the South or by fact in the North and West. In every city and town, blacks had their own neighborhoods, commercial districts, and social institutions. They ran their own newspapers, magazines, radio stations, and numbers rackets. They produced their own "race" movies and "race" records and formed their own professional baseball leagues. They had their own colleges, churches, labor unions, fraternal groups, hospitals, cemeteries, restaurants, life insurance companies, bars, parks, YMCAs, swimming pools, jazz joints, funeral parlors, taxicabs, doctors, dentists, and even police.

In 1948 the United States was the richest and most powerful country on the planet. However, black Americans were not sharing equally in the country's postwar prosperity. They were disproportionately poor, under-educated, and discriminated against in both the rural South and the urban North. The average annual salaries of black high school grads and college grads were roughly half of comparably educated whites. Naturally, their personal and economic success stories were fewer in number, and even the best, brightest, and most talented blacks were systematically denied equal access to opportunity or unfairly treated in the workplace. Top universities had few if any black professors or students. Black medical doctors were rare, black corporate execs even scarcer. Duke Ellington, Louis Armstrong, Ella Fitzgerald, and other great black musicians popular with whites were plentiful. Black movie stars, pro golfers, and NBA players were not. Joe Louis was an all-American hero, but there were only two blacks in Congress and no black staffers or black secretaries in the Truman White House. No big city had a black mayor.

America was where a colorblind Constitution and the rule of law were supposed to guarantee every individual the equal right to live, speak, worship, work, vote, and travel freely, where your property rights were protected and where no matter how rich or poor you were you had the right to peacefully pursue your own happiness without fear from your government or neighbors. In reality, America had yet to live up to its founding principles and ideals for many of its people. Women, homosexuals, Latinos, Jews, and American Indians still had steep uphill legal roads to travel before they became free and equal citizens. And for fourteen million blacks—one in ten Americans—the Land of the Free was more like an extension of the feudal Mississippi Delta. From Boston to Atlanta to Los Angeles, practically everything of importance or great value in government, business, education, and entertainment was owned and operated by white people—white men, mostly. Interracial marriage was against the law in every state of the South and would technically stay that way until the restriction was declared unconstitutional by the US Supreme Court in 1967. In the North, blacks in cities like Pittsburgh were subjected to a range of blatant and subtle extralegal discriminations and social indignities in employment, in housing, and in their daily lives. They too had fewer and steeper paths to achieving the American Dream. But at least in the North they were equal to whites under the law. In the Jim Crow South, eighty-three years after the end of the Civil War, it was the law itself that hurt blacks and made certain they stayed third-class citizens in their own country.

In 1896 legal segregation had been given five decades of extended life by the Supreme Court of the United States. In the fateful *Plessy v. Ferguson* decision, the justices ruled 7–1 to uphold the constitutionality of "separate but equal." The imprimatur of the highest court didn't hide the fact that the South's system of segregation was conspicuously un-American. Swedish economist Gunnar Myrdal pointed out that obvious, yet ignored, truth to the country in *An American Dilemma: The Negro Problem and Modern Democracy*, his epic 1944 study of the black population and white-black relations.

Myrdal was a Swedish scholar and politician hired in 1938 by the Carnegie Corporation to come to the United States and do an in-depth sociological study of the American Negro. His fifteen-hundred-page book was not light reading, but it sold one hundred thousand copies and greatly influenced the country's future racial policies. It was heavily relied upon in *Brown v. Board of Education of Topeka*, the landmark 1954 Supreme Court case that ruled "separate but equal" schools were "inherently unequal" and therefore unconstitutional. Myrdal and his team of researchers, including future Nobel Peace Prize winner Ralph Bunche, traveled extensively through the South gathering data and observing blacks. Coincidentally, Myrdal himself spent time with John Wesley Dobbs in 1938. In what would be a mini-preview of his trip with Sprigle, Dobbs drove Myrdal around Georgia and introduced him to members of the South's thin top-layer of black professionals and middle-class businessmen and farmers.

Observing segregation through the unbiased eyes of a European liberal, Myrdal said he was immediately "shocked and scared to the bones by all the evils I saw, and by the serious political implications of the problem which I could not fail to appreciate." Treating one-tenth of the population as inferior and denying them their basic civil and political rights violated what he called "the American Creed," the ideals of liberty, equality, and justice for all that he believed Americans of all races, classes, and religions held in common.

Myrdal famously warned that the mistreatment of millions of blacks under Jim Crow was "a moral problem" America was going to have to solve. He didn't think solving it could be possible, however, until the majority of white people found out how horrible life was for the average black person in the South. There was "an astonishing ignorance about the Negro on the part of the white public in the North," he said.

Whites outside the South, Myrdal quickly realized, knew almost nothing about black people. Racist stereotypes predominated: They were criminals with low sexual morals and low intelligence who were good dancers and children of nature. Hollywood moviemakers exploited and perpetuated the worst racial stereotypes. *Amos 'n' Andy*, America's most popular radio show in the late 1920s and 1930s, reinforced the stereotypes even if it softened them with its humor and universal working-class values. Myrdal had no doubt that if the white public in the North could learn the facts about the conditions of black Americans, they'd "be prepared to give the Negro a substantially better deal." "To get publicity," Myrdal said presciently in 1944, "is of the highest strategic importance to the Negro people." But for that to happen, he said blacks would need a lot more help from the northern white press than they were getting.

What life was like for blacks under Jim Crow was no mystery to the four million blacks living in the North. Powerful national black papers like the *Pittsburgh Courier* and the *Chicago Defender* had been railing about the horrible situation in the South for decades. They exposed lynchings and other injustices in sensationalized news stories. They editorialized hard and long for federal civil rights legislation and other political, social, and economic reforms that would bring equality to blacks.

But white people in the North didn't read black newspapers. And the mainstream press in Pittsburgh and elsewhere did nothing to cure their white readers of their ignorance about black Americans. White papers rarely covered the growing black communities in their own urban backyards, much less black news from the South or around the country. The average white in the North had no way of knowing how impoverished or un-American daily life was for blacks in the South. The Big Media of the day—daily newspapers, news magazines, and network radio—had no moral or commercial interest in telling them. For more than half a century the best white print journalists in the North and South, including Ray Sprigle, had neglected, ignored, or not noticed the unconstitutional and shameful elephant in the national newsroom.

The Delta's big sky was more cloudy than blue and the air blasting through the Mercury's open windows was hot and sticky. The damp warm earth stretching to the horizons was brown except for a few trees and the thin green lines of a million baby cotton plants. Sprigle and Dobbs had a long muggy day ahead. Their first stop was going to be a segregated cemetery near Clarksdale, just off Highway 61. Dobbs had arranged a meeting there with a relatively wealthy dentist who had a tragic story to tell about two victims of the Jim Crow South's cold-hearted race laws.

The brown fields on both sides of two-lane Highway 61 were scattered to the horizons with ragged little columns of men, women, and children in overalls, printed cotton dresses, and wide straw hats. Sharecroppers. All of them were black. Some were in their seventies, some as young as five. Heads bowed, eyes to the ground, they mechanically worked their long hoes in short chops as they moved among the rows of baby cotton plants they'd be taking personal care of until picking time in the fall. If there hadn't been telephone wires strung along the highway and Pepsi-Cola signs nailed to the fronts of the few "colored cafes" and general stores they passed, it could have been 1880.

Despite their obvious differences, the two senior citizens were getting along famously. They were alike in many important ways—intelligent, self-educated, big talkers, political animals, fellow Republicans, and good fathers and husbands. A team of equals, they were worldly, accomplished men of influence at the top of their games. Both were celebrities, insiders, and newsmakers in their home states and were also known around the country. Both liked to drive their cars faster and eat more than they should, and both had long histories of stirring up trouble for people or institutions that deserved it.

Based on what Sprigle and Dobbs were seeing as they crossed the Delta, Jim Crow and his petty racism looked as invincible as ever. But up North in the corridors of federal power, the constitutional and moral legitimacy of segregation was coming under serious attack. Liberals led by Minneapolis mayor Hubert Humphrey were pressing for a strong civil rights plank to be hammered into the Democratic Party's presidential platform in July. Northern progressives were finally serious about replacing "states' rights with human rights," as Humphrey aptly put it. They intended to make Negroes equal citizens under the law, especially in the South where a hardened web of state and local segregation laws, devious voting requirements, and legalized discrimination guaranteed they'd remain separate and unequal Americans forever.

Black leaders, the NAACP, and the black press had been demanding federal action on civil rights and voting reform in the South for decades without success. Powerful entrenched southern Democrats in the US Senate had always been able to thwart Republican anti-lynching bills and other anti-discrimination bills with their filibusters and parliamentary maneuvers. Now Humphrey and his allies were asking the Party of Franklin Roosevelt to stand up to its powerful segregationist wing. The liberals were determined to force the Democratic Party to join the twentieth century and, after sixty years of enabling Jim Crow, make it live up to the letter and spirit of America's ideals.

It would take Congress, the US Supreme Court, and the yet-to-be-born civil rights movement another sixteen turbulent, often bloody years before the Southland's cherished apartheid was outlawed. But the process of strangling old Jim Crow to death had already begun at the presidential level. The previous summer President Truman had surprised the country by suddenly making civil rights a federal priority. In a historic speech on the steps of the Lincoln Memorial, he didn't spell out what specific steps his administration would take, nor did he say when or where Washington would begin focusing its legal powers to eradicate racial discrimination. But every southern politician from Richmond to Little Rock understood the road the president was headed down when he said, "We can no longer afford the luxury of a leisurely attack upon prejudice and discrimination. There is much that State and local governments can do in providing positive safeguards for civil rights. But we cannot, any longer, await the growth of a will to action in the slowest State or the most backward community. Our National Government must show the way."

The Mississippi Delta's authoritative source for news about civil rights threats from Washington, and everything else of importance to the region's white minority, was the *Delta Democrat-Times*. Its offices were in a brick building on Main Street in Greenville, the Delta's biggest and wealthiest town with thirty thousand people. The daily paper was owned and edited by Hodding Carter Jr., a Pulitzer Prize–winning editorial writer and prolific freelancer who at age forty-one had made himself well known in the northern press as a moderate voice "of the New South." Carter was smart, wealthy, sophisticated, dark-and-handsome, and, unlike most white southern Democrats, a liberal. A self-described redneck from Louisiana, he had received a fine northern education in Maine at prestigious Bowdoin College. He spent a year at Harvard as a Nieman Foundation journalism fellow and vacationed regularly at his summer house on the Maine coast. But he loved the Deep South and had made a second career out of doggedly explaining and defending its culture, history, ideals, habits, and artificial ecosystem of racial separation.

The contents of the *Delta Democrat-Times* each day reflected Carter's sharp opinions and scrappy spirit. He was an excellent, versatile writer. He could be lighthearted and satirical. But when he wrote editorials on serious political subjects, he didn't pull any punches. Whether he was calling for Germany to be "erased as a nation" after World War II, scolding local planters for trying to fix the wages of cotton pickers, blasting a powerful southern senator for his crude racism, or telling northern liberal do-gooders to do good in their own backyards not his, it was always clear where he and his paper stood.

Carter's news judgment was radically inclusive for a white southern newspaper—he covered black people and looked out for their interests. He didn't just run articles that reported on their minor criminal acts. He put photos of famous blacks like Jesse Owens on his front page, knowing he'd get heat—and hate—from white readers and his less enlightened white friends, advertisers, and subscribers. He editorialized in favor of better housing for Greenville's eighteen thousand black residents and railed against the decision of the Daughters of the American Revolution not to let black performer Marian Anderson sing at Constitution Hall in Washington, DC. He even praised President Truman in 1947 for his early rhetorical calls for civil rights reform, saying his promise to put the Bill of Rights into full practice for everyone was "sound and courageous." As an unwavering segregationist, he especially liked Truman's promise that individuals and local governments would be protected from "dictatorial pressure from Washington."

Though Carter lived in a secluded corner of the very Deep South, there was nothing parochial about him. The town's most famous citizen, he was intellectual, reasoned, well traveled, and connected with the elite national press. He even wrote poetry, novels, and nonfiction books. He was already part of the country's nascent debate on civil rights, and he was active in professional journalism circles. He knew who Ray Sprigle was. He knew Sprigle had won his Pulitzer Prize after coming down to Alabama in 1937 and digging up the documents that proved FDR's newly appointed Supreme Court justice Hugo Black had been an active member of the Ku Klux Klan. Carter had never met Sprigle—not yet. He wouldn't find out why he was snooping around his beloved Delta until August, when Eleanor Roosevelt, *Time* magazine, and half the major newspapers in the country were talking about the trouble the famous Yankee reporter had stirred up.

Chapter 2

Ray Sprigle, Star Reporter

Eight months before setting off with John Wesley Dobbs, Ray Sprigle woke up in his western Pennsylvania house with troublemaking on his mind. September 25, 1947, was going to be a cool, cloudy day. Rain dripped through the leaves of the old hardwood trees that covered most of his 103-acre farm. His bosses at the *Post-Gazette* had already endorsed his idea to disguise himself as a Negro and infiltrate the Jim Crow South. He still didn't know how he was going to safely dye his pale skin. But later that afternoon in Pittsburgh's largest black neighborhood he was going to meet secretly with the executive secretary of the National Association for the Advancement of Colored People, Walter F. White. White was in town to give a pep talk to the local NAACP branch. Sprigle wanted to brief White about his trip idea and ask him to find a southern black man brave enough to be his guide.

Sprigle had no trouble getting a private meeting with the most influential civil rights leader in the country. The *Post-Gazette*'s star reporter was one of America's elite newspapermen. He had burst onto the national scene ten years earlier for confirming rumors that President Roosevelt's recent Supreme Court pick, former US senator Hugo Black of Alabama, had been a member of the Ku Klux Klan. Sprigle's bombshell, which hit the front page of every daily newspaper in September of 1937, became the political scandal of the year. His investigative series in the *Post-Gazette*— energized by his and his conservative publisher's deep hatred of FDR and the New Deal—began in typical Sprigle fashion with a bang and plenty of spin.

Hugo Lafayette Black, Associate Justice of the United States Supreme Court, is a member of the hooded brotherhood that for ten long blood-drenched years ruled the Southland with lash and noose and torch, the Invisible Empire, Knights of the Ku Klux Klan.

He holds membership in the masked and oath-bound legion as he holds his office in the Nation's Supreme tribunal—for life.

For Supreme Court Justice Hugo Lafayette Black bears the proud distinction that not a half dozen other men in the United States can claim. The cloaked and hooded Knights of the Klan have bestowed upon him the solid gold engraved Grand passport that betokens life-membership in the mysterious super-government that once ruled half a continent with terror and violence.

Sprigle backed up his charges with great reporting. He had outfoxed a platoon of other big-city journalists who had descended upon Justice Black's hometown of Birmingham looking for proof of his KKK past. Using a generous expense account, private detectives, and his natural schmoozing skills, Sprigle got his hands on the KKK membership papers Black had signed in the mid-1920s. He also procured the transcript of a speech the then newly elected US senator gave at a Klan gathering during which he thanked them for their support and professed eternal fealty to the principles of Anglo-Saxon supremacy.

Justice Black rejected demands from the NAACP, Catholic groups, and others that he immediately resign from the high court. In a brief primetime radio broadcast heard by more than a third of the country, he didn't explain or apologize. He tersely admitted he had joined the Klan but said he had resigned and never rejoined. Ironically, the former klansman went on to become a long-serving liberal jurist and friend of the NAACP who was consistently pro–civil rights.

Sprigle's authoritative exposé of Hugo Black made him famous far beyond Pittsburgh, where he was already a celebrity. It launched his name into the pages of *Time*, *Newsweek*, and a thousand newspapers. *Life* magazine did a multipage spread of him reenacting his sleuthing in Birmingham. He was interviewed in a Pathé newsreel that was shown in hundreds of movie theaters. The *New York Times* editorial page praised his reporting

Ray Sprigle set off a national story by proving former Senator Hugo Black of Alabama had been a member of the KKK. COURTESY OF THE *PITTSBURGH POST-GAZETTE*

as "the best of the year," but in Pittsburgh the local franchise of the KKK had a different opinion. In the dead of a foggy night, the Klan burned a fifteen-foot cross at a crossroads not far from the driveway to his farm and left a wooden tombstone bearing the message "Kastigate the Kallous Kallumniator Ray Sprigle." Sprigle's fellow ink-stained wretches had the last word on his Hugo Black series, however. In the spring of 1938 he was given his profession's ultimate prize—a Pulitzer Prize for reporting.

Hard to find and difficult to access, Sprigle's land leaned against a steep hillside on the outskirts of Coraopolis, an Ohio River community twelve miles west of downtown Pittsburgh. Halfway up the slope on about four flattish and cleared acres sat his white two-story house and a garage, a small barn, a well, a pond, and the meadow where the *Post-Gazette* editorial staff held its annual summer beer blasts. To reach Sprigle's "feudal estate," as his admiring coworkers called it, you had to scale a three-quarter-mile gravel and dirt driveway that was cut into the side of a cliff. In winter and spring a car needed tire chains to traverse the snow or mud.

Sprigle, his wife, Agnes, and twelve-year-old daughter, Rae Jean, shared their isolated paradise with a bunch of tasty chickens, two ponies, a dozen or so cats, and a crazy English mastiff who preferred scrambled fresh eggs to dog food. Sprigle had bought the place in 1925. He called it his "farm," or his "ranch," and he had a few calluses on his hands. He cut grass with a scythe, cleared brush, grew vegetables, tended a pear orchard, and at various times raised chickens and bred bulldogs. But he was no farmer and no farmer's son. His father, Emanuel, was a carpenter and contractor in Akron, Ohio, where he also served as president of city council. Sprigle and his younger brother, Harold, were raised in an upper-middle-class home where Democratic reform politics was practiced more rigorously than the doctrines of the German Reformed Church.

Martin Ray Sprigle was born August 14, 1886. One of his fondest childhood memories was "helping" his father build a speaking platform for William Jennings Bryan, the populist Democrat and silver-tongued orator whose presidential campaign train stopped in Akron in 1896. Family lore says Bryan accidentally stepped on the young Sprigle's hand, but Ray barely noticed. He was too swept away by the orations and populist message of "The Great Commoner"—especially his deep concern for the underdog. Though Sprigle grew up and became a conservative Republican, for the rest of his life he considered Bryan his "unvarnished" political hero.

Sprigle went off to study at Ohio State University in 1905 but lasted only a year. He was asked to leave by school authorities after he turned up the heat of a bonfire at a football rally by adding someone's barn. A failing grade in Greek didn't help, either. Because the only thing Sprigle really ever liked about school was writing—and he was a talented scribe—he went from Ohio State straight into newspapering. At age twenty he was in Columbus covering the state penitentiary for the *Ohio Sun*, playing cards with prisoners through the bars of their cells, and acquiring a taste for police, crime, and corruption stories that would last half a century. For several years he worked as a reporter at papers from Ohio to Arkansas, sometimes for only a week, and usually specializing in crime.

Meanwhile, he also tried his hand at fiction. He was good at it and had met lots of colorful real-life people to fictionalize. By 1911, at twenty-five, he had sold three short stories to *Red Book*, a top New York pulp-fiction magazine. The editor, who said later he thought he had discovered "the American Gorky," told Sprigle to come to the Big Apple and possibly work for him at *Red Book*. Sprigle, on his way east with dreams of becoming a great writer of social realism like Russia's Maxim Gorky, got only as far as the copy desk of the old *Pittsburgh Daily Post*. When he stopped in to say hello to a friend, he was invited to work a shift as a copy editor on the understaffed news desk. Though he continued to write and publish fiction, he took a job with the *Post* and never made it to New York City.

Pittsburgh was a hard place for a young and single journalist to leave. In 1911 it was a newspaperman's dream—a crowded industrial city rife with political corruption, prostitution, vice, Eastern European immigrants, radical politics, and labor ferment. Sprigle was a wiry dandy who wore a derby and spats and carried a walking stick. Slaving six ten-hour days a week, he quickly rose to become city editor of the *Post*, the city's staunch Democratic paper. Meanwhile, his nights were filled with adventure and talk of social revolution. He was boarding in one of downtown Pittsburgh's many brothels above an illegal bistro. Forty years later he described the smoky "speakeasy" as "a romantic madhouse" where off-duty prostitutes, madams, homosexuals, and "the self-baptized saviours of the world hung out." Most of its denizens, i.e., most of his friends and associates, he confessed, were "the motley mob of Socialists, Communists, Syndicalists, Anarchists, idealists, bums, thugs, criminals, hoodlums and heroes that made up the Industrial Workers of the World—the IWW or the Wobblies."

At that formative time in his life, Sprigle's soft spot for underdogs and the oppressed included Socialists, anarchists, and violent union organizers. He didn't just drink beer with the Wobblies. For about two years he functioned "as a sort of unofficial organizer, ghost writer and general handyman" for them. His unholy mix of journalism and social rebellion came to a dramatic end, however, when he used his connections at city hall to get a blank parade permit, which he filled out himself so his Wobbly friends could march through downtown without being clubbed by police.

Unfortunately, when two thousand grateful demonstrators reached the end of their route, outside the *Post*'s offices, they stood in the street and cheered their comrade Ray Sprigle by name. When his bosses put two and two together, Sprigle was sacked. He worked at several papers in Pittsburgh and Chicago before being forgiven by the *Post* and rehired as a reporter a couple of years later. He soon fell out of love with the nasty Wobblies and their dreams of overthrowing the employing class. In 1917 he enlisted in the Army. He had hoped to become a war correspondent, but the closest he got to France was a training camp in Virginia, where he ran the camp paper for ten months.

In 1922, back in Pittsburgh and again the *Post*'s city editor, Sprigle finally settled down. At age thirty-six he married Agnes Trimmer, the tall young woman he had been talking to on the streetcar every morning for several years as they rode to work. She did the etching on expensive gold-dipped glassware for a company that catered to the wealthy and superstars like actress Lillian Russell. "Mother was a perfect match for Daddy," their daughter Rae said in 2016. "She was majestic and commanding. She was five-foot-eight, unusual for a woman of her generation. The only person she respected was Daddy. She read voraciously and was addicted to politics."

Prohibition was in full swing. Women could vote but no one could legally drink. It was a decade of speakeasies, organized crime, flappers, jazz, sex, soaring and crashing stocks, silent movies, strikes, race riots, Republican presidents, Babe Ruth, the rise and fall of the KKK, the birth of commercial radio and talkie newsreels, and exploding newspaper circulations. Pittsburgh was growing into the fifth biggest newspaper market in the country. The city's three largest daily newspapers—in order, the working-class *Press*, the Republican *Gazette Times*, and the Democratic *Post*—were fiercely competitive.

Muckraking journalism sold papers, and city editor Sprigle and his staff made the most of his adopted city's rich muck. He mounted aggressive campaigns against speakeasies, gambling joints, and brothels and went after crooks, bad cops, and corrupt politicians. The *Post* went from neighborhood to neighborhood, taking photos of buildings and printing them in the paper with big white arrows pointing to the illegal bars, gambling dens, and whorehouses. Also provided were the property owners' names and handsome portraits of the police inspectors who were not doing their jobs. Sprigle was causing so much trouble that the most famous madam in town sent a pair of thousand-dollar bills to his desk, but he declined Nettie Gordon's bribe and continued his crusade.

In 1927 Sprigle's newspaper career—and the rest of his life—was altered when Paul Block, a friend and business associate of William Randolph Hearst, bought the *Pittsburgh Daily Post* and another Pittsburgh daily. By the time Block and Hearst were finished swapping the four Pittsburgh newspapers they owned, Block had created the *Pittsburgh Post-Gazette*. Like its owner—and like Sprigle, its portly forty-one-year-old city editor—the new morning paper was Republican and conservative.

Though an editor, Sprigle occasionally still reported stories. He went undercover for the first time in 1928 during a long state-wide strike by twenty thousand coal miners. Realizing he knew nothing for sure about the strike his paper was covering every day, or coal mining, he got himself hired as a strikebreaker. For a week he ate, slept, lived, and worked underground in a fenced off and heavily protected mine camp with six hundred other "scabs." Heavily promoted in advance, his six-part series "Down in a Mine Pit" promised readers it would tell the truth in an impartial and un-sensationalized way, and it did.

The series was a huge success journalistically, and it would become a model for Sprigle's future undercover ventures. The heavy Page 1 headline ("Editor Lands Job to Dig Coal and Truth in Mines") and large photo of Sprigle dressed in his miner's gear did a great job of selling the story to readers. Sprigle wrote in the first person, telling his story in an engaging way, exactly as it happened to him. His series didn't outrage the public or bring about reforms in mine safety, and it was deemed to be evenhanded. But

as a spying journalist he delivered tons of detailed information about coal mining and miners that average readers never could have learned otherwise.

Nearly two years later Sprigle found himself a central player in a crime story that sounded like one of his fictional tales for *Red Book* magazine. It started in late December of 1929 when a Pennsylvania state trooper was shot dead and another was wounded north of Pittsburgh. The killers—blonde ex-waitress Irene Schroeder and her lover Glenn Dague— were identified, but they disappeared. The hunt for the fugitives was the biggest newspaper story in western Pennsylvania for two weeks. It had died down when Sprigle, working at his desk on a Tuesday night, read a two-paragraph Associated Press wire story from Chandler, Texas. Two men and a "blonde gunwoman" had shot and kidnapped a deputy sheriff, dumped him out of their car, and fled west. As he wrote when retelling the story twenty years later, "That was all. But to me there was only one blonde gunwoman in all the world. And she was my Irene."

Sprigle made a few calls and soon learned the shootout actually occurred a thousand miles away in Chandler, Arizona, where the sheriff's office told him a posse of fifty deputies, local cowboys, and Maricopa Indians was at that very moment surrounding the three fugitives in the rugged desert canyons. Sprigle was still on the phone when word came in that the trio had been captured and were being brought in on horseback. Schroeder and Dague would not give their real names. But when Sprigle heard that a sales slip found in their car had been made out to a "James Crawford" of New Concord, Ohio—Schroeder's brother—he shouted, "That's them! That's them!"

Sprigle immediately hopped a train to Columbus, Ohio, and a plane to Phoenix. But it still took him three days to get to the jail where Schroeder, aka "the trigger blonde," and Dague were the center of a media circus. The first Pittsburgh reporter on the scene, he wrote the big scoop for the *Post-Gazette*. He rode on the train with the killers back to Pittsburgh, writing stories all the way. He covered their trial. Then he was an official witness at their back-to-back executions in Pennsylvania's electric chair. As he described it, Schroeder—after sneering "over at us newspapermen"—"surged desperately under the terrific power of 2,000 volts. The heavy, flaccid breasts rose, firm, rounded and pointed like a girl's." After the executioner switched off the third jolt, "a wisp of smoke rose from the blonde head."

Covering the Schroeder-Dague case was a great thrill for a true-crime fan like Sprigle. The story was later turned into an NBC radio network drama, and he would always say he considered it the greatest achievement of his newspaper career. Going to Arizona also changed Sprigle's life in several ways. He fell in love with the Southwest, made friends with the Maricopa Indians, and drove there each year on family vacations. It was also where he lost his nondescript 1930s businessman's hat and discovered the wide-brimmed Stetson that became his signature lid for the rest of his life. The last name "Crawford" was a less obvious legacy of his Wild West adventure. It became his lucky alias, and he used it for the first time a year later when, posing as a homeless derelict named Ed Crawford, he booked himself into a Pennsylvania state mental hospital.

Starting on March 6, 1931, Sprigle gave more than two hundred thousand *Post-Gazette* readers a gripping personal tour of life inside Mayview, a sprawling campus of large brick buildings where thirty-four hundred men and women were warehoused under conditions that were closer to a concentration camp's than a refuge for the poor, sick, and homeless. Another Sprigle special, perhaps the most emotionally powerful one he'd ever write, "Over the Hills to Mayview" was a brilliant account of a grim reality the public knew nothing about and could never see. Mayview was one of several gigantic institutions of its kind in the Pittsburgh countryside. It was:

> a great hospital ward, where idiots, insane, the tubercular, paralytics, victims of social diseases, sufferers from virulently communicable skin diseases are pitchforked together, hit-or-miss, cheek by jowl in a long, low basement room, locked—day and night. In that fetid, hot, almost airless prison, these men on the high hospital beds use a common comb, drinking cups in common, from time to time a common towel, a shaving brush in common, and a crowded lavatory in common.

He lived for a week at the state hospital. His series ran on Page 1 for six straight days. What he wrote about, and how he wrote it, was shocking, heartbreaking, Dickensian. It began with an editorial disclaimer saying it was just one man's story, one man's experiences, and it did not pretend to be an expert technical analysis. The disclaimer also said "it was not meant to be an attack on the institution or its management," but the series couldn't help but be exactly that. At the time, Mayview, which was administered for the state by the corrupt Allegheny County government, was being audited. Its officials were in the papers every other day for having been caught rigging bids for furniture, faking food purchases, and other malfeasances. Its annual recreation budget was five hundred dollars. And while its inmates ate sticky cooked cereal and rarely saw an egg, its superintendent recently had been caught dining at his own table on caviar and winter strawberries.

In January of 1932 Sprigle left newspapering for politics. The previous fall, despite being a journalist, he had worked hard to elect his good friend and neighbor, "Buck" McGovern, to one of three Allegheny County commissioner positions. McGovern, a reformer and cost-cutter, and another Republican formed the majority, which meant they ran the county government and got to dish out the fat patronage jobs. McGovern appointed Sprigle the new Allegheny County property and supplies director. Sprigle was well prepared for the job, thanks to two decades of observing corrupt political machines and his faithful adherence to the precepts of his reform hero, William Jennings Bryan. The position paid a handsome sixty-eight hundred dollars a year—about $120,000 today. Overnight it made him one of the most powerful men in local government. When half a dozen other departments were consolidated into his, he was in charge of everything the county owned, from the courthouse to paperclips and five asphalt plants. The former city editor was the chief of the county police, the county purchasing agent, and sales agent.

Wielding his power from a desk in a spartan cubbyhole in the county building, Sprigle wasted no time shaking things up and paring them down. He sold county junk he found stashed in closets and real estate the county didn't know it owned. He cut county jobs and rejected bids for new furniture at the county airport because it was too expensive for a waiting room. One of his first moves was to institute time clocks for county employees—incompetent political hacks renowned for spending more time sleeping than working. He decreed that county officials, including judges, could no longer use expensive embossed stationery. He put the county building's watchmen in new uniforms and gave them badges. He declared a war of extermination on the armies of cockroaches in the basement. He steam-cleaned the county jail and morgue. All that was done in the first month.

For four years Director Sprigle's official actions, antics, and fiery political speeches put his name or face in the papers every week. He was occasionally criticized, but he was treated tenderly by his old newspaper buddies, who took advantage of his cheerful troublemaking and natural public relations skills. He ignored the constant, not-always mild complaints he got for fouling the air with his corncob pipe during commissioners meetings, which he continued even after the time he set a wastebasket on fire and filled the room with billowing yellow smoke.

His most publicized antic, which brought him national attention in the press, revolved around his futile efforts to drive off the several thousand starlings and Belgian pigeons that had taken up residence on the roof and windowsills of the county building. Sprigle tried noise, but his greatest success, albeit fleeting, came when he ordered Roman candles to be shot at the roosting pests each night at midnight. With a quiver of long Roman candles in his suit pocket, he was photographed firing the first shots of the battle himself. Director Sprigle did many more important things, including catching nine cement companies who were colluding to fix their county bids and personally auctioning off two county asphalt plants in the courthouse lobby.

Meanwhile, he earned his political appointment by being a loyal Republican Party firebrand at public meetings and on the radio. At one mass meeting he assailed the state legislators that represented the 12th District, his own district, as "a collection of bums, owned, absolutely, body and soul, by the public utilities." He blasted local and state politicians and railed about the rotten politics of Pennsylvania and the "gang of drunks" who met in hotel rooms and selected candidates that disgraced the state Republican Party.

In the fall of 1935, the Roosevelt Revolution finally arrived in Pittsburgh, sweeping Republicans out of their city and county offices. Sprigle, who had told a local columnist he was hankering to get back into newspapering, was welcomed back at the *Post-Gazette* as a general assignment reporter, the position he'd hold until the day he died. Supported by publisher Paul Block, who paid him well and deployed him in his escalating war against FDR like a piece of artillery, Sprigle quickly became the *P-G*'s star product. In 1936, starting with the case of a murdered seventeen-year-old girl, he wrote thirty-eight articles. Most began on Page 1. He kept up that pace, with time out for his Pulitzer story on Hugo Black, until Hitler turned his bombsights on England.

World War II kept Sprigle busy. With great fanfare the *Post-Gazette* flew him by way of Lisbon to London in June of 1940 during the first weeks of the Battle of Britain. Almost daily, for four months, as Spitfires and Messerschmitts dueled over southern England and German bombers terrorized London, he cabled feature stories to the *Post-Gazette* about British civilians coping with "the nightmare of total war." During the Blitz, he joined the thousands of families who spent their nights in subway shelters as bombs shook the earth six stories above them. He interviewed bombing victims and farmers and firefighters and rode a slow train through the blacked-out city during an intensive German air raid.

He was never in real danger. What he wrote about the first week or two of the nightly bombings in September was good dramatic stuff: "The clouds are lit with flames of scattered fires. The night is filled with the constant roar of hundreds of guns that shatter the sky with bursting shells from darkness until dawn." But during the day London was just a bustling metropolis going about its business. With no German invasion imminent, he was actually getting bored. In a rare letter to his wife, Agnes, he wrote that London under siege wasn't as harrowing as the American press was making it out to be. Cranky that he had been ordered to stay an extra three months, he wondered if his war stories—which his publisher and patron Paul Block said he liked—were really any good.

Sometimes I think they are all right and then again as I look over some of them I think they smell. It doesn't seem to make much difference what Mr. Block thinks of them, he doesn't even buy the paper. I wonder what the readers think.

The difficulty I have is to find unusual or newsworthy things to write about. Back there you can't even imagine how humdrum things are in England even with a war going on. Nobody seems to care very much, no one is worried or alarmed.

Now I know from what I get in *Time* and the few papers from the states I can get that people back there must have an idea that we are all running around in circles here. And I have an idea that they expect that in my stories too. Well I can't write that stuff because it isn't true. I know you've been getting some cockeyed stories about raids on London. All these raids do is make a lot of people lose sleep. But not anymore. I stayed up for Saturday's raids in order to write a story . . . But now I just turn over when the sirens sound and go back to sleep.

Sprigle, well into his fifties and earning the equivalent of ninety thousand dollars a year in today's dollars from the *Post-Gazette*, returned to Pittsburgh in October and spent the rest of the war years on the home front. He was grinding out front-page reports about the snafus in the food, whiskey, and oil and gasoline rationing programs and touring defense plants around the country like Chrysler's tank factory in Detroit. In April of 1945, however, with Germany weeks away from surrendering, his enterprising journalism created another national news sensation. Knowing that thousands of tons of meat were being bought and sold each week in the Pittsburgh area without the required wartime ration coupons, he decided to go undercover to investigate.

He recruited an anonymous partner in the meat business to give him access to the black market and assumed the alias of a small-time butcher named Alois Vondich. To disguise himself Sprigle shaved his moustache, removed his false teeth, and donned old clothes and a sixty-nine-cent chauffeur's cap he bought from Sears. Bankrolled with a two-thousand-dollar budget by the *Post-Gazette*, he rented a truck and in less than a week illegally purchased more than a ton of beef, ham, bacon, pork, and lamb.

His seven-part front-page series, opening the day after President Roosevelt died, began with the sentence "Pittsburgh's war-born black market in meat operates openly, brazenly and insolently." Any city in America could have been substituted for Pittsburgh, but Sprigle turned his hometown into the nation's capital of illegal meat sales. He showed how local farmers and established meat merchants operating the lucrative black market laughed at the ineffectiveness of the Office of Price Administration (OPA), the federal agency that supposedly enforced the wartime price-control and rationing system that affected almost every good and service.

After just one article appeared, Sprigle and his editor were served a subpoena by the local office of the OPA. Sprigle was threated with jail if he didn't reveal everything he had learned as "Alois Vondich." He refused, saying everything he knew was going to be in his newspaper series. He was looking forward to the PR value of serving a stint in jail, but the OPA backed down. A week later a US Senate investigative committee came to Pittsburgh to quiz Sprigle for a day and hear from other witnesses. In the end the OPA was shamed in the national press as a toothless and incompetent bureaucracy, and Sprigle won the National Headliners Award for the best public service story of 1945.

When *Time* magazine wrote about Sprigle's series in "Meat Makes News" on April 30, 1945, it called him "a hard-digging, hell-for-leather newsman" and helpfully explained that his last name rhymed with "wiggle." Praising his handiwork and his refusal to cooperate with the OPA, *Time* noted that he had won a Pulitzer in 1938. Perhaps confusing Sprigle with his alter ego Alois, the country's number one newsweekly caricatured Sprigle as "a gaudy, rustic-looking eccentric" whose personal trademarks were a tan ten-gallon Stetson and a "fuming corncob pipe." It neglected to mention that when he wasn't dressing up as a scruffy butcher, he wore expensive tailored suits to work and counted the governor of Pennsylvania among his close friends. Or that by producing two decades of world-class journalism in Pittsburgh, he had made "Sprigle" a household name and made his hat and pipe so iconic he'd be greeted by drunks on the street.

Sprigle's house had been built on weekends as a party house by a swinging proctologist and his friends without the knowledge of the doctor's wife. After he bought it Sprigle and his carpenter father had worked hard to fix it up. It was airy, full of light, and had beautiful hardwood floors and a huge fireplace. It was lived in, and it looked it. Books, pets, and weapons were everywhere. A loaded .45 revolver always sat on the back of the buffet in the dining room. It was a perfect house for big parties and picnics. His daughter, Rae, remembered seeing judges, politicians, and department store magnates mixing with county cops and the woman who owned the local grocery store.

Born in 1935, Rae grew up to be a professor of medieval politics and intellectual history, married Bob Kurland, a brilliant chemical physics professor and pioneer MRI researcher, and kept alive her father's love of good journalism, concern for the underdog, and belief in the principles of conservativism. She said her father was very much the head of the family. He made a good living in 1947 for a newspaperman—about one hundred thousand dollars a year in today's money—but cared more about food and his wardrobe than money. Except for T-bone steak dinners, an occasional Cuban cigar, and his expensive suits, he lived simply, buying a new Ford with a radio every two years and usually taking the bus to and from work.

Rae's mother, Agnes, didn't drive or have a job, but she took care of the family finances, the cooking, and the house. She made Rae do old-fashioned things like walk around the house fifteen minutes a day with a book on her head and do laps around the yard for exercise. She also was the best shot in a family that did a lot of shooting. Whereas her father didn't care about sports, Rae and her mother regularly listened to Pittsburgh Pirates baseball games and Joe Louis fights on the radio. "Mother loved Louis," Rae said. A Roman Catholic who had suffered discrimination because of her religion, her mother understood bigotry and didn't stoop to racial stereotyping. Rae said she was as fair-minded and tolerant as her father, who once refused a membership offer from a country club because it excluded Jews and made it a point to always call "Whitey," the lone black cop in Coraopolis, "Mister White."

In 1947 Rae was a precocious seventh grader. She knew her father was a well-known newspaperman, but as far as she was concerned his "first and foremost role in life was being a daddy." At an early age he taught her two important life lessons—"Keep your eyes on the ground so you don't step on a copperhead" and "All guns are loaded." His mornings revolved around her, she said in 2016. "He would pack my lunch every day. He peeled the oranges and scooped the seeds out of my grapes. Every day at school I ate an elegant packed lunch." In addition to teaching her to shoot and swear like a newspaperman at an early age, he helped her with her schoolwork and drove her to the bus stop each morning. Then he'd return home and

take a cold shower at an outdoor faucet by the garage—even in winter—
and putter around his farm until it was time to go to work.

——

Except for his clandestine afternoon meeting with the NAACP's Walter
White, Sprigle's agenda on September 25 was that of a typical Thursday.
At 10:00 a.m. he drove into Coraopolis, parked his car at a gas station,
and rode the bus downtown to the *Post-Gazette* building. Because the
P-G was a morning paper, most of the writing work was done in late
afternoon and into the evening. Just like in the old movies, the newsroom was a dirty, noisy, unhealthy but democratic workplace—for men.
Only the publisher and editor had private offices. Phones rang. Teletype
machines and typewriters banged against cheap paper. Everyone smoked
something. The smell of printer's ink and hot lead hung in the air. Many
of the men had half a whiskey bottle in their desk drawer.

Sprigle's oak desk sat in an open room of equally messy desks. "Sprig"
was the star and usually the center of attention. Everyone who worked
with him liked him. He was good-natured. He was one of the boys—
a reporter, not an editor. He was just older, wiser, better dressed, and
far better-paid. Sprigle's voice boomed. His pipe fumed. He joked. He
cursed—everyone did. It was a newspaper office. His desk was cluttered
with old newspapers, wire baskets, thick pencils, a can of Granger pipe
tobacco, a phone. Years of yellowed copy paper were impaled on a deadly
spike. Typewriters were shared by reporters, but Sprigle had his own. It
was borrowed so often, he had to get tough and attach a warning: "This
is my typewriter, bought and paid for with my own money, so keep your
goddamn hands off it."

After he checked his mail and said his hellos, Sprigle went to lunch.
It was always a working lunch. Meeting with cronies and insiders was
where the tips, gossip, and story ideas came from. Afterward he'd walk up
Grant Street to his main hangout, the Allegheny County Prothonotary's
office. *Prothonotary* was an old-fashioned word for chief of clerks. Sprigle's best friend was county prothonotary Dave Roberts, a Democrat who
was a powerful part of the political machine that ran the county. Sprigle
would hold court in Roberts's office most of the afternoon. That's where

Norm Wolken, the young deputy prothonotary, met him in 1944, when he was thirty-two and Sprigle was fifty-eight. They became good friends.

"Ray was bigger than life, physically and otherwise," Wolken said in 1998. "He would come in all the time. He would rant about FDR—'that crippled, syphilitic bastard in the White House.' He liked to talk politics and tell stories of the old days and just shoot the breeze. I admired him a lot. He was not a ladies man. I never saw him take a drink. He was humorous and always had a retort to fit the situation. His gruffness was a front. His best quality was that there was no bullshit in his makeup. He called it as he saw it. He was very anxious to expose bad situations, but he was not a moralist. I brought him home to dinner several times to give him his Jewish food. He had a very large appetite. He could probably eat two-dozen blintzes at a sitting. He'd order another steak for dessert."

Norm Wolken and Dave Roberts, Sprigle's trusted friends, were among the handful of Pittsburghers who knew he was planning his trip to expose the truth about Jim Crow. "He was talking about how to dye his skin," Wolken recalled. "He liked challenges and risks. That's why he did his southern trip—because it was risky. He was a classic journalist looking for a good story. If it was about something wrong, he enjoyed it even better."

CHAPTER 3

Pittsburgh in White and Black

Pittsburgh was feeling pretty good about itself in the fall of 1947. The capital city of what Franklin Roosevelt called "The Great Arsenal of Democracy" was still basking in the glory of supplying most of the steel America needed to win World War II. Its population was about to hit its all-time peak of 676,000. It was the twelfth largest city in the USA and the busy hub of a productive metropolitan area of 2.6 million. It was true that it was noisy, shockingly dirty, ugly, dense with people, clogged with traffic, polluted with industrial wastes, and pocked with hard urban poverty. But it had enormous corporate and private wealth, top-flight universities, and major-league culture and sports.

The population and industrial capacity of "The Steel City" had surged in the first half of the century. Its founding nationalities—Germans, Irish, and English—had been swamped by waves of Italians, Poles, and Eastern European immigrants who came in the late 1800s and early 1900s to work in the fiery mills and factories. Pittsburgh and dozens of smaller steel-and-coal towns orbiting it also were home to Hungarians, Serbs, Croats, Greeks, Syrians, and Jews. Many were foreign-born or the children of immigrants. In 1947 Pittsburgh's metropolitan population was 90 percent white, predominantly Catholic, and heavily Democratic. Its huge blue-collar workforce was religiously pro-union. Inside Pittsburgh's crowded city limits were a dozen middle-class urban neighborhoods, thousands of fine homes, and many mansions. There were also scores of ethnic working-class neighborhoods built on the sides of cliffs, on the top of hills, or stretched out in ravines and hollows or along the rivers. There was no single large black ghetto. But about 112,000 blacks, including many recent migrants from the South, lived within the city or nearby in tight neighborhoods in smaller towns throughout Allegheny County.

For over a year a series of overlapping major strikes had tormented the citizens of Pittsburgh and the rest of the country. In the Pittsburgh region alone, 120,000 steelworkers and coal miners walked off their jobs. By September of 1947, however, labor peace had arrived. Pittsburgh's industrial economy was back to making products for moms and dads instead of generals and admirals, the unemployment rate was low, and at night the surrounding hills and river valleys still glowed eerily with the fires of the area's signature industry.

Pittsburgh was a major corporate-headquarters town. It was home base for U.S. Steel, the corporation *Life* magazine called "the most fabulous giant yet produced by the industrial revolution." Gulf Oil, Pittsburgh Plate Glass, Mellon Bank, Alcoa, H.J. Heinz, and other major American corporations were headquartered in the compact downtown triangle formed where the Allegheny and Monongahela Rivers join to create the Ohio. But despite its wealth, or because of it, Pittsburgh was an environmental wasteland. Its three rivers, barely visible beneath fleets of barges loaded with coal and coke, were little more than free sewers for the fiery mills and open-hearth furnaces that hugged their banks for miles. The air was loaded with so much soot that downtown streetlights sometimes had to be turned on at noon.

But with the war over, the "Smokey City" had finally started the long-overdue process of cleaning up its air. The average Pittsburgher had no reason to think the city was headed anywhere but up, and yet beneath the permanent fog of smoke and steam its sprawling four-hundred-acre steel mills were sliding toward obsolescence. Over the next three decades, metropolitan Pittsburgh would be forced to de-industrialize by national and global economic forces beyond its control. Its mighty steel industry would collapse. It would hemorrhage population, become the unofficial capital of the Rust Belt, and then slowly recover by diversifying its stagnant economy, so that health care, education, and government became its chief job providers. But in the fall of 1947 it was still a prosperous industrial city living off its glorious past, a place where hourly wages of nearly two dollars and generous benefit packages made the region's union steelworkers the highest paid blue-collar workers in the world.

～～

To say the city's largely unskilled black workforce was not sharing equally in the industrial bonanza of Pittsburgh is an understatement. Pennsylvania was one of the most progressive states in the union. Under the law its half-million blacks were equal to whites. But the state's anti-discrimination laws were rarely enforced, particularly against the largest companies. Discrimination in employment, housing, education, and social relations—practiced by public and private institutions and individuals—was a daily fact of life for Pittsburgh's black citizens.

Job opportunities for blacks in the North were far better than in the Jim Crow South, yet they were far from equal. In both public and private employment, black men and women in Pittsburgh were rarely able to get good blue-collar jobs and seldom able to advance if they got one. They were hired last, fired first, and invariably paid less. There was a distinct color line in Pittsburgh's steel and construction industries. About 40 percent of the area's employers, including some of the largest, barred black employees outright. U.S. Steel didn't hire black brick masons and had no management positions open to blacks. Jones & Laughlin Steel didn't hire black carpenters or bricklayers. Black women and girls were not hired in defense plants during World War II, though tens of thousands of white women were. In the mills black men got the lowest, dirtiest, and most dangerous positions. They were janitors and laborers or they worked in the hellish coke ovens and furnaces—the "man-killing" jobs.

The unions that controlled the best industrial jobs made things worse for black workers. They were practically lily-white and intent on staying that way. Of fifteen hundred union blacksmiths, twenty-one were black Americans. Of thirty-three hundred union millwrights, one was black. The ironically named Brotherhood of Electrical Workers Local 5 had one black among its fourteen hundred well-paid members. Low-skill blacks needed to be trained, but there were no black apprentices in the electricians, pipefitters, ironworkers, or plumbers unions.

Meanwhile, white-collar jobs for black men were practically nonexistent in business, finance, real estate, education, and medicine. By the end of World War II, the city's integrated public schools had hired just two full-time black teachers. No black doctor practiced at a local hospital until 1948. In retail, and in any job that interacted with the white public, black employees simply were not accepted. The city's private trolley company and bus lines were all white. So were the staffs of its daily newspapers and dominant radio stations. Department stores, utility companies, hospitals, hotels, and grocery store chains had quotas on black employees or did not hire them at all. It took protest marches organized by the Urban League, the NAACP, and others at Christmas time in 1946 to force the big downtown department stores to finally begin hiring black women as sales clerks.

Legal segregation in housing didn't exist in Pittsburgh, but its urban and suburban neighborhoods were nevertheless segregated. As in other northern cities, real estate agents and private housing developers wrote restrictive covenants into the contracts of white homebuyers that prohibited the resale of their homes to someone of a different race. Federal housing policy enforced segregation by requiring builders to include restrictive covenants in their new developments. White landlords kept their apartment buildings segregated. Less subtly, real estate agents simply would never show a black couple a house for sale in a white suburb.

Other common but no less degrading varieties of Jim Crow–like private discrimination existed throughout Pittsburgh. Black shoppers couldn't try on clothes in downtown department stores. Black baseball fans had to sit in certain sections of Forbes Field, where the Pittsburgh Pirates played. Black kids were expected to swim only in the city's traditionally all-black public swimming pools, and as late as 1945 blacks had to sit in the balcony at neighborhood movie theaters. The best hotels in the city refused black guests no matter how famous, which is why Jackie Robinson, Paul Robeson, Louis Armstrong, and other notable visitors regularly had to stay in the Hill District, the city's largest and most important black neighborhood.

The Hill District occupied the high ground in the center of Pittsburgh, but it was the city's most depressed neighborhood. Nicknamed "Little Harlem" for its nationally famous jazz scene and jumping nightlife, it was a predominately poor but vibrant urban neighborhood of about forty thousand blacks and ten thousand whites. The Hill's disorderly maze of residential streets, business districts, rundown apartments, and junked-up alleys looked over at the stumpy skyline of downtown from a steep but walkable slope. The area was originally settled by immigrants from Ireland, Germany, and Eastern Europe. Blacks began arriving in trickles from the South and elsewhere in the 1880s, but their numbers dramatically swelled after 1910, thanks to a steady stream of rural southern blacks seeking manufacturing jobs. By the late 1940s the Hill District contained the largest concentration of blacks in metropolitan Pittsburgh. It was also home to two dozen nationalities, including Italians, Russian Jews, Greeks, Eastern Europeans, and Syrians.

An unregulated, loosely policed city within the city, the Hill's bustling, self-sustaining, partially subterranean economy provided almost everything its human melting pot needed. Its schools, shopping districts, nightclubs, gambling dens, and whorehouses were integrated. Blacks owned and operated hotels, bars, movie theaters, restaurants, groceries, drugstores, clothing stores, photography studios, florists, bookstores, funeral homes, and social clubs. There was a black YMCA. A cheap, efficient but illegal system of unlicensed cabs called "jitneys" took care of the transit needs of everyone from grandmothers to bar hoppers. Rising above the dense human commerce and poverty were the spires and pointed roofs of two dozen churches and several synagogues.

The Hill District was home to the *Pittsburgh Courier*, the country's largest and most widely distributed black newspaper. But during the 1930s and 40s, it was more famous around the country for two things—baseball and jazz. The Pittsburgh Crawfords and the Homestead Grays, two of the best teams in the history of the professional Negro baseball leagues, were based in the Hill District. Until the integration of Major League Baseball put them out of business, the teams fielded some of the game's greatest players, black or white.

Jazz and the Hill had a long and special relationship. Its black community was an incubator of a dozen seminal musicians including Earl "Fatha" Hines, the father of modern jazz piano, and baritone crooner Billy Eckstine, who in 1947 was poised to become white America's first major black pop singer. And because Pittsburgh was about halfway by train from Chicago to New York, it became a regular stop for the big bands of Count Basie, Duke Ellington, Woody Herman, and stars like Nat King Cole, Billie Holiday, and Ella Fitzgerald. The touring black musicians performed for white audiences in the major hotels downtown or were booked into the Hill's nightclubs and ballrooms, where they jammed all night long.

Unlike venues downtown or in the suburbs, where blacks were usually excluded or made to use their own dance pavilion, the Hill's entertainment complex was colorblind. Its integrated clubs and dancehalls were one of the few places in Pittsburgh where blacks and whites constantly socialized. White jazz fans were greatly outnumbered by blacks, but places like the Savoy Ballroom and the block-long Crawford Grill were packed on weekends with integrated dance crowds from every part of the city. The ballrooms, nightclubs, cabarets, and after-hours bars lining Wylie and Center Avenues kept the Hill's sidewalks lit up and jumping all weekend long.

Despite its energy and glamour, however, by 1947 Little Harlem was in terrible socioeconomic shape. The Lower Hill, where sixty-four hundred black and sixteen hundred white people lived, rented, worked, went to school, and worshipped, was particularly distressed. You could buy everything from refrigerators and Italian ice to marijuana, kosher hot dogs, and live chickens on its teeming streets. Violence was rare. The sidewalks were generally safe for kids, women, old folks, preachers, numbers runners, or a friendly game of craps. Men played checkers outside late into the night and people slept on fire escapes in the summer, but there was nothing romantic about its ratty urban poverty.

The Lower Hill's rough apartments and tenements were overcrowded, rundown, dirty from years of smoke and soot. Part of it was a classic urban slum. Communal faucets in the hallways and outdoor privies were common and private bathrooms were rare. Decades of malign neglect by city hall had made things worse. Streets—many not paved—were maintained poorly at best. Police and fire protection, as well as health and sanitation services, was inadequate.

Making matters worse, many of the Hill District's middle-class blacks and professionals had moved to better black city neighborhoods. Most of the blacks left behind were poor or lower-middle working class. They were maids, garbage men, waitresses, bartenders, musicians, jitney drivers, and small-time criminals. Their everyday hopes and struggles were richly and warmly captured by award-winning playwright August Wilson, who was born on the Hill in 1945. His mother was a black cleaning woman and his father was an immigrant German baker. All but one of his ten plays were set in the Hill District, each in a different decade of the twentieth century. His most famous work, *Fences*, about a former Negro League baseball player who had become a city garbage man in the 1950s, won a 1987 Pulitzer Prize and became a 2016 movie starring Denzel Washington.

The Hill's rich urban culture was preserved journalistically over time by the *Pittsburgh Courier*'s star staff photographer, Charles "Teenie" Harris. He filled the pages of the Pittsburgh edition each week with photos documenting the lives of the Hill's black residents at work and at play. His collection of eighty thousand black-and-white images of everyday people and celebrities, taken on sidewalks and in nightclubs and churches with precision and love from 1935 to 1975, makes up one of the greatest visual records of the black urban experience in mid-century America.

For most of Pittsburgh's older, squarer, law-abiding white population, Little Harlem was an unknown and scary place they'd never dare to go. Along with the great jazz scene, it was where poverty, vice, violence, and black people dwelled. The city's three daily newspapers—the *Press*, the *Post-Gazette*, and *Sun-Telegraph*—had a combined circulation of more than seven hundred thousand a day. Other than small news items about crime, police raids on gambling operations, and house fires, they rarely mentioned the Hill or its "colored" residents.

Like their counterparts across the country, the white editorial staffs of the papers paid about as much attention to black America as they paid to black Africa. They barely covered national or local civil rights topics. They didn't do profiles of black leaders or write reviews of homegrown jazz stars when they came to town. In their sports pages they covered the legendary Homestead Grays and Pittsburgh Crawfords like they were a pair of church-league teams. Black enterprise, black institutions, and black social problems received token attention, at best. If they seriously cared about civil rights, institutionalized racial discrimination, or black workers being automatically shut out of most of the best jobs in their hometown because of their skin color, the white papers didn't editorialize about it.

The white papers didn't care about the Hill District's present or its future. In 1947 city hall was quietly making plans to raze and redevelop Pittsburgh's worst slums, which meant bulldozers and wrecking balls were coming for the unsuspecting people living in the city's poor and politically defenseless neighborhoods. The Hill was the planners' first target and the white newspapers were enthusiastic propagandists and cheerleaders in the brutal crusade for civic progress and urban renewal. To the square white men who made the important decisions in town—the entrenched Democratic Party machine, zillionaire businessman Richard King Mellon, and a handful of lesser Republican corporate honchos, boosters, and newspapermen—the Hill was not hip or culturally exciting. It was not a self-reliant community of hustling people, black and white, who needed to be given a helping hand by government or have their lives improved with new jobs or better housing. It was a cancerous slum that threatened the future growth, health, and beauty of their cosmetically challenged city. Pittsburgh's powerbrokers had plans for a new cultural center for rich white people like themselves and a dozen identical upscale apartment towers. Within a decade a hundred acres of the Lower Hill would be clear-cut to the sidewalks and thousands of people who called it home, most of them poor and black, would be gone without a trace.

In 1936, two months after he left politics and returned to newspapering, Ray Sprigle looked into the origins and inner workings of the Hill District's biggest "industry" and most sophisticated business enterprise—the illegal daily numbers game. It was the only time in his long career that he had dealt in depth with Pittsburgh's black people or their institutions. In his six-part investigation, cheerfully headlined "We've got your number!," Sprigle explained, in his usual entertaining and illuminating way, how the massively popular gambling game worked, how it corrupted the city's politicians and police, and how two black bootleggers got rich after bringing it to Pittsburgh.

During the previous decade betting on the numbers had become a daily ritual in the city's working-class culture, white and black. Similar to gambling games in Italian, Irish, Jewish, and black neighborhoods in cities like New York and Atlanta, it was supported by the nickels, quarters, and dollars of the poor and rich. It involved picking a three-digit number that was randomly generated each afternoon by certain closing sales figures on the New York Stock Exchange. When a gambler placed a nickel or dollar bet with his local numbers writer, his number was written on a slip of paper and picked up by a runner who took the slip and the money to a "numbers bank." The odds of winning were 999 to 1. But if the number picked by the player "hit," a nickel or dollar bet returned a payout of 600 to 1.

In 1936 the numbers rackets flourished throughout the city and suburbs. The Italian Mob and the Jewish Mob had their own operations. But Sprigle said the one on the Hill run by two black "businessmen" was the city's first, largest, and, according to what he had determined, the most honest and most trusted to pay off winners. The numbers game had been imported to western Pennsylvania from the East Coast in the mid-1920s by Hill District bootlegger and restaurant owner Gus Greenlee and his partner, barber William "Woogie" Harris. These "colored businessmen," as Sprigle described them, built a lucrative gambling empire employing hundreds of numbers writers, runners, and pickup men.

Beginning his series like a work of fiction, Sprigle traveled back in time to 1926 to re-create a scene in Morals Court where a judge was trying to figure out what to charge "two colored men" with after they were picked up for writing numbers. The new gambling game was sweeping the Hill District, but there were no statutes against it yet, so the judge fined each of the men fifty dollars for operating a lottery. Sprigle waited until the last few paragraphs before revealing the identity of those two scuffling "colored men" who had to borrow the money to pay their fines. They were numbers barons Harris and Greenlee, who by 1936 had become the Hill District's wealthiest men.

As Sprigle went on to detail, the forty million dollars in pennies, nickels, and dollars (about $680 million today) collected by the numbers rackets between 1926 and 1936 had subsidized the campaigns of many corrupt Pittsburgh politicians and fed millions in graft and protection money to the police. The wealth generated by the game, which had spread from the Hill into every white and black borough and neighborhood in the county, was enormous. When Sprigle wrote his series he estimated that as many as five thousand people—blacks and whites—were working well-paying full- or part-time jobs in the numbers business, which at the time was decentralized, highly competitive, but rarely violent.

Grossing a reported twenty-five thousand dollars per day when the average American salary in the middle of the Great Depression was seventeen hundred dollars a year, Gus Greenlee's operation made him the city's richest black man. To launder his illicit income, "Big Red" became a legitimate businessman, a banker, and a philanthropist. He bought the Crawford Grill and made it a world-famous jazz club and his local headquarters. He owned a stable of professional boxers. He provided mortgages and loans to Hill District residents and businesses who were automatically denied credit by the white banks. He got into local politics, handed out Thanksgiving turkeys, opened a soup kitchen, helped families with college tuition bills, gave money to hospitals, and funded the local branch of the NAACP.

Greenlee was loved and renowned in the Hill District, but he earned his national fame from what he accomplished as an executive in the legitimate world of professional black baseball. After buying the Pittsburgh Crawfords in 1930, he played a leading role in the growth and respectability of the major Negro baseball leagues. To build a powerhouse team he signed stars like legendary catcher Josh Gibson, aka "the Black Babe Ruth," and pitcher Satchel Paige. When the Pittsburgh Pirates wouldn't let his team use the locker rooms at Forbes Field, where they played their home games, he built a seventy-five-hundred-seat lighted baseball field at the top of the Hill for one hundred thousand dollars.

After he quit the numbers in the mid-1930s and turned it over to his partner Woogie Harris, Greenlee supposedly went legit. He guided the Negro baseball league to its greatest heights and largest attendance figures until the mid-1940s. Then, when Branch Rickey, the owner of the Brooklyn Dodgers, was thinking about signing black players, Greenlee was one of the first men he called. The integration of the major leagues put black baseball leagues out of business, and Greenlee spent the rest of his life running his nightclubs and fighting with the IRS over unpaid income taxes. When he died in 1952 after a long illness, *Pittsburgh Courier* sports columnist Wendell Smith said if the "big, robust, dynamic man of Pittsburgh" hadn't come along "there probably wouldn't be a Negro player in the big leagues today."

Sprigle's series showcased his ability to write colorfully and authoritatively about a complicated and serious subject. As always, it was full of his opinions and asides. But it was free of subtle prejudice or racist stereotypes. He thought Gus Greenlee and Woogie Harris were American success stories deserving of the era's romance surrounding self-made businessmen. In the second article of the series, which featured huge photos of each racketeer, Sprigle went out of his way to tout their character and community spirit.

There's nothing high hat about Woogie. He still runs his barbershop as of yore. It is the leading tonsorial parlor in the Hill. Woogie is there every day, no hired managers for him. He meets his friends there and personally sees to it that they get service and courtesy from his barbers. Both Woogie and Gus are leading citizens of the colored community of Allegheny county. They are the first to respond to calls for charity. More than one colored church owes its continued existence to the liberality of Gus or Woogie.

At the end of his lively primer Sprigle didn't hop up on a soapbox and spoil everything by preaching about the sinfulness, criminality, or stupidity of gambling when the odds are 999 to 1 against you. Instead, he used a conversation with a police official to hint that he believed cracking down on a massively popular illegal activity would bring harmful unintended consequences by overwhelming the police and courts and driving the real crooks running the rackets into more harmful criminal activities. Sprigle wrote nothing else about blacks in Pittsburgh or anywhere else after his numbers racket series. Two years later he traveled back and forth several times to Birmingham, Alabama, to prove Hugo Black had been a member of the KKK. He saw how unfairly blacks were treated in that citadel of Jim Crow, but he didn't mention it then or later.

⌐⌐⌐

Writing about black people was as rare for Pittsburgh's three white papers as it was for Sprigle. They were happy to cede the black-American market to the Hill District's most politically influential institution, the *Pittsburgh Courier*. The *Courier*, which had its offices and printing plant on the Hill, was an impressive business success story. In 1947 it was not just the country's largest selling black newspaper. It was also a popular and important source of news and opinion for black Americans in the North and across the South. A weekly, like 99 percent of the nation's mostly much smaller black papers, it published a national edition, a Pittsburgh city edition, and local editions in twelve cities from Detroit and Miami to New York, Los Angeles, and Seattle.

The *Courier* was at the peak of its power and reach. Its total circulation had climbed to nearly four hundred thousand, with each copy said to be passed along to two or three people. Its presses on Center Avenue ran every day. A single copy sold for twelve cents and an annual subscription was five dollars, in advance. It employed four hundred people, had bureaus in Washington and elsewhere, and had correspondents around the country and the world. In India, after reading the reports of the *Courier*'s great World War II correspondent Frank Bolden, Mahatma Gandhi invited Bolden to be his house guest for two weeks.

The *Courier*, the *Chicago Defender*, the *Afro-American* in Baltimore, and the *Journal and Guide* in Norfolk, Virginia, were the largest and healthiest of roughly 175 black papers that collectively reached more than five million black Americans a week. Like the more progressive *Defender* and other black papers, the *Courier* dedicated its news and opinion pages to fighting for black civil rights and equal economic and political opportunity. That meant exposing and protesting discrimination in the North and South, demanding equal job opportunities for blacks, pushing for federal and local civil rights reforms, and pointing out racism and white hypocrisy in politics and the mainstream media.

The *Courier*'s national edition linked urban black Americans into a national market, but it also penetrated into the deepest parts of Dixie. Like other black papers, it was marketed and distributed through an arrangement with the porters of the Brotherhood of Sleeping Car Conductors. Porters on trains sold subscriptions and delivered bundles of the *Courier* to cities and small towns throughout the South, where it was often available on Sundays at black churches. White authorities in Georgia and Alabama, needless to say, did not appreciate the *Courier*'s marketing prowess or its seditious content. To prevent their papers from being seized and burned by county sheriffs and other local supremacists, porters often threw their bundles off the train before they reached the station.

Only in the Jim Crow South could an American think the *Courier* was radical or subversive. It was a patriotic, capitalist, middle-class Republican paper. It didn't endorse or encourage socialism or unions and emphasized economic self-reliance and self-improvement. There was nothing un-American about the conservative values on its masthead— "Work, integrity, tact, temperance, prudence, courage, faith." Its official editorial policy was to inform its readers, not lead them, but the *Courier* was as biased and opinionated as a newspaper could be and still maintain its journalistic credibility.

A 1945 *Fortune* magazine article describing the narrow, subjective, self-interested focus of America's black press fit the *Courier* perfectly.

The pictures in Negro newspapers are of Negroes or of mixed Negro-white groups. The news is news of Jim Crow regulations ...; it is news of Negroes winning scholarships, of Negroes in battle, of Negroes denied commissions, of Negroes running for local office, of Negroes sitting on committees with white men, of white men speaking up for Negroes, of white men embarrassed because they have neglected Negroes. And, except when it is news thus angled, there is no news of national affairs, of the war, of Congress, of the President, of industry. The Negro press deals single-mindedly with the problems of being a Negro in the United States, the prospects, the troubles, the triumphs, and the despairs of all those for whom the fact of being a Negro outweighs, for a part of the time at least, all other concerns.

Serving as a supplement to the national and local news carried in the much larger dailies, the *Courier* covered what black readers wanted but what the white papers in their cities would never provide. Its reporters and correspondents attended southern lynching trials and infiltrated Klan meetings, then passionately reported what they saw and heard. Its editorials and black political columnists discussed the top issues of the day, questioning Truman's commitment to civil rights or criticizing the NAACP's Walter White for being too fond of the New Deal. Floating along the bottom of the front page was "Your Public Conduct," a two-by-four-inch message board of tips like "Neatness is an index to character" or "Rank does not make quality— what you have in you makes you great. Show it!"

The *Courier*'s society pages reported the births, weddings, parties, civic achievements, and deaths of upper- and middle-class blacks in Pittsburgh as well as in other cities like Atlanta. In 1930 a small item announced that John Wesley Dobbs, "one of the best known and most popular men" in Georgia, and his wife were sailing with their daughter Irene to France, where she was to get a master's degree in French. Between 1924 and 1947 the *Courier* had reported more than a dozen times on Dobbs's political or Masonic activities, the accomplishments of his talented daughters, and his visits to Pittsburgh. In 1940, when he attended a conference of southern black leaders, the *Courier* quoted what he said in his speech calling for blacks to be able to serve in the armed forces. "All Negroes love their country. We stand ready to defend her. We want to serve in the Army, in the Navy and in the Air as valiantly as we have served in the cotton patches and on the railroad tracks."

On July 4, 1947, Dobbs was in Richmond, Indiana, speaking to the Shriners, the "fun and fellowship" wing of the white Masons. As high degree Masons, he reminded them, they were obliged to address the economic, political, and social concerns of all Americans. As the *Courier* reported, Dobbs told the Shriners that "people of color particularly were 'demanding the same rights of freedom everywhere—in Mississippi, same as in Minnesota, in South Carolina just like in South Dakota—nothing more or less.' Listing programs that should be of paramount interest to Shriners, Mr. Dobbs called for 'eternal war against racial segregation and discrimination on public carriers and in public places,' increased Governmental aid to housing and farm projects and governmental aid to medicine and hospital facilities."

Though it was engaged in a worthy moral and political crusade for equality, the *Courier* could look and feel like a tabloid. Because it got so few local and national ads, it had to rely on subscriptions and newsstand sales for most of its revenue. Its journalists excelled at sensationalizing its front pages with huge shouting headlines, oversized photos of dead bodies of escaped black prisoners, or pictures of cute kids and sexy swimsuit models.

"U.S. MAY TRY S.C. LYNCHERS," "8 CONVICTS MURDERED!" and "DIXIE 'TERROR REIGN' SPREADS" were some of its Page 1 headlines in 1947. Another was "BARRED FROM HOSPITALS: White Institutions Refuse Dying Athlete," which described how members of the track team from Clark College were denied admittance to white hospitals in Tennessee after their bus was sideswiped by a truck. Sometimes using red-ink headlines and banners, the *Courier* jammed its front page with the news of civil rights victories in the courts, black students who won prizes or scholarships, and Jackie Robinson's every rookie exploit and honor. Its news stories were often followed with one-line bold-faced mini-editorials like "END JIM CROW IN WASHINGTON."

When it came to national politics, the *Courier* was far more conservative and Republican than liberal and Democratic, but it didn't believe in tying itself or the interests of blacks to any single political party or person. The *Courier* was proud to say that in 1932 it had been one of the few black papers with the vision and courage to break from the Party of Lincoln and endorse Democrat Franklin Roosevelt. But by 1940 its owners were unhappy with FDR's neglect of black Americans and the way he kowtowed to the racist southern Democrats that controlled Congress. The *Courier* switched its endorsement to liberal Republican challenger Wendell Willkie, "a man who embraced perhaps the finest type of Americanism of our day and generation."

For the 1944 election, with World War II in the bag and FDR clearly ill, the *Courier* endorsed Republican New York governor Thomas Dewey for president. In a long editorial, "THE PRICE WE PAY," which appeared on the front page of its October 22 national edition, the paper praised Dewey as "honest, fearless, capable and efficient" and said he was "the best man at this time for America and Negro Americans." The editorial worried what would happen if FDR died and his new Border State VP choice, Senator Harry Truman of Missouri, became president. Truman had replaced ultraliberal but loony vice president Henry Wallace on the ticket and was the choice of the big-city bosses and southern Democrats, which, the *Courier* warned, would only mean "MORE SEGREGATION. MORE JIM CROWISM. CONTINUATION OF THE VICIOUS POLL TAX SYSTEM!"

The person responsible for the Dewey endorsement was the same man who had written every one of the *Courier's* unsigned editorials since 1926—the brilliant conservative intellectual George Schuyler. Schuyler (SKY-lar), who lived in New York City, was arguably the country's most talented and prolific black newspaperman from the mid-1920s to the mid-1960s. He has been largely forgotten by blacks and whites. But at one time the *Courier's* star columnist and was the most debate-provoking, most politically incorrect black social commentator and cultural critic in the country.

During the 1920s Schuyler was considered the preeminent satirist of the Harlem Renaissance. In the 1930s he was known as "the Black H. L.

Mencken" for his skepticism, iconoclasm, and political satire. He became widely known among whites and blacks after writing two satirical novels, including the highly praised and much discussed *Black No More*. The 1931 book, premised on the ability of blacks being able to quickly change their skins white, condemns and mocks America's obsession with race. It makes fun of white and black people, skewers the KKK and the NAACP with equal ferocity, and savagely caricatures W. E. B. Du Bois, Marcus Garvey, and other important blacks.

Schuyler was not merely the dominant political and intellectual voice of the *Courier* for forty-four years; he also wrote scores of articles in national magazines, went on speaking tours, and appeared on the radio. In addition to his weekly "Views and Reviews" columns and editorials, he wrote articles for the paper under his own name and pen names, took long investigative trips to Africa and South America for the *Courier*, and traveled by car across the South to carefully report on the conditions and progress of blacks. When he spoke for the *Courier*, Schuyler's most radical opinions were toned down or missing. But under his byline in his columns, he was mercilessly provocative.

Race was his favorite target. He satirized, questioned, or criticized every significant black or white person who had anything to say about the issue. Married to a white woman from Texas, he ridiculed the science and the morality behind anti-miscegenation laws. He believed race was an artificial social construct and argued that it was the individual that mattered, not his skin color or caste. As he said in one column, "it's a pretty good policy not to think so much about a person's color and to think more about his or her character."

There was nothing tame, conforming, simple, or politically correct about what Schuyler thought about race or much else. A recovered Socialist, he disliked communism, socialism, fascism, Western and Soviet imperialism, Zionism, organized religion, FDR, the New Deal, bureaucracy, partisan politics, herd-thinking, hero worship, and mass protests. He assailed Negro intellectuals and elite whites. He accused FDR's agricultural policies of being racist and helping wealthy landowners in the South at the expense of sharecroppers, white and black. Like Booker T. Washington, he believed black Americans, North or South, would achieve the equality and greater progress they sought by succeeding individually in the capitalist free market, not through collective political action, social protest, and federal civil rights legislation. In the 1960s his savage criticism of Martin Luther King Jr. as a Communist-influenced troublemaker and opposition to the civil rights movement in general would end his incredible *Courier* career, wreck his reputation, and make him a pariah to most of his race.

The *Courier*'s news coverage and fearless opinions were always targeted at a black audience, but the paper occasionally influenced white society. Locally, it led successful fights for things like the legalization of a black cab company for the Hill District. Its most notable national campaign occurred early in World War II. Seizing on an idea proposed by a young man in a letter to the editor, the *Courier* created and led the national "Double V" for victory campaign. It put a domestic civil rights spin on the ubiquitous wartime slogan and hand-signal, "V for Victory," which was the Allies' call for winning the fight against Axis aggression, slavery, and tyranny in Europe.

The *Courier*'s "Double V" campaign cleverly—and patriotically—threaded a dangerous wartime needle. It combined the fight black soldiers were waging for freedom overseas with the fight for freedom that blacks still needed to win at home. In his January 31, 1942, letter proposing the double-victory idea, cafeteria worker James G. Thompson of Wichita, Kansas, said that some important questions needed answering.

> Being an American of dark complexion and some 26 years, these questions flash through my mind: "Should I sacrifice my life to live half American?" "Will things be better for the next generation in the peace to follow?" "Would it be demanding too much to demand full citizenship rights in exchange for the sacrificing of my life?" "Is the kind of America I know worth defending?" "Will America be a true and pure democracy after this war?" "Will colored Americans suffer still the indignities that have been heaped upon them in the past?"

The *Courier's* editors took the idea and ran with it. The "Double V" promotion included "VV" logos, lapel pins, posters, and songs and was picked up by other black papers across the country. It was supported by movie stars Humphrey Bogart and Ingrid Bergman, as well as Wendell Willkie. The campaign became so popular and persuasive it almost backfired. The military banned black newspapers from their libraries. The country was at war and, as Schuyler editorialized about, war gives even the most democratic governments the excuse to throw fundamental freedoms into the fire, round up untrustworthy citizens, or see enemies of the state under every other bed. Though a subsequent FBI investigation of black newspapers turned up no signs of disloyalty, J. Edgar Hoover felt the publishers of black papers who took part in the "Double V" campaign were subversives who should have been indicted by the Justice Department for treason.

After the war the *Courier* played a leading role in the campaign by black papers and others to integrate Major League Baseball. Its sportswriter Wendell Smith pushed hard for baseball to drop its racial barrier and recommended Jackie Robinson to Dodgers owner Branch Rickey as the best choice, character-wise, to become the black to break modern baseball's color barrier. Smith, who also went to bat for other black players, later traveled and roomed with Robinson on several Dodger road trips and helped him find lodging in towns where his white teammates stayed in segregated hotels.

When it came to racial matters, the *Courier* didn't pretend to be objective or neutral about war, baseball, or anything else. It mixed facts and straight journalism with biting anti-segregationist commentary and constantly promoted heroic or successful blacks like Joe Louis or the local businessman. An example of how it applied its race-centric spin to news events occurred in Pittsburgh on September 9, 1947, when the downtown business district was rocked at lunchtime by a tremendous explosion that shattered office windows, set cars on fire, and knocked down pedestrians a block away. The *Island Queen*, the largest river excursion boat in the world and capable of carrying four thousand passengers, had blown up while it was moored at a wharf on the Monongahela River. A welder had accidentally ignited the oil in the ship's fuel tank. No passengers were on board. But nineteen crewmen died and eighteen were injured in the explosion and fire that quickly consumed the luxurious steel and glass-enclosed pleasure ship.

For days the *Pittsburgh Press*, the *Pittsburgh Sun-Telegraph*, and the *Post-Gazette* plastered their front pages with photos and stories about underwater divers and salvage crews searching the twisted hulk for the charred remains of the missing. The papers didn't point out that six of the nineteen dead crewmen were black, or that the opulent Cincinnati-based cruise ship was for white passengers only, but the *Courier* did. In "6 Killed in Luxury Boat Explosion: Lily-White Steamer Blows Up at Dock as Thousands Look On," it praised the two heroic black Pittsburgh police officers who risked their lives to pull the dead and injured from a burning river boat that "virtually flew the scarlet, hated flag of segregation and jim-crowism."

Chapter 4

"Mr. NAACP"

A lot of Pittsburghers were unpleasantly surprised during their dinners when an unfamiliar voice with a slight southern accent suddenly popped from their Philco console radios. The regularly scheduled program on KDKA at 6:15 p.m. was "Supper Music," a fifteen-minute block of gentle background noise. Before anyone with an addiction to dinner music had time to leap from the table and turn the knob to "Song Time" on WCAE, a serious man started blabbing at them about segregation in the South, discrimination against Negroes, and the string of Supreme Court cases his civil rights organization had won.

Most of KDKA's regular listeners were white. They had no idea why the executive secretary of the National Association for the Advancement of Colored People was being interviewed on their favorite radio station. The NAACP had nothing to do with their lives. Even if they read their morning and afternoon papers every day, they had probably never heard of Walter F. White or seen his photo. In the previous twelve months his name had not appeared once in the *Pittsburgh Post-Gazette*, the liberal-minded morning paper, and it had appeared in just a single news story in the *Pittsburgh Press*, the working-class afternoon daily. The *Pittsburgh Courier* carried a story about White and the NAACP in almost every issue, but white people didn't read black papers.

White had been asked to come to Pittsburgh by the head of the local NAACP branch to boost the morale of its 2,813 members. He was going to speak to as many of them as possible at a mass meeting later that evening at the Central Baptist Church in the heart of the Hill District.

It was a PR coup for the local branch to get fifteen free minutes of airtime for White on the most popular radio station in Pittsburgh, but "Mr. NAACP" deserved it.

Though he was far from a white household name, White was at the peak of his amazingly successful career. Since taking charge of the NAACP in 1931, he had built it into the country's top civil rights organization. It had grown to nearly 580,000 members and mounted dozens of legal, legislative, and publicity campaigns to fight racial discrimination, stop lynchings and mob violence in the South, end segregation in the US military, and stamp out racial stereotypes in Hollywood movies. The public face of the NAACP, White was a one-man lobby for black Americans and a tireless crusader for winning their full civil rights in the South and North.

During his sixteen years with the organization, he had given thousands of speeches around the country. He had personally sweet-talked, pleaded with, pressured, and extracted promises and pledges from presidents, congressmen, army generals, business executives, and movie moguls. If the Pittsburghers whose suppers were being interrupted could have seen what the fifty-four-year-old White looked like, they would have been very confused. Mr. NAACP's eyes were blue, his graying hair was once blond, and he was whiter looking than most of the white people they knew. White was less than one-fourth black, but he had been raised as a middle-class Negro in Atlanta and had chosen to live his life as one. His skin was so pale he could easily infiltrate the Ku Klux Klan—which is exactly what he did more than once in the 1920s.

Before he rose to become the NAACP's national director, White had been its top undercover investigator. It was his Caucasian looks, courage, and easygoing nature that allowed him to venture into rural areas and small towns following a lynching, pretend to be white, and gather key information from klansmen and other locals that could have gotten him killed if he was found out. A small, slight man who packed a .45 for protection, he investigated forty-one lynchings and eight race riots. White described some of his most harrowing adventures in "I Investigate Lynchings," which appeared in the January 1929 issue of the *American Mercury*, the weighty intellectual magazine edited by H. L. Mencken.

White was a prolific writer and skilled propagandist whose tireless civil rights work had not gone unnoticed. He had been on the cover of *Time* in 1938 and been damned by segregationist politicians on the floor of the US Senate. By the fall of 1947, however, he was much better known for what he did than what he wrote. John Gunther, the great journalist who had toured every state for his encyclopedic book *Inside U.S.A.*, included him among the sixty-four men who ran America. White scoffed at that personal honor, saying with false modesty that he was chosen as a symbol of both the progress made by Negros and "the growing intelligence of Americans on racial issues and their increased acceptance of the Negro as an integral part of the American commonwealth."

Mr. NAACP may not have been one of the men running America, but he knew most of those who did. He lived in Harlem, home to half of New York City's seven hundred thousand blacks, in the elite and wealthy "Sugar Hill" neighborhood with the likes of Duke Ellington, Thurgood Marshall, and NAACP founder W. E. B. Du Bois. (Regarding Harlem and New York City, John Gunther remarked that there was less discrimination against blacks there than in any other city in the country. "They have better chances in education, jobs, social evolution, and civil service," he said. "They are the nearest to full citizenship of any in the nation.") White was also a close friend of Wendell Willkie, the ex-Democrat turned liberal Republican presidential candidate who, after being crushed by FDR in 1940, became an enthusiastic supporter of White's lifelong quest to end segregation in America.

In time, White had gained access to the highest government places. During the war he often visited FDR and Truman in the White House to urge them to integrate the military or use federal power to end discrimination in jobs, housing, and schools. More importantly, he was a friend, close adviser, and conspiratorial ally of Eleanor Roosevelt, the country's most visible white civil rights warrior and a member of the NAACP's national board. As first lady, Mrs. Roosevelt had become an outspoken public champion of racial equality and a lonesome, nagging conscience for black issues behind White House doors. During the buildup to World War II, for instance, she, White, and other national black leaders, including A. Philip Randolph, the charismatic and tough president of the Brotherhood of Sleeping Car Porters, joined forces to persuade President Roosevelt to outlaw discrimination against blacks in the armed forces, defense industries, and the new government agencies spawned by the New Deal.

In 1940 hundreds of thousands of new jobs making bombers, tanks, and warships were closed to blacks. They were specifically excluded from government-initiated training programs because they were thought to be untrainable and fit only for labor gangs or janitorial work. Meanwhile, the expanding armed forces were almost entirely white. In the half-million-man Army of 1940, there were forty-seven hundred blacks in four segregated units. Of these, there were only twelve black officers. In 1939, every one of the Navy's 2,807 black enlisted men was either a waiter in dining quarters or kitchen personnel, and all of the Navy's 19,477 officers were white. The US Marines, the Tank Corps, the Signal Corps, and the Army Air Corps had no black men in their ranks.

To meet the manpower needs of the war more blacks were drafted or allowed to enlist in the Army and Navy, but black Americans were not thought by the military brass to have the physical, mental, or moral character for combat. Still, about a thousand black men died in the fighting, most serving in all-black non-combat units. By V-J Day, approximately 1.2 million were in military service. They dug ditches, served meals, drove trucks, and supported all-white fighting units; most were trained in segregated camps in the Deep South. When the war was over, the armed forces were still segregated in every way. As historian Stephen Ambrose said in his book *Citizen Soldiers*, the irony of American soldiers fighting "the world's worst racist, Adolph Hitler, in the world's most segregated army" was too obvious to be missed.

After World War II, Walter White and Mrs. Roosevelt went to work on Harry Truman to secure the civil rights goals that were sidetracked or put on hold by the war: the desegregation of the military, the end of legal segregation in the South, and the passage of federal legislation to outlaw racial discrimination in hiring, housing, and voting. Though never considered a liberal on race or civil rights issues, Truman, falsely accused of being a former member of the KKK, was serious about ending the prejudice and inequality black Americans faced in the Jim Crow South and elsewhere.

In September of 1946 White and other civil rights activists went to see Truman at the White House. White shocked the president with details of recent lynchings in Georgia and Louisiana and the gruesome violence directed against returning black World War II soldiers who had the impertinence to want to vote in the Deep South. Apparently, Truman knew almost nothing about the degree of bigotry or hardship blacks faced in the South. White said in his 1948 autobiography, *A Man Called White*, that the president's response was, "My God! I had no idea it was as terrible as that. We've got to do something!"

Several months later, Truman formed the President's Committee on Civil Rights. Its mission was to identify discrimination wherever it existed in the country and recommend how to end it. "I want our Bill of Rights implemented in fact," he instructed the committee. "We have been trying to do this for 150 years. We're making progress, but we're not making progress fast enough." While Truman's blue-ribbon committee did its work, White kept the slow federal desegregation train on track. He invited Truman to appear before the NAACP's annual convention in Washington and urged him to make an important speech on civil rights. Truman agreed that eliminating discrimination in America was the fair and right thing to do, but the politics were tricky—especially for a battered president who already looked destined for early retirement.

Championing civil rights from the White House may have been several decades overdue, but it created serious political risks for Truman and the Democratic Party. If the president pushed too hard, it would enrage the white Democratic voters of the South. It would also blow up the winning coalition FDR had cleverly put together: labor unions, city political machines, blue-collar workers, farmers, southern states, and liberal intellectuals. In presidential elections Democrats would no longer be able to count on getting all of the Electoral College votes from the "Solid South." If Truman were genuinely serious about advancing a civil rights agenda, he would have to figure out how to hold on to the White House without the help of his party's fundamentalist segregationists.

White was probably not telling the president anything he didn't already know when he made the argument that the timing was right to dump the party's morally challenged southern wing. By 1947, thanks to the Great Migration, there were 2.5 million black voters living in northern cities; White and the NAACP believed blacks could hold the balance of power in key states like Illinois in the coming presidential election. Outlawing segregation and other forms of discrimination against blacks by federal decree would have another benefit, White argued. It would strengthen Truman's anti-Communist foreign policy. The Soviets and other despotic nations would no longer be able to use America's flagrant discrimination against its own minorities to discredit and weaken its moral authority in the United Nations and overseas.

White's lobbying paid dividends. On Sunday afternoon, June 29, 1947, President Truman and Eleanor Roosevelt rode from the White House to the Lincoln Memorial, where he was to address the closing session of the NAACP's thirty-eighth annual conference. The president, Mrs. Roosevelt, and White walked together to the top of the memorial steps. Waiting there, facing an integrated crowd of more than ten thousand, were the national media, liberal Republican senator Wayne Morse of Oregon, Supreme Court chief justice Fred Vinson, the Marine Band, and assorted dignitaries and guests.

Mrs. Roosevelt and Morse spoke first. Then it was White's turn. After listing his association's many legal and legislative successes in the fight for civil rights, he asked the ambassadors of other countries in attendance "to tell your countrymen that although the stories of lynching and denial of justice to Americans because of race, creed or national origin are tragically true, those outrages do not accurately represent the majority of American citizens." It was a strong but positive speech delivered in a clear, throaty, slightly black-sounding southern accent. White noted the substantial progress on civil rights that had been made, but said the NAACP believed "there will never be complete equality until the courts and America abandon the myth of separate but equal accommodations."

White then introduced Harry S Truman, the first president ever to address the NAACP. Blending advice and input from White, Mrs. Roosevelt, and others with his own sense of fairness and contempt for discrimination, Truman said it was time to guarantee the "civil rights and human freedom" of every American. Quoting Lincoln, mentioning Mrs. Roosevelt, paying honor to the ideals of the Declaration of Independence, the Constitution, the Bill of Rights, the Emancipation Proclamation, and promising certain entitlements courtesy of the modern welfare state, Truman, the plainspoken man from Missouri who still casually dropped the n-word into his private conversations, staked his claim as the first modern civil rights president.

> We must make the Federal Government a friendly, vigilant defender of the rights and equalities of all Americans. And again I mean all Americans.
>
> As Americans, we believe that every man should be free to live his life as he wishes. He should be limited only by his responsibility to his fellow countrymen. If this freedom is to be more than a dream, each man must be guaranteed equality of opportunity. The only limit to an American's achievement should be his ability, his industry and his character. The rewards for his effort should be determined only by these truly relevant qualities.
>
> Our immediate task is to remove the last remnants of the barriers, which stand between millions of our citizens and their birthright. There is no justifiable reason for discrimination because of ancestry, or religion. Or race, or color.

After pledging his support for securing the equal civil rights of every citizen, Truman said, "We cannot wait another decade or another generation to remedy these evils. We must work, as never before, to cure them now. The aftermath of war and the desire to keep faith with our Nation's historic principles make the need a pressing one." He never said the word "Negro." His twelve-minute address was slyly vague and understated, but the world heard his message. It was delivered during radio primetime—late afternoon. The major networks—CBS, NBC, ABC, and Mutual—and most independent stations broadcast the speeches of White and Truman live from coast to coast. The State Department beamed their words overseas via short wave.

Several of Truman's best lines drew moderate applause from the crowd, praise that could be heard through the radio. White was slightly disappointed that the speech's conclusion was followed by "hearty but not overwhelming" applause, but nevertheless he was pleased. Tens of millions of people, including black American soldiers stationed on the island of Tinian, heard the president of the United States promise to wage a war against bigotry and inequality in his own country. White claimed in his autobiography that it "was by far the largest single audience in history to hear the story of the fight for freedom for the Negro in the United States."

The next day the white northern press did its job, more or less, to publicize news of Truman's surprise civil rights pledge. The top front-page story on June 30 for many smaller papers, and larger ones like the *St. Louis Post-Dispatch*, was not about civil rights. It was about Truman's decision that day to sign a bill extending federal rent controls. The *Chicago Daily Tribune* hid "Truman Seeks Improved Laws on Civil Rights," its abbreviated Associated Press wire service story, on Page 21. The *Pittsburgh Post-Gazette* did a much better job, placing its coverage of Truman's speech on top of Page 2 with a great photograph taken from above and behind the president as he looked out over the crowd. But the editors of the *New York Times* clearly recognized history as it was being made. They placed "Truman Demands We Fight Harder to Spur Equality" on Page 1, quoted Truman extensively, and generously quoted Walter White and Mrs. Roosevelt as well. The article was accompanied by a full transcript of the president's speech.

Later that week the *Pittsburgh Courier*'s national edition spared no ink and little ballyhoo in carrying the historic news to black America. Across the top of the front page, under the huge all-capitalized headline "TRUMAN RAPS PREJUDICE," its Washington correspondent wrote, "Lashing out at backward states and communities which failed to safeguard the rights of ALL AMERICANS, President Truman condemned the twin evils of race prejudice and segregation Sunday afternoon in a nationwide radio address. . . . The president recognized the grip mob rule has on certain sections of the country and urged teeth for federal laws to effectively meet the evil."

Walter White's speech and those of Senator Morse and Mrs. Roosevelt were amply quoted in the *Courier*. In its photo of Truman at the top of the Lincoln Memorial steps, Walter White sits only a few feet behind the president. White said in his autobiography that as the president sat down next to him he asked how he liked the speech. After White told him he thought it was excellent, Truman replied, "I said what I did because I mean every word of it—and I'm going to prove that I do mean it."

❧

KDKA was presenting White as a public service. Though the interview sounded like a spontaneous news Q&A, it wasn't. His questioner was *Pittsburgh Courier* executive editor P. L. Prattis, a seasoned and highly respected journalist who saw no conflict of interest in also being a local NAACP official. In what was essentially a free infomercial from KDKA, White explained to the radio audience that the NAACP was a nonpartisan organization whose members were composed of all races, creeds, colors, and political beliefs. Its national headquarters were in New York City, where he lived in Harlem, plus it had offices in Washington and Los Angeles and 1,509 local branches.

The NAACP's work, White expounded, was divided roughly into three categories: educational, legal, and legislative. By educational, White meant informing white Americans about the true nature of black Americans. Reinforcing what Gunnar Myrdal had written in *An American Dilemma*, White said that, because of segregation, many Americans held "an altogether erroneous picture of the Negro as being a comic, menial or shiftless character." Overcoming that stereotype by correcting false or prejudicial statements about Negroes and publicizing the accomplishments of black artists, scientists, and businessmen, he said, was one of the NAACP's important jobs.

In his explanation, White singled out the "traditional discrimination" blacks faced in obtaining a quality education as "one of the greatest of the Negro's handicaps." Nine million of the country's fourteen million blacks still lived in states where segregated schools were required by law. And that, he said, "always means inferior facilities and the expenditure on Negro schools of one-fourth or less from public tax monies of the amount spent for the education of whites." He also touched on the importance of the NAACP's recent victory in the Supreme Court's sweeping decision to outlaw the South's white-only primary elections, which were designed to disenfranchise blacks. "As a result," he said, "in the more enlightened Southern states, Negroes are now voting with a remarkable freedom and even in some backward states those who share the beliefs of the late Senator Bilbo are recognizing that they cannot much longer keep the Negro from the polls."

The name "Senator Bilbo" needed no explanation for KDKA's more informed listeners, white or black. It was a passing reference to the notorious US senator from Mississippi who had died a month earlier. A fiery orator, ex-governor, and proud member of the KKK, Theodore Bilbo was a faithful representative of the primitive values and fears of the white voters of Mississippi. He regularly filibustered civil rights bills in the Senate, where he was free to flaunt his uncensored racism without shame or fear of being impeached.

Bilbo was such a flagrant and ugly racist that his last name had become synonymous with southern white supremacy and bigotry. It was not by accident that "Senator Bilbo" was dropped into the script of *Gentleman's Agreement*, the acclaimed 1947 Academy Award–winning movie about anti-Semitism in New York City and upscale Connecticut. Even if they recognized Bilbo, few of KDKA's white listeners were aware of the depths of his racism or what his presence in the US Senate for twelve years said about America's political system and the white voters of Mississippi who elected him. Yet White didn't beat up on Bilbo or the South for their public or private sins. Instead he paid tribute to the white southerners who were writing him letters of approval or who were supporting the NAACP's legal campaigns to "equalize" the pay of black teachers and per-student expenditures with white schools.

When Prattis asked about the NAACP's legal and legislative successes, White rattled off an impressive list that demonstrated how hyperactive his association was and on how many fronts it was fighting in the civil rights battle.

> We have won twenty-two of twenty-four cases, involving basic citizenship rights, in the Supreme Court, including the right to a fair trial in a court not dominated by mob hysteria, residential segregation, the right to vote and the right to equal pay for equal work. At the October term, we shall argue a case involving not only Negroes, but other minorities. This covers restrictive covenants in deeds to property by means of which individual property owners enter into private agreements, which they ask the courts to enforce in violation of the Fourteenth Amendment. As for our legislative program, we actively support federal aid to education and health, anti-lynching, anti–poll tax, Fair Employment Practice and all other legislation which affects the Negro, not as a Negro but as an American citizen.

Throughout the interview, White was generally upbeat and optimistic about the future of the civil rights struggle and the improving economic and political conditions for blacks in the South. No one will ever know how many white Pittsburghers listened to White's interview in its entirety or what they thought about it. But if Mr. NAACP hadn't been given his free airtime on KDKA, the white people of metropolitan Pittsburgh never would have known he passed through their midst. Despite Prattis's efforts to drum up publicity, the three daily papers didn't mention White was coming. They didn't interview him or report what he said in his pep talk to the hundreds of NAACP faithful who packed Central Baptist Church's sanctuary to hear him. The only one-on-one encounter the country's most effective civil rights leader had with the mainstream white press during his whistle stop in Pittsburgh was the secret meeting he had earlier that day with its greatest newsman, Ray Sprigle.

CHAPTER 5

Learning to Become a Negro

For six months Ray Sprigle had been thinking about doing another of his patented undercover stories. The idea that came to him was to travel through the Deep South for thirty days—posing as a black man—and report what life was like for the ten million black Americans living under Jim Crow. His motives were purely journalistic. He wasn't an early civil rights crusader or even a liberal Republican; he was a seasoned newsman looking for a great story to tell. As he later told *Editor & Publisher*, "I wanted to find out what the Negro thought and I knew the best way to do it was to pose as a Negro."

In nearly forty years as a reporter and editor, Sprigle had shown little interest in black Americans or their problems. Other than his 1936 series on Gus Greenlee and the numbers racket in the Hill District, he had written practically nothing. He had made scores of trips through the South, but was as ignorant of Jim Crow as the rest of the North. As he said, he had always traveled in the white world. In 1937 he had seen segregation at its meanest when he was investigating Hugo Black's KKK past in Birmingham, but that was for only five days. He owned hundreds of books yet hadn't read Gunnar Myrdal's *An American Dilemma: The Negro Problem and American Democracy*. He had heard a few horror stories about returning World War II soldiers being beaten and even killed in the Deep South because they sought to vote or tried to assert their rights. When it came down to it though, his motivation for wanting to publicize the plight of black Americans was not complicated. He had always been a friend of the underdog and ten million of them were living below the Mason-Dixon Line.

For an old newsman with muckraking in his heart, the Jim Crow idea was a no-brainer. With his speech on the steps of the Lincoln Memorial, President Truman had put the issue of civil rights on the front page of the *New York Times*. The routine legal, social, and economic abuse of millions of citizens in the South by their own governments for sixty years was not news, sadly, but it was an ongoing American travesty. It had been crying out for an in-depth, first-person exposé by a skilled writer and reporter, yet no major northern newspaper or magazine had ever done one.

Going undercover came naturally to Sprigle: His trademark was pretending to be someone else, infiltrating a closed or specialized subculture, and then reporting what he found. He knew he'd get great material if he snuck into the Jim Crow South. Though it would be his most ambitious and potentially most dangerous secret mission, he was prepared. His health was pretty good, and his mind was as sharp as ever. He weighed nearly 220 pounds and ate lustily, but he was in decent physical shape thanks to his weekend chores as a "gentleman farmer." Most important, at sixty-one he still had his youthful thirst for adventure and hadn't lost his itch to make trouble.

Sprigle had already persuaded his reluctant bosses, *Pittsburgh Post-Gazette* publisher Bill Block and editor Andrew Bernhard, that he could come up with a proper disguise and not get himself hurt or killed. Now, as he began to seek ways to stain his white Pennsylvania Dutch skin black, or at least brown or bronze, he needed the blessing and help of Walter White and the NAACP.

Sometime in the late afternoon, before White went to KDKA's studios for his radio interview, Sprigle met with him at a small three-story brick apartment building in the Hill District. Also there was Ira Lewis, the president of the *Pittsburgh Courier*. White knew exactly who Sprigle was—he held no grudge against the newsman who had caused him and his good friend, Supreme Court justice Hugo Black, so much trouble ten years earlier.

Sprigle and White didn't know each other personally, but in 1937 they had each been key players on opposite sides of the controversy over the Alabama senator's appointment to the Supreme Court by FDR. After Sprigle's series of syndicated front-page articles shocked the entire country with proof that Justice Black had been a member of the KKK, civil rights leaders and the black press immediately demanded that he resign from the high court only weeks after he was confirmed. It became the biggest news story of the year and would earn Sprigle his Pulitzer. Amid the controversy, Justice Black took off to England on a "vacation" to avoid the press. In the ensuing transatlantic media circus, which Sprigle joined and the new justice did his best to dodge, Black was asked by the *Baltimore Sun* if he had any lingering affinity for the Klan's core principles. His retort was that his secretary was a Catholic, his law clerk was a Jew, and one of his closest friends was "Walter White of the NAACP."

Overnight White became the center of the circus. Besieged by reporters, he strongly defended Black and said he thought he'd make an able justice. White and the NAACP took a lot of heat from their friends and allies, but White knew Black well. He had dealt often with him when the justice was in the Senate and he had a good handle on his views on racial, economic, and political issues. It was true Black had voted in lockstep with the other southern senators, working to kill anti-lynching bills and happily taking part in civil rights filibusters. But White felt he was at heart a fair-minded Alabama lawyer who had made amends in the US Senate for the intimacy he had with the KKK early in his political career. As White wrote in *A Man Called White*, in the Senate Black never "descended to the cruel and cheap vilification of the Negro of which most of his Dixie colleagues were guilty."

While White and the NAACP obviously disagreed with Senator Black's argument that federal anti-lynching laws were unconstitutional because they impinged on the rights of states, White thought Black was honest about his beliefs and not a racist. His KKK ties were not automatic deal-killers. Everyone at the time knew that no one was elected dog-catcher in 1920s Alabama without pandering to the Klan. White thought Black was the first of a new breed of liberal southern politicians. He wrote that his "superiority of intellect and character over most of his colleagues from the South" was so obvious that to him he seemed "to be an advance guard of the new South we dreamed of and hoped for when that section of the country emancipated itself from the racial, economic, and political bondage which fear, prejudice, and a regional inferiority complex had created." White believed Black's relatively liberal views would make him sympathetic to civil rights issues as a Supreme Court justice. He turned out to be right, and since 1937 he and Justice Black had become close personal friends.

The apartment building where Sprigle and White had their clandestine meeting was owned by Daisy Lampkin, the national field secretary of the NAACP and a lifetime activist in the civil rights and suffragette movements. She always kept one of her units vacant so that notables like her friend White had a nice place to stay when they came to town. Lampkin, in her mid-sixties, was one of Pittsburgh's most accomplished black citizens. She was a dynamo recognized throughout the national civil rights movement for her great oratory, her superior fund-raising and recruiting skills, her organizing abilities, and her huge hats. She had helped to found the Pittsburgh chapter of the NAACP and was a longtime vice president of the *Pittsburgh Courier*. In 1924, when a group of black leaders met with President Calvin Coolidge at the White House, she was the only woman in the room.

When White heard Sprigle's idea, he jumped at the chance to help. The PR benefits of having one of the most famous white reporters in the country expose the conditions blacks faced in the segregated South would be enormous. White would have no trouble finding Sprigle someone to guide him safely and discreetly through every level of black society. The toughest problem Sprigle faced, or so Sprigle thought, was how to pass as a black man. His German-American skin burned much better than it tanned. But White told Sprigle not to worry too much about acquiring a darker color. Tens of thousands of Negros in America were light-skinned or had European looks. White's own skin was as pale as Sprigle's, yet he was accepted as a Negro everywhere he went. If you tell people in the South you are a Negro and behave like you are one, he told Sprigle, nobody with white skin will argue with you.

There's no written record of what Sprigle and White discussed at Lampkin's apartment, but a week after their meeting, on October 2, 1947, White told Sprigle in a letter that he had asked his brother-in-law, Eugene Martin, to find the newsman a guide. Martin, a graduate of Atlanta University, was the wealthy vice president of the Atlanta Life Insurance Company, a successful black-owned company that sold low-cost insurance door-to-door to blacks in seventeen states. After urging Sprigle to let him know if there was anything else he could do to help, White wrote, "It is an exciting idea and if it turns out one-half as well as you and I hope, I predict for you another Pulitzer prize."

White wasn't just blowing smoke in Sprigle's direction. That same day, he wrote to his brother-in-law Eugene Martin, "Here is one of the most exciting ideas I have run across in a long time and I hope it titillates you as it did me. I had a long talk with Ray Sprigle in Pittsburgh when I was there last week to speak. I believe the kind of story he plans and is capable of doing will be a sensation. So far as I know, nothing like it has ever been done before. So, won't you give your best thought and assistance to the project, writing Mr. Sprigle directly? . . . As for his background, he is the famous Ray Sprigle who won the Pulitzer prize for exposing the Ku Klux Klan and Hugo Black's membership in the organization."

White's brother-in-law wasted no time contacting Sprigle. He suggested that Mr. J. Richardson Jones, Atlanta Life's former publicity director, would make a perfect guide. "He not only knows the race problem, but has displayed unusual ability in social and public relations in a practical way, as pertains to the races. He is affable and pleasant, and you will have no dull moments in traveling with him." In their exchange of letters, Martin advised Sprigle to work out his itinerary well in advance. "You see," he wrote, explaining how difficult traveling by car in the South was for blacks, "stopping places for Negroes are often harder to obtain than stopping places for whites. Our travelling men usually write ahead and even then they have trouble finding a decent place to stop."

Sprigle told Martin he was having a great deal of trouble finding a safe way to darken his skin. First, he said, he tried dyeing a square foot of his Nordic chest with "that old reliable stain of boyhood memory, the juice of walnut hulls." The juice worked, except that after a day or two his darkened skin fell off. After recovering from that experiment, and before consulting a pair of chemists, Sprigle experimented on himself with iodine, Argyrol, pyrogallic acid, and potassium permanganate. They each stained his skin, but if he perspired he'd find himself "striped like a tiger or spotted like a leopard."

Martin got a laugh out of Sprigle's efforts. "You see," he wrote, "I have never realized before what a real problem it is for a white man to become a Negro." He was pleased to see Sprigle was interested in darkening his skin so he could get down to "the grass roots" and "get into the thick of things as a Negro." He agreed that Sprigle needed "a little tan of some kind to step down suspicion as to your racial identity. I know this to be true, for we are often having fun or pathos over the incidents that often happen to members of our race who are mistaken for whites. Many of them are so fair that it is hard for either race to believe they are Negroes, and there is often suspicion both ways if they are strangers."

A simpler and safer solution for becoming less white, Martin suggested, was getting a deep suntan. He had seen many persons at the beach that previous summer who "had gotten such excellent sun tans that they would have little trouble in passing for Negroes. I saw one life guard who was almost brown." Martin agreed that a little colorizing would help Sprigle's chances of passing for a light-skinned black man. But he said it was much more important that he be able "to really act the part of a Negro. You possibly know that high treason in the South, and the thing Negroes get in trouble about, is a show of a little manhood. In spite of great progress, the hang-over of slavery is so great that even Negro women and men are not accorded the courtesy of Mr. and Mrs. by the superior race. Most assuredly your problem is not so much color or lack of color as it will be mannerism."

Martin was excited about Sprigle's project and believed it could "result in much good to many people." Though he warned "You're going to learn that it's hell to be a Negro in the South," he thought it would be "fraught with more fun than danger, unless you should forget that you were a Negro and disobeyed the segregation ordinances of the South." Martin was a life insurance executive, but Sprigle would have been impressed by his writing and his sense of adventure. "Segregation is, of course, nothing more or less than the extended arm of slavery, a caste system that circumscribes the life and liberty of the Negro and the darker races of men. I believe you will get great fun out of the project, for what can be more thrilling than to be in the thick of a great fight, a noble cause, rather than on the sideline looking on?"

By the end of October Sprigle was consulting with two chemists who must have thought he was nuts. They gave him a list of possible stains and dyes to use on his skin. When told a solution made by boiling mahogany bark might work, Sprigle ordered a hundred pounds of it from Central America; the gunnysacks filled with bark sat on his porch for years. The various chemicals sounded deadly but were not particularly dangerous, a chemist said, but they affected everyone differently. A staining dye called "methyl phenylene diamine sulphate" would create a shade somewhere between brown and black, depending on its concentration. The developing chemicals used by newspaper photographers in their darkrooms could also work, depending on a person's sensitivity.

"Whatever you do," the chemist cautioned, "run a patch test on some sensitive part such as the inside of the arm, by moistening a piece of cotton with the proposed solution, squeezing it almost dry and taping it on for 48 hours. If some of the things suggested should happen to make you sensitive you might turn into the fellow who fell into the poison ivy patch face down." Actually, as Sprigle learned later, and after he decided a deep Florida tan was the best method, "there was one little drawback" to those chemical potions. "It seems that if you covered yourself thoroughly with one of them you'd find yourself thoroughly dead in from 15 minutes to 15 days, depending upon your resistance."

At the last minute it turned out, for reasons unknown, that Mr. Jones, Atlanta Life's former PR man, could not serve as Sprigle's guide. In the spring of 1948, as Sprigle was getting ready to fly down to St. Petersburg for three weeks to grill his tender skin dark brown, Eugene Martin had to find a suitable replacement for Mr. Jones in a hurry. He reached out to Grand Master John Wesley Dobbs, the head of Georgia's Prince Hall Masons and one of black Atlanta's most venerable political and civic leaders. Martin sent a special delivery letter to his friend asking if he'd be willing to help Sprigle.

Dobbs was staying at the Pythian Bath House in Hot Springs, Arkansas, and immediately whipped off a four-page handwritten letter on official Prince Hall stationery. Saying he was "inclined to accept the proposition," he added that he thought the project "is feasible, possible, necessary, and ultimately, highly important and useful in getting nearer the truth of conditions in our country." Noting that he owned a 1947 Mercury with seventy-five hundred miles on it, Dobbs said that "in driving the gentleman around with me, he would be fully protected. He could be a friend or distant relative. My mother's father was a white man, naturally there are relatives on that side. Nobody would question my word about it. I know the people and, as suggested, would do most of the talking. I don't think there would be anything to worry about along that line."

Dobbs warned Martin that "This matter must be kept a profound secret until over." Then he accepted the same financial arrangements offered to Mr. Jones: five hundred dollars for a month (five thousand dollars in today's money). "I am willing to take the gentleman around with me," said Grand Master Dobbs, whose Prince Hall duties, political activism, and career as a traveling public speaker had given him a network of black professionals from Savannah to the Delta. "I will look after his protection and security if he will be willing to endure the hardship of accommodations that we will face in cheap hotels and private boarding houses." He didn't think there was any need to start the trip in Pittsburgh. He could pick Sprigle up in Florida when "the tanning" was over and begin there, or they could meet in Washington, DC, where he was scheduled to be for official Prince Hall business in early May.

On April 1, a few minutes after Martin's secretary finished typing a letter to Sprigle telling him he had recruited Dobbs, Sprigle called from Pittsburgh. Martin described Dobbs's qualifications and personality over the phone and assured Sprigle that he was "a very excellent man to help out in this interesting project." Martin said Dobbs had many contacts in the little towns as well as the big cities, and he knew "how to talk with all classes of people and get them to talk with him." In a handwritten note attached to his typed letter, Martin wrote, "I'm glad you wish a person who can talk. Mr. Dobbs loves to talk and he usually says something when he talks. . . . Mr. Dobbs is congenial, pleasant and light brown in color."

Sprigle's primary color, despite his chemistry research and self-testing, was still pale white. He had given up trying to stain his skin and, two weeks later, he rode a train a thousand miles straight south from his farmhouse to St. Petersburg, on the west coast of central Florida. He booked lodging at the modest Carleve Hotel, where fully appointed rooms with showers went for about nine dollars a night. Billed as the most modern hotel in "The Sunshine City," it didn't have a pool or air-conditioning and was closed between May 1 and November 1, but it got lots of sun and was just three blocks from Tampa Bay. Like almost every Florida hotel, the Carleve made it clear that its clientele was "restricted," which every seasoned traveler and anyone who'd seen the movie *Gentleman's Agreement* knew meant Jews were not accepted. As for any black person, it was a given that the state's Jim Crow rules applied. As a survey prepared in 1947 by the Civil Rights Division of the Anti-Defamation League of B'nai B'rith said matter-of-factly, "The traditional pattern of civil rights in the South prevailed in all areas of Florida. The Negro was completely banned from places of amusement, resorts and public accommodations."

Sprigle shaved his thin gray hair down to his skull and lopped off his signature modest moustache. His skin was used to western Pennsylvania, where the clouds usually outnumbered the weak northern sun. He immediately overcooked himself. It was for only ninety minutes, but he said he spent his first night at the Carleve Hotel "standing up and rubbing soothing unguents into my flaming epidermis." His scorched skin peeled from head to toe, but it slowly became a darker red. His daughter, Rae, sent him several letters reminding him to stick to his diet, not get too much sun, and take his medicine for his chronic but mild bronchial asthma. She knew why he was in Florida. In her seventh grade social studies class during a discussion of race relations and civil rights, she had blurted out, "Do you know what my Daddy is going to do? He's going to disguise himself as a Negro and go to the South."

Rae had heard her father and mother discussing the Jim Crow story, which is something they always did when he was planning a big project. Though a very bright thirteen-year-old, she wasn't privy to the details or hazards of the trip. She wasn't happy that her father was going to be away for a long time. When he went on the road for extended periods, there was never much communication from him—that was the way he always operated. The Sprigle family telephone—like approximately 75 percent of phones in the USA—was a party line, so he always had to be careful about calling home. Letters from him were a rarity as were telegrams. This was even true in 1940 when he was in London for four months covering the Blitz. In that case it didn't make sense to write a letter that might take a week or more to cross the ocean. As a foreign correspondent he had a quicker method of proving to his family that he was surviving the German bombing raids: transatlantic cable. Every other day the front page of the *Post-Gazette* carried one of his fresh updates on the Battle of Britain, a story about civilian life during wartime, or a first-person account of Messerschmitts attacking barrage balloons on the coast of the English Channel. During his southern road trip, he was going to have no contact with his family and there would be no proof-of-life Ray Sprigle bylines in the morning paper.

After burning himself for three weeks in Florida, Sprigle returned home for a few days to say his goodbyes to Agnes and Rae and make last-minute arrangements. He was aware of the danger he was courting in the Deep South and prepared accordingly. He had already typed up an updated version of his will and given it to his lawyer. He didn't dare take his .45 automatic along for protection, but he accepted an offer of help from his racketeer friend Hymie Martin.

Martin was a very large and colorful Pittsburgh "gambling entrepreneur" and local representative of the Cleveland mob. He was a career criminal and had an arrest record dating to the early 1920s. He had never been convicted of anything serious, though he came close in 1931 when he was arrested in Pittsburgh and accused of murdering a Cleveland councilman. Photographed by the *Post-Gazette* after his arrest, "Pittsburgh Hymie" was described in the caption as "a prominent figure in local bootleg and racketeering circles throughout the city." Martin was found guilty of the murder and given life in prison, but he went free after a second trial in which several witnesses conveniently changed their stories.

Martin was one of Sprigle's most trusted sources in the local underworld and occasionally dropped by the farmhouse for some quiet conversations. Sprigle told him his travel plans and he gave him the names and phone numbers of fellow criminals who lived in various southern towns. In case Sprigle got involved with the local branch of the KKK or anyone else, he would have someone to call that he could trust. The *Post-Gazette* arranged a less shady way to protect its star reporter: During his travels Sprigle was to phone his editor every forty-eight hours to show he was all right. If the call didn't come, the paper was to immediately alert the FBI.

CHAPTER 6

Teaming Up with Mr. Dobbs

So at last I scurried back north to Washington, met my companion who was to pilot me through four weeks of life as a Negro, and that night we were on our way south, just a couple of Negroes Jim Crowing it through the Southland.

—RAY SPRIGLE, *IN THE LAND OF JIM CROW*

How the two collaborators greeted each other will never be known. What is known is that on Friday, May 7, 1948, Ray Sprigle and John Wesley Dobbs met each other for the first time somewhere inside the monstrous granite caverns of Washington, DC's Union Station. As they sized each other up, thousands of commuters and travelers surged through the station's concourses or sat on the long mahogany benches under the high vaulted ceiling of its waiting room.

Sprigle had traveled 240 miles by train that day from Pittsburgh. When he boarded his passenger coach, he was a free, famous, and fairly affluent white American. When he got off in Washington, he was James Crawford, a light-skinned black American of modest means who was subject to the local ordinances and indignities of Jim Crow. Sprigle had traded his tailored suits and business shoes for an ordinary gray suit coat, a stiff cotton shirt, baggy cuffed dress pants, wide suspenders, and unshined ankle-high work shoes. An oversized checkered newsboy's cap hid his bald, well-tanned head and drooped over the heavy black frames of his eyeglasses. In his pockets were his corncob pipe, a pouch of Granger tobacco, a small spiral notebook, several pencils, and a travel wallet with his "James Rayel Crawford" Social Security card. Everything else he was taking into the South, including some tablets and fake paperwork to prove he was "a smalltime writer and smalltime office holder," he carried in a worn leather doctor's bag. His new skin color, in his own words, was "a passable coffee-with-plenty-of-cream shade."

Sprigle's partner Mr. Dobbs needed no disguise. He was his usual self—bigger than life. With his shiny set of luggage and three-piece suit, he looked like a cross between a movie star and the Ambassador of Ethiopia. He wore a gold Masonic stickpin and a subtle cloud of cologne. A watch dangled from his vest pocket. He looked, acted, and spoke like a man who played hardball with white politicians, taught black history to college kids, gave speeches on national radio, and had his own parking space when he went to see the Atlanta Black Crackers play at Ponce De Leon Park.

Dobbs had just finished four days of Prince Hall Masonic business in Washington, which, except for federal property, was nearly as Jim-Crowed as his hometown of Atlanta. About a third of the District's eight hundred thousand residents were black. Its schools, movie theaters, department stores, hotels, and other businesses were strictly segregated. There were no

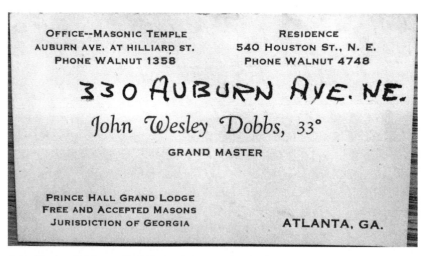

John Wesley Dobbs mailed his business card to Sprigle before they met.
COURTESY OF SENATOR JOHN HEINZ HISTORY MUSEUM

"Colored Only" signs posted, like in Georgia, but every black person in DC knew the unwritten rules. Most downtown restaurants didn't serve blacks, but if they did, these second-class customers had to eat standing at a counter. At post offices lines of blacks and whites were separated by partitions. The National Theatre was for white audiences only. So were the first-run movie houses in the major business area on F Street.

Blacks and whites could eat together at the lunch counter in Union Station and in the cafeterias of federal buildings. Otherwise the capital city of the strongest and freest democracy in the world was just another segregated southern town. Foreign visitors regularly expressed shock at the extent of the discrimination they found. Perversely, blacks from countries in Africa and elsewhere were accepted at fashionable hotels and allowed to eat in places where American blacks were not.

Washington's public spaces were strictly segregated in large part because the district was governed by Congress, and Congress was controlled by racist committee chairmen from the South like the recently departed Senator Bilbo of Mississippi. Bilbo and his fellow Democrats shared a disturbing enthusiasm for keeping the races separated in Washington—Bilbo even bragged about it to his constituents.

Though Republican presidents Teddy Roosevelt and William Howard Taft had introduced some minor discriminatory policies during their administrations, the Jim Crowing of DC began in earnest in 1913 when Woodrow Wilson came to town. The leader of the Progressive Movement, raised in Georgia and South Carolina, was the first southerner elected president since Zachary Taylor twelve years before the Civil War. Wilson was a Democrat who had won a three-way race against Bull Moose candidate Teddy Roosevelt and Republican incumbent Taft. During the election he promised blacks he'd be their champion and treat them fairly, but when he got to Washington he turned 180 degrees. He purged blacks from important federal positions and outraged black leaders by segregating the federal government's departments, offices, hospitals, eating tables, locker rooms, and public toilets.

Segregation in DC slowly became more prevalent in the private sector as well. The places blacks could live and work became increasingly limited. Powerful real estate interests made sure blacks couldn't move into the district's new suburbs, forcing them to stay in designated city neighborhoods that became overcrowded, low-rent slums. Kids straying into white neighborhoods on their bikes were told by cops to go back where they belonged. The city's real estate board of "ethics" stated "no property in a white section should ever be sold, rented, advertised or offered to colored people." By 1948 Washington was at the height—or depth—of its Jim Crow era: It had a large black ghetto, its public schools were segregated by race, and black housing stock was being "redeveloped" out of existence by urban renewal projects for the benefit of white middle-class residents. Meanwhile, most of the blue- and white-collar jobs open to blacks in and out of government were lousy.

Sprigle didn't get a chance to experience Washington as a newly minted black man. At 5:10 p.m., he and Dobbs boarded the Silver Comet, a stainless steel streamliner bound for Atlanta via Richmond, Raleigh, and the Appalachians of South Carolina. It was owned by Seaboard Air Line Railroad, which was an important New York to Miami railway along the Atlantic coast that hauled humans from the dreary Northeast to the sunny resorts of Florida and delivered timber, oranges, lemons, and limes to the North. The Silver Comet was one of about two hundred trains a day that entered or left Union Station. It was a typical passenger train of the age—diesel locomotives, baggage cars, passenger coaches, Pullman sleepers, a dining car, and a forty-eight-seat observation car at its tail.

Like every train heading into the South, the Silver Comet was a Jim Crow train. In keeping with a Virginia law that decreed "no white and black persons shall occupy contiguous seats," it had two coaches set aside for black travelers. In case of disputes, it was up to the train conductor to decide if a passenger was white or black. If he had any doubts about Sprigle's race when he saw his ticket, the conductor didn't show it. Dobbs had a little trouble locating the Jim Crow cars until he ran into the stylish daughter of a friend of his who pointed the way. Both black coaches were filled, but Sprigle found them surprisingly pleasing. They weren't overcrowded and everyone was quiet and polite, even the lone drunk. Everything was in perfectly fine condition. The reclining seats were comfortable. The seats had numbers. The washroom was "luxurious" compared to ones Sprigle had encountered on some unsegregated trains.

After claiming their reserved seats, Sprigle and Dobbs set out in search of the dining car. Sprigle—now James Crawford—was hungry and he was buying. The two large men had to squeeze through the middles of about six Pullman sleeping coaches. Proving how widely known he was among the black upper class, Dobbs ran into three people he knew: a doctor, a minister, and a businessman. They were black Americans, but that night they were going to be sleeping in their berths in the Pullman coaches, only feet away from sleeping white people. Sprigle was shocked to learn Jim Crow's rules didn't apply in the Pullmans. He found out later that it was because a US Supreme Court ruling a few years earlier had ordered the Pullman Company to end all discrimination against blacks on interstate railroads. Unlike some southern railroads, southern governments and southern educational institutions, Sprigle said, Pullman regarded a decision by the Supreme Court as the law of the land and obeyed it. As a consequence, he said, "If you've got the price you ride Pullman, no matter how black you are."

The coexistence of integrated sleeping cars and segregated passenger coaches on the same train was the first example of "the many absurdities—idiocies might be a better word—" Sprigle noticed in Jim Crow's machinery. Minutes later more absurdities manifested themselves. When they reached the packed dining car, they discovered a long line of white people. They were waiting for tables to open up, but Dobbs waltzed right past them. Sprigle feared there was going to be trouble—and they were barely thirty minutes into Virginia territory. But Dobbs "knew the ropes" of being a black man and he didn't. At the end of the gently swaying dining car, behind some curtains, were two empty tables. "They were for us colored folks," Sprigle said. "So we sat down while the white folks stood. Just what protection that curtain affords the white folks I don't think that any living human has ever figured out. We could watch them eat and they could watch us eat. There weren't any curtains around the Negro waiters who served their food with black hands."

Sprigle was greatly impressed by the waiters, who "yes-sirred" them like crazy throughout the meal and brought their food out fast and hot. In the tiny spiral notebook he carried to keep track of his expenses, he entered the cost of their dinners in pencil. Earlier in the day under "May

7" he had written down the decimal-free price of his breakfast—"105 B"—and his lunch—"270 L." For his and Dobbs's dinners on the train he wrote "450 D-2." The prices were so low they hardly seemed worth recording. But the $8.25 Sprigle spent for four meals that Friday would equal a healthy $82.50 today.

After dinner they returned to their Jim Crow–assigned seats and continued telling each other their life stories. Sprigle had already realized how kind the gods of journalism had been to him. Instead of having to live and travel for a month with an affable but anonymous insurance man named Jones who liked to talk a lot, fate had delivered John Wesley Dobbs. Dobbs was destined for the history books. He was a classic American success story who had lifted himself out of deep rural poverty and overcome the South's soul-grinding system of discrimination. In thirteen years Martin Luther King Jr. was going to speak at Dobbs's funeral and his friend Thurgood Marshall was going to be one of his pallbearers. The street he lived on in Atlanta's best black neighborhood was going to be renamed after him and a giant sculpture of his head was going to be placed on the sidewalk of Auburn Avenue, the Main Street of black Atlanta.

Sprigle made his living extracting the relevant or interesting facts of any person's story, no matter how humble or boring they were. But Dobbs's remarkable life was a feature writer's gold mine. He was born in 1882 on a farm about thirty miles northwest of Atlanta, near the Kennesaw Mountain National Battlefield. Like so many of his generation, his parents were ex-slaves. He was also the grandson of a white slave owner named McAfee who had fathered his mother Minnie during the first years of the Civil War. After his parents split up when he was two years old, Dobbs was raised nearby on a farm in Marietta by his paternal grandparents.

Living with more than a dozen young uncles, aunts, and cousins in two log cabins, he grew up barefoot and poor a hundred yards from a railroad line. The ghostly faces looking out the windows of passenger coaches were the only white people he saw. He went to a black school three months a year, but when he was nine he joined his single-mother Minnie in Savannah and began school there full time. When a white woman learned he was to be pulled out of school because his mother could no longer afford to buy him the clothes or shoes he needed, the woman gave him a job so he could buy them himself.

For the rest of his life Dobbs never stopped working. His jobs included delivering the *Savannah Evening Press* and shining shoes at a barbershop. At age fifteen he moved to Atlanta and accomplished something fewer than 10 percent of all Americans—white or black, North or South—did in his era: He got a high school diploma. He was intelligent, hardworking, and driven at an early age to become a successful black man in a white man's world. He started college at what would soon become Morehouse College, but had to quit after only a few months to tend to his sick mother. Knowing a federal job was one of the few places a black man in the South could escape Jim Crow's reach and earn enough to achieve a middle-class lifestyle, he took a civil service test. In 1903, at age twenty-one, he became a US Post Office clerk who sorted mail on the Nashville & Atlanta railroad. It was a highly respected position that not only paid him the princely starting salary of eight hundred dollars a year, but also allowed him to carry a Colt revolver. The only black man working on the train, he stayed at his job for thirty-two years, eventually becoming the boss of a crew of white men. In 1906 he married Irene Ophelia Thompson, bought a house on Houston Street in Atlanta's best black neighborhood for $2,767, and began filling it with a piano, hundreds of books, and six children, all girls.

Though he never received his college degree, Dobbs never stopped educating himself. He studied literature, history, and philosophy all his life. On his layovers in Nashville, the young mail clerk spent his nights reading. In a notebook he called his "Armory of Ideas," he wrote down quotes he liked from the writings of Aesop, Frederick Douglass, Jefferson Davis, Booker T. Washington, and W. E. B. Du Bois. He also made up quotes of his own including "I cannot conquer age; all other fights I can win," which became his mantra for the rest of his life. He memorized long stanzas of English poetry and passages from Shakespeare, but most of all he was a history nut. He studied black history and learned it so well he taught it in college classes and once presented a lecture on CBS national radio. He read books about Napoleon, the Romans, the Greeks, and Abraham Lincoln, his greatest hero and the reason he was a Republican. He visited Lincoln's birthplace in Kentucky so many times that the guides knew him by name. Eternally thankful for what Lincoln and the Union armies did to end slavery, he would faithfully stop at Civil War battlefields in the North and South to pay his respects to the Union dead.

In 1911, at age twenty-nine, Dobbs changed his life forever by joining the Prince Hall Masons, the black version of the Masons fraternal group that appealed to socially conscious middle-class black men like him. The Prince Hall Masons were started in the late 1700s in New England because white Masons wouldn't admit blacks. They established lodges and temples in cities across the country, though most were concentrated in the South where the majority of blacks lived. To be admitted, you needed recommendations from Prince Hall members. Plus you needed what Dobbs already possessed—a good reputation in the community, a strong belief in God and Christian values, and an initiation fee of $7.50. Dobbs quickly worked his way up through the ranks of the Atlanta grand lodge. In the mid-1920s, while still a mail clerk, he became head of the lodge's financial department, a position that paid him more than his government job.

In 1932, three years before he retired from the Post Office, Dobbs was elected the grand master of the Prince Hall Masons of Georgia. He made full use of his near-dictatorial powers and his managerial skills to increase the membership and clout of the state's masons. The duties of the grand master—visiting local lodges and settling any disputes over money or membership issues—meant he traveled extensively on Prince Hall business. "The Grand," as he was reverentially called, was greeted like a celebrity in black communities throughout the state. A thunderous and dramatic orator, he delivered well-constructed speeches at Prince Hall affairs in Cleveland and Detroit. Whether he was addressing hundreds of Masons, a church congregation, or just "preaching" to a few citizens he'd cornered on the sidewalk, he always pushed the same subversive political message—the key to the advancement of the his race was the ballot box. He was always the consummate "race man"—a black man who devoted his life to bettering and defending his race by confronting—peacefully— the institutions, people, and ideas that held them back.

After Dobbs retired with a pension from the Post Office in 1935, he concentrated on building his race into a political force the city's white power structure had to reckon with. On February 12, 1936, by no accident Lincoln's birthday, he called a public meeting at Atlanta's largest black church and announced the formation of the Atlantic Civic and Political League. In a rousing two-hour speech at Big Bethel A.M.E. Church, he proclaimed that the city's ninety thousand blacks were never going to get decent public schools for their kids, black police officers for their neighborhoods, equal pay for their teachers, or decent city parks for their old folks unless at least ten thousand of them registered to vote. Until they could deliver a large bloc of black votes to white politicians on Election Day, they were never going to have the political leverage they needed to improve their lives. On the day Dobbs started his organization and named himself its president, there were six hundred registered black voters in Atlanta. Three years later there were nearly three thousand.

Though he was a Lincoln man to his soul, Dobbs had an eight-year fling with FDR and the New Deal Democrats. In the fall of 1936 he was invited to join Roosevelt's re-election campaign by the Democratic National Committee and went north to speak to black voter groups in Rhode Island, New Jersey, Delaware, and Maryland. In a 1939 interview with an oral historian for the Library of Congress, as part of the Federal Writers Project, Dobbs said he accepted the "assignment and duty because of my sincere belief in the progressive principles advocated by the New Deal administration, especially as they related and are interpreted toward the uplifting and betterment of living conditions for poor people regardless of race, color, or creed."

Through the war years Dobbs never stopped banging the drum for black voter registration in Masonic halls, churches, college campuses, and at the Butler Street YMCA, where Atlanta's black leaders often met to plan and argue. By 1944 he had soured on President Roosevelt, deciding he had not been so progressive after all when it came to helping poor blacks or challenging the power of segregationist Democrats in the Senate. He returned to the Republican fold, becoming a Georgia delegate committed to New York governor Thomas Dewey at the GOP national convention. Dobbs favored the moderate-to-liberal Dewey largely because of his strong civil rights record. In 1946 he cofounded the Atlanta Negro Voters League, which also urged blacks to register and vote.

During this time Dobbs took his moral and political message on the road. In the summer of 1947, for example, he was paid to speak at least eight times at black colleges and Prince Hall Mason events from Ohio to Atlantic City to Savannah. In the fall of 1947, a few weeks after Sprigle and Walter White had their clandestine meeting in the Hill District, the *Courier* reported that Dobbs had visited Pittsburgh to dedicate the cornerstone of a Prince Hall lodge and speak at a Baptist church. Neither the *Courier* nor the white papers reported what he said to the churchgoers, though it wasn't hard to guess.

A month before he met Sprigle in Washington, DC, Dobbs had proudly watched an event on Auburn Avenue that he had worked for years to achieve. In payment for the promise he made—and kept—to deliver a bloc of ten thousand votes to incumbent white mayor Bill Hartsfield in a Democratic primary election, eight black policemen made their debut on the streets of Atlanta. They could only patrol black neighborhoods, the only whites they could arrest were drunks and vagrants, and they were stationed in the basement of the black YMCA. But integrating the police force was a major symbolic victory for Dobbs and his allies. It proved the foundation of segregation could be cracked if blacks learned when and where to hit it with their votes. When Dobbs watched black cops walk down Auburn Avenue in their uniforms for the first time, at his side was his ten-year-old grandson, Maynard Holbrook Jackson Jr., the future mayor of Atlanta.

Sprigle was a worldly and intelligent man, not easily impressed. He had met and interviewed hundreds of political and corporate big shots in his career. His friends included US senators, the governor of Pennsylvania, and future Pennsylvania Supreme Court justice Michael Musmanno, the author and presiding judge for one of the war crimes trials held in military court at Nuremberg in 1947. If Sprigle had any doubts that the man sitting next to him on the train did not belong in their league, they would have disappeared if he read the transcript of Dobbs's long interview in 1939 with the Library of Congress.

Dobbs was fifty-seven at the time. He told his interviewer about his poor beginnings, his early love of learning, his struggle to educate himself, and how much his many jobs taught him about human nature and getting ahead in life. He said he was "a great believer in self-help. All I wanted was an opportunity to work." He expressed his love of America, the Constitution, and "people's human rights." He said his immediate goal was "to awaken the Atlanta Negroes to their civic and political consciousness" and get them to exercise their vote for their own benefit. But his ultimate ambition was for every black American to be made a full and equal citizen with all of the same rights and privileges guaranteed by the US Constitution. "Over the doorway of the nation's Supreme Court building in Washington, DC," he said, "are engraved four words, 'Equal Justice Under Law.' This beautiful American ideal is what the Negroes want to see operative and effective from the Atlantic to the Pacific and from the Great Lakes to the Gulf—nothing more or less."

Later in that long Library of Congress interview, during which he impressed the interviewer by reciting forty-nine lines of Edwin Markham's poem "The Man with the Hoe," Dobbs said he was embarrassed to be talking so much about himself and his accomplishments. But he said, "Whatever I have accomplished, if there is anything, I have done it from sheer determination and because I looked up and saw the stars. I have struggled to be useful to mankind. . . . I made up my mind at an early age to do something and I guess I can sum it all up by saying I can compare myself with the two ships: 'One ship sails east, the other sails west by the same wind that blows. It's the set of the sail and not the gale that determines the course as she goes.' I set my 'sails' to rise above poverty and ignorance and whatever the 'gale' I still kept my mind on what I wanted to accomplish in life, and each day I have tried to do those things that would reflect credit on me, my family, and my race. I have devoted my life and my talents to helping pave the right road for my people."

While Sprigle and Dobbs slept side-by-side in their Jim Crow seats, the Silver Comet hurtled them across South Carolina and eastern Georgia at an average speed of forty-eight miles an hour. At 7:40 in the morning, 605 railroad miles south of Washington, their shiny streamliner pulled into Atlanta's Terminal Station. The ride cost Sprigle $36.70. Before he even got out of the railroad station, he made a rookie black man's mistake. Walking a few paces ahead of Dobbs, who he quipped was loaded down "with more bags than an actor," Sprigle saw a line of taxis at the curb outside and hurried to claim one. Dobbs yelled at him to stop. Sprigle had forgotten what color he was and whose country he had entered. He had no idea he was headed out the white exit. He retreated. To leave the station they had to pass through the small littered waiting room with the "For Colored" signs above its doors.

Outside the black exit there were no Jim Crow taxicabs. They had to call one. While they waited, Dobbs had a mischievous idea. He led Sprigle around to the front of the train station and they boldly strolled through the white entrance. Nothing happened. They did it again. It was clear to Sprigle that Dobbs was disappointed they hadn't been stopped by a policeman. Usually there was one posted at the white entrance, and his only job was to shoo blacks around to the colored entrance. Dobbs pronounced that the only reason they were able to break the law without consequence was because of the usual "police inefficiency." He warned Sprigle not to think Jim Crow was getting soft or lazy when it came to enforcing its basic door laws. "There'd have been no unpleasantness unless we had refused" to use the colored door, Dobbs explained. "They wouldn't even have called us 'nigger' as they would have a few years ago. But if you have any idea you can walk through the white folks' entrance to a railroad station—you just try it at any station in the South outside Atlanta. And I'll stand back and watch—and bail you out."

Sprigle understood Dobbs was joking. But he never had any intention of challenging Jim Crow's ordinances for the next four weeks. He had been given plenty of advice to do exactly the opposite. He was not even a one-day-old black American. He had just taken his first steps on pure Jim Crow soil. But already he found himself feeling contempt for the white race and starting to think like a black man. White people, he said, felt "entirely alien to me, a people set far apart from me and my world. The law of this new land I had entered decreed that I had to eat apart from these pale-skinned men and women—behind that symbolical curtain. For 300 years these people had told each other, told the world, told me, that I was of an inferior breed, that if I tried to associate with them they would kill me." For the first time in his life he was the underdog. He wasn't bothered that he couldn't ride in the same railroad coach with whites or eat in a restaurant with them. What he resented was their "impudent assumption" that "he wanted to mingle with them, their arrogant and conceited pretense that no matter how depraved and degenerate some of them might be, they, each and every one of them, was of a superior breed."

Before the pair of delinquent seniors could get into serious trouble with Jim Crow, a taxicab with "For Colored" printed on its doors arrived. Fifteen minutes and two miles later they had crossed Auburn Avenue—Atlanta's "Black Broadway"—and were standing at the curb in front of a deceivingly modest house. Four shallow steps made of white marble led up to a sidewalk that ended at a wide front porch. There was no doubt who owned the three-bedroom home. Into the top marble step was carved "J.W. Dobbs, 540 Houston Street N.E."

CHAPTER 7

The Poor, Poor South

Men talk of the "negro problem." There is no negro problem. The problem is whether the American people have honesty enough, loyalty enough, honor enough, patriotism enough to live up to their own Constitution. We intend that the American people shall learn the great lesson of the brotherhood of man and the fatherhood of God from our presence among them.

—FREDERICK DOUGLASS SPEECH,
CHICAGO WORLD'S FAIR, 1893

If Ray Sprigle didn't read John Gunther's *Inside U.S.A.* in advance of his trip, he should have. The 1947 huge bestseller contained everything important about the South that Sprigle could possibly need to know. If he wondered how many black, brown, and white people were hung, shot, or beaten to death by mobs between 1882 and 1944 in Mississippi (573), Georgia (521), or Texas (489), or wanted to compare the number of rural homes without toilets or privies in Massachusetts (303) to the number in Alabama (78,562), he could have found the answers buried in Gunther's dense, useful, and entertaining tome.

Written during 1946, reported and researched in 1944 and 1945, *Inside U.S.A.* was—and still is—a priceless time capsule of postwar America. Its nearly one thousand pages of facts, background, analysis, and commentary included 160 pages on the ten states from Virginia to Texas that Gunther lumped into the South. When he called the region the "problem child of the nation" and said it was underlain by "the harassing pressure of the Negro problem," he wasn't merely repeating what he had read in Gunnar Myrdal's *An American Dilemma*. John Gunther was a famous foreign correspondent and best-selling author of other *Inside* books on Europe, Asia, and South America. He didn't do his journalism in libraries. After deciding to treat his homeland like a foreign country, he traveled to every state and major city and sought out the white male powerbrokers who ran them.

Gunther reported and editorialized on everything, everyone, and every place with intelligence, a sharp wit and withering prejudice. He nailed California for its "crackpotism," Pennsylvania for its filthy politics, and New York for its "get-rich-quickism." He made enemies of whole cities by calling them the ugliest or dirtiest in America. He pissed off big-time politicians like Governor Earl Warren of California and spotted up-and-comers like Congressman Jack Kennedy. To the lovers and defenders of the South, he was just the latest in a parade of clueless Yankees to come down to their world and tell them what was wrong with the way they treated millions of black people. But *Inside U.S.A.* was an incredible one-man display of high-quality drive-by journalism.

He started his ruthless assessment of the South's economic, social, and racial problems with a sympathetic caveat. He said it was impossible for an outsider—whether from Mars or Jersey City—to understand the South without understanding what happened during the War Between the States and the era of Reconstruction that followed. The damage from the war itself was straightforward—the loss of a quarter of the male population and billions worth of property, chief of which included formerly enslaved humans. But he said, "To this day the South has never recovered from Reconstruction. This was one of the most cruelly outrageous episodes in all the wantonness of history. . . . the roots of white supremacy, the Negro problem, and a dozen other inflamed and derivative issues, are all to be found in what occurred in Reconstruction days."

The arrival of the carpetbaggers, the division of the South into five Union army military districts, the enfranchisement of millions of ex-slaves, the disenfranchisement of white southerners, the dictatorial control of the northern military over social and economic matters—they all took a serious and lasting toll on the white southern psyche and soul.

Federal troops didn't leave some states until 1877. Gunther compared what Atlanta was like in 1870 to what Budapest and Warsaw must have been like under the Nazis in the 1940s and what postwar Germany was then undergoing under Allied occupation. To sum up what happened to Dixie, he quoted historian James Truslow Adams: "The war left the South prostrate; Reconstruction left it maddened."

Gunther understood the South's pain, but he showed no mercy in criticizing its many defects and shortcomings. He cracked that not only did the region lead the country in every socioeconomic and educational problem, it also resented being told about any of them. Unlike other regions that were more diverse, the states of the South could be painted with a broad but generally accurate brush. There were ten million mostly poor and lawfully oppressed black Americans in the South. But Gunther noted that the primary common feature of the region was that its majority population was made up of poor, native-born white Anglo-Saxons who pretty much thought, worshipped, and hated alike. Immigrants and the foreign-born in the South were rare. Except for Florida and Louisiana, 90 percent of southerners had two American-born parents. In Arkansas, the figure hit 98.7 percent, which caused the politically incorrect Gunther to wonder "what peculiar characteristics the Celts and Gaels, when transported, contribute to a civilization."

The "most salient and pervasive item" in Gunther's list of woes was poverty. The South was like an underdeveloped country, and he piled on the raw numbers to prove it. Its average annual income per capita was $716 in 1944 compared to $1,117 for the whole country and $1,459 on the West Coast. Reportedly eleven million of twenty-six million southerners had cash incomes of less than $250 a year. With those dismal Third World incomes, it's not surprising that the states of the South placed dead last in dozens of per-capita consumer categories, from bank deposits to the number of farm tractors, cars, and telephones they owned. Whereas the North measured the number of radios per family, the South still counted the number of families per radio.

The reason for the South's pathetic economic statistics—compounded by the stupidity that, as Gunther said, segregation demanded there be two sets of everything, from insane asylums to playgrounds—was that its population was so rural. Seventy percent of southerners lived in the sticks, not cities, which was nearly the reverse of the Northeast and the West. Despite its famous Georgia peaches and Florida oranges, its major crops by far were cotton and tobacco. Both quickly depleted the soil, which, combined with backward farming practices, is why the South had the ignominious distinction of losing more of its land to erosion than any other region.

The South's crops were raised by the cheap labor of millions of share-croppers and tenant farmers, black and white. They lived impossibly hard and impoverished lives. Most were too destitute, too unskilled, and too uneducated to improve their lives by migrating north or west or to a southern city or town. But sharecroppers had the worst arrangement. Landlords provided them with about ten acres of land and a "house" as well as the seeds, fertilizer, and tools they needed to raise whatever crop the land owner decided. The 'croppers worked in the fields as supervised laborers until harvest time, when the landowner sold all the crops. After deducting the cost of the supplies, the landlord gave the sharecropper between a third and half of the profits generated by his ten acres.

As Gunther said, sharecroppers were no better than peons or serfs. They had nothing to offer or bargain with but their labor. They lived in dilapidated shacks, old buses, or packing crates. They had no cash and too many children, which they couldn't educate because they couldn't afford to buy them decent school clothes. Most sharecroppers lived harvest-to-harvest. Many were constantly in debt to their landlords and couldn't move elsewhere. Some were able to save money and buy their own farms or at least improve their lives by becoming a tenant farmer. Tenant farm-ers rented a piece of someone else's land and grew and sold their own crops on it, usually using their own animals and tools. The risk of bad weather or low cotton prices was borne by the tenant, who paid his rent in cash or with a share of the crop he raised.

When Gunther was in Atlanta, a guide took him ten miles into the countryside to visit two tenant farmers, one white and one black. In terms of poverty, squalor, and hopelessness, their lives were nearly identical. As Gunther said, he was seeing the tenant farming system at its "most forlorn and slapstick." Actually, it was so primitive it was only about ten years and a couple hundred dollars a year up from slavery. The white farmer owned a horse, which made him better off, but to rent eighteen acres he paid the landowner one hundred dollars a year—half his annual income. The black tenant's place—six acres planted in cotton and a little corn— reminded Gunther of what he had seen in Paraguay or remotest India, where civilization was a thousand years behind the West. "No bathroom, no radio, no running water, no electrical light, no gas—of course. A crude table, a dipper in a cracked white pail, flies buzzing around, hog meat hanging from the ceiling in white sacks, a small hand-turned phonograph, old trunks and tools are features of the two room house." The black tenant did have a few assets—seven old hens in the yard, two roosters, and ten children.

Meanwhile, the South's white and black schools, which Gunther also visited to see for himself how laughably unequal they were, were the worst in the nation in terms of money spent per student and per teacher. They also had the lowest high school enrollment rates. Southern states ranked among the lowest in white literacy, so it was no surprise they had the fewest libraries per capita. In terms of public health, the South had the fewest hospital beds per capita, the fewest doctors, and the highest rates of infant mortality, maternal childbirth deaths, and venereal disease.

As for crime and civil liberties, Gunther said, "The South is probably the darkest place in the nation." That may have been a cheap or inadvertent racist pun, or a failed joke, like the title of Chapter 41, "The Negro in the Woodpile." But he was serious. Most southern states and cities had murder rates ten times those of New England's. Gunther believed writers like William Faulkner, Thomas Wolfe, Eudora Welty, and Richard Wright were proving that the South was no longer the cultural desert Mencken said it was, but the rest of Dixie remained a cultural wasteland. There were no major symphonies, no important philosophers, no renowned painters or sculptors.

Gunther dealt bluntly with every aspect of southern life, past and present, and had no sympathy for its racist Jim Crow laws, white-rigged political system, militant Protestantism, puritanism, or crude biases against Jews and Catholics. He scoffed at the myth of the existence of a southern aristocracy that loved and took care of the land, saying that the "idea that all old-line southern planters were, or are, of a superior social

class is of course nonsensical." The number of wealthy plantation owners who had been substantial slaveholders was minuscule and the typical
southern cotton farmer was more likely to exhaust the land he owned and
then move west and ruin some more.

Somehow Gunther managed to find a few kind things to say about
the sorry conditions of the post–World War II South, which, like the
sorrier lives of its black citizens, were unknown to most northerners. He
noted that southerners had a disproportionate love of the military. They
enlisted at a much higher level compared to other Americans in peace
and war and were much more enthusiastic about fighting Germany and
Japan and sticking up for the British. The South's economy was more
diversified than most people thought. It wasn't just cotton, tobacco, lum-
ber, and Coca-Cola. It had textile mills in the Carolinas, a few steel mills
in Alabama, and some shipbuilding in Virginia. He grudgingly admitted
it had some powerful college football teams. And he said Atlanta, the former "Workshop of the Confederacy," had twenty-five hundred factories,
a very busy airport, and seven of the country's thirty-two accredited black
colleges to balance its terrible white and black slums.

An entire chapter in *Inside U.S.A.* was devoted to segregation and the
South's mistreatment of blacks—the 10 percent of Americans Gunther said
the other 90 percent knew existed but largely ignored. He began by con-
fessing he didn't realize the "grim enormousness" of the problem of legalized segregation until he saw it up close. "It has to be seen to be believed,"
the native of Chicago and world traveler said, apologizing for using a trite
phrase that any honest first-time observer from Sweden or Mars would use.

Gunther was no social scientist. But he noted that the absence of
large blocs of immigrants to form a buffer zone between poor whites and
poor blacks was a constant source of social and economic friction. It was
the "undereducated semi-mountaineer Scots-Irish" who believed "most
firmly in 'white supremacy,' and are therefore a continual exacerbation
to the Negro problem." He thought all the problems of the South were
"interlocked." The future of agriculture was connected to the future of
poor black sharecroppers and tenant farmers, which was connected to
"the luckless, miserable group of millions known as poor whites." Poor
whites lived in cities and towns, too. But their "gross poverty" was most

conspicuous in "the rural slums of the South," which he declared were "almost beyond doubt the most revolting in the nation."

Gunther took on every angle and sensitive complexity of "the Negro problem," including what blacks thought of those who try to pass for white and why fear of sex between the races was the underlying reason for whites wanting to keep blacks separated as much as possible. He didn't hold back. He even reprinted a sizeable chunk of an essay by the always shocking George Schuyler of the *Pittsburgh Courier*. Identified by Gunther as "one of the nation's outstanding journalists," Schuyler asserted "there is actually no Negro problem" in the South or anywhere else, but "there is definitely a Caucasian problem." Schuyler figured out how to simultaneously needle and offend white liberals and the folks Gunther called "white supremacy addicts."

> Continual reference to a Negro problem assumes that some profound difficulty has been or is being created for the human race by the so-called Negroes. This is typical ruling class arrogance and . . . has no basis in fact. It has been centuries since any Negro nation has menaced the rest of humanity. The last of the Moors withdrew from Europe in 1492. The so-called Negroes . . . have passed few if any Jim Crow laws . . . set up few white ghettos, carried on no discriminatory practices against whites, and have not devoted centuries of propaganda to prove the superiority of blacks over whites . . . While we may dismiss the concept of the Negro problem as a valuable dividend-paying fiction, it is clear that the Caucasian problem is painfully real and practically universal. Stated briefly, the problem confronting the colored peoples of the world is how to live in freedom, peace, and security without being invaded, subjugated, expropriated, exploited, persecuted, and humiliated by Caucasians justifying their actions by the myth of white racial superiority. The term Negro itself is as fictitious as the theory of white racial superiority on which Anglo-Saxon civilization is based, but it is nevertheless one of the most effective smear devices developed since the Crusades . . . Of course "white" and "Caucasian" are equally barren of scientific

meaning . . . There are actually no white people except albinos who are very pale pink in color . . .

Though Gunther seemed to miss the satire and said he thought Schuyler's views were extreme, he added it wasn't because the voice of the *Courier* was some kind of wild-eyed communist. He was "a prosperous and perfectly respectable citizen" that, Gunther correctly assumed, "often votes Republican." Gunther didn't buy Schuyler's clever twist on the nonexistence of "the Negro problem." He was genuinely shocked at how black Americans were being treated in the Jim Crow South, even though he had prepped for his visit by reading Gunnar Myrdal's indispensable *An American Dilemma.* Gunther saw evidence everywhere that supported Myrdal's hypothesis "that the Negro problem is above all one of morals, heart and conscience." He also believed, as Myrdal did, that any "seeming inferiority" exhibited by southern blacks was not innate to their "race." Agreeing with Schuyler, he said "race" was a bogus sociological or political distinction with no scientific validity. Any statistical inferiority blacks exhibited as a group, he said, was a result of hundreds of years of poverty, discrimination, lack of education, and "the appalling uglinesses" that occur when a whole community is ostracized and becomes unseen, unheard, and practically nonexistent to the larger society.

Inside U.S.A. was an instant bestseller in 1947, selling half a million copies at a pricy five dollars each. *Time* magazine's unsigned review was mixed. It praised Gunther's personalized journalism for being "highly readable" and said his writing was "brisk and breezy," but it also complained, without specifying, that it was "glib, superficial, exaggerated, full of impressions passing as insights and facts palmed off as truths." Still, *Time* concluded it was probably his best book, certainly the best since his 1938 bestseller *Inside Europe*, which used the same drive-by, I-am-here technique to chronicle the events and dictators that were taking the world to war.

Fifty years after originally reviewing *Inside U.S.A.*, Gunther's fellow liberal and old friend Arthur Schlesinger Jr. read it again to see how well it held up. The great New Deal historian, presidential insider, and speechwriter was still impressed. Writing for *The Atlantic* in 1997, Schlesinger said *Inside U.S.A.* was "an astonishing tour de force" that "foresaw dilemmas and paradoxes that were to harass and frustrate Americans for the rest of the century."

Schlesinger was in sync with Gunther's liberal politics. Gunther was a fellow New Dealer, a fellow progressive who trusted the federal government to plan, manage, and trespass upon the economy of a free society far more than a conservative Republican or libertarian would like. But he also recognized that it was the country's system of free enterprise—albeit grossly manipulated by politicians of both parties for the benefit of their friends in business, labor, and agriculture—that was to thank for "the equality of opportunity" that was "still a pivotal keystone of American life and thought."

Gunther saw America's many political and economic positives and glaring negatives. He understood there were a lot of good reasons we had become the world's greatest economic and military power. But at the end of what he called "this long, detail-choked and multicolored journey," he concluded that America was great largely because "it was founded on a deliberate idea—a complex and enveloping idea including equality of opportunity for all, government only by the consent of the governed, and the Bill of Rights; the form and spirit and texture of the United States is based on individualism, civil liberties, and the democratic process." It is embarrassingly obvious today that America clearly was not living up to its founding creed as it applied to ten million black citizens in Dixie. It was obvious to Gunther too. But he—like Myrdal, Walter White, and other early civil rights advocates—knew he had to loudly spell it out to millions of his oblivious countrymen.

His tour of the southern states convinced Gunther that Gunnar Myrdal was right. At the end of *Inside U.S.A.*, he concluded that "the most gravid, cancerous, and pressing of all American problems is that of the Negro, insoluble under present political and social conditions though capable of great amelioration." In 1947 he could see small but encouraging signs of improvement. Blacks were being admitted to the American Bar Association and the American College of Surgeons for the first time, and Jackie Robinson was going to play for the Dodgers. Black Americans and their leaders were more unified and more aggressive in demanding their civil rights than ever before. Gunther saw their political strength was growing and quoted Walter White's claim that black voters held the balance of power in seventeen states. He could see America's blacks were headed in the right direction, but he could also see it would take generations for true progress. And he was right when he advised the country to prepare for what he said was inevitable—"Negro equality under democracy."

It had been a rough first hundred years for Atlanta. Established in the foothills of the Appalachian Mountains as an early railroad stop in the 1840s, it had only ten thousand citizens when General Sherman and his Union army marched through in the fall of 1864 on their way to Savannah. Sherman's troops burned everything except the churches and hospitals to the ground, but the city rebounded quickly. Doubling and redoubling its population into the twentieth century, Atlanta's energetic booster class promoted their city as the capital of "the New South." They sought to make it a modern commercial and industrial hub that didn't rely on Georgia's agrarian economy yet preserved the framework of white supremacy.

Atlanta was strictly segregated starting in the 1880s and stayed that way. As it prospered and grew, poor blacks and poor whites moved in from the surrounding countryside and competed for work and places to live. By 1900 the city held within its borders ninety thousand of the Atlanta area's 420,000 people. Blacks made up a third of the city's population. They got the lowest-paid jobs and they were concentrated in two neighborhoods on the east and west sides of town. Jim Crow laws and social discrimination prevented most of them from gaining economic and political success in the white world or moving to other parts of town. A tiny percentage made good livings working for whites as barbers, tailors, and shoemakers or found work as masons, carpenters, and plasterers. With their businesses located downtown on Peachtree, Broad, and Marietta Streets, a small black business elite developed that was middle-class by white standards but upper-class compared to the majority of blacks. Many of them moved into the nice homes in the Fourth Ward on streets flanking Auburn Avenue, where black professionals, clergy, educators, and self-made men like John Wesley Dobbs were living.

As in Pittsburgh and other black urban population centers, Atlanta's blacks created a parallel society that had its own economy, social institutions, entertainment venues, and sports teams. Strong black churches like the Big Bethel A.M.E. took root along Auburn Avenue and elsewhere and supplied schools, mutual aid societies, and welfare services with their gospels. By 1900 Atlanta had become the South's center for black higher education. Five private colleges—Clark, Spelman, Morehouse, and Morris Brown colleges and Atlanta University—had been founded by local black churches or white mission societies from the Northeast.

In 1905 the city became the national center of the debate over ending segregation. It started when Atlanta University economics and history professor W. E. B. Du Bois, the first black to receive a PhD from Harvard, challenged the position Booker T. Washington took in his "Atlanta Compromise Speech" of 1895. Washington, a former slave who advised presidents and industrialists, was the founder of Tuskegee Institute and at the time the most popular black man in America. Believing that politics should be left to the mainstream white population, he had proposed a compromise in which the millions of poor blacks in the South would accept segregation and their second-class social and political status in exchange for receiving basic education and economic opportunities, justice in the courts, and financial help from northerners for black schools and businesses.

Du Bois, who thought Washington had sold out the political freedom of black Americans, emerged as the country's leading intellectual spokesman for their full citizenship and equal political rights. From 1905 onward, black leaders across the country were split between "conservatives" who thought Washington's economic way was best and "radicals" who followed Du Bois. In 1909 Du Bois cofounded the National Association for the Advancement of Colored People in Atlanta and became editor of its monthly magazine *The Crisis*. For the next half century, in addition to writing more than twenty important scholarly history books about the experiences of blacks in the United States and Africa, he was a major civil rights figure, prolific left-wing political commentator, and peace activist. An avid socialist who looked too kindly on Soviet and

Chinese communism and believed capitalism caused racism and poverty, he was still making news and causing the US government trouble in 1963 when he died in exile in Ghana at age ninety-five.

— ~

Early in the new century two historic tragedies set back the progress of Atlanta, dramatically affected its swelling black population, and threatened the health and safety of John Wesley Dobbs. On Saturday, September 22, 1906, "The Atlanta Race Riot" erupted and made news around the world. It was sparked by sensationalistic white newspapers and their incendiary, vague, and racist front-page reports of black men attempting to assault white women in different parts of town. The rioting by whites raged on and off for several days. Gangs of armed young men and boys roamed through every part of the city, beating, stabbing, and shooting black men at random. They dragged many of their victims out of trolleys, supposedly, according to one newspaper, because the mere sight of a crowd of "negro brutes" in the presence of white women drove them to kill.

Jim Crow laws prohibited blacks from owning guns, so most were defenseless. But not Dobbs. On the second night, a mob stalked into his residential neighborhood in the Fourth Ward, which was also the neighborhood of thirteen-year-old Walter White and his family. Waiting in the darkened house he shared with his new wife, Irene, on Auburn Avenue, Dobbs sat behind a bolted door with his US government–issued Colt revolver in his lap and plenty of ammunition on the floor. In another middle-class home a few blocks away, Walter White's father handed him a gun he had purchased that day and told him to shoot the first white man who stepped on his property.

A *New York Times* story on Sunday, September 23, was filled with shocking details of the "lynching fever which seized upon the white people of Atlanta" the previous night. The stack of headlines above the article didn't go out of its way to inform readers that it was white people who were doing the rioting and murdering, but it summed up the first day of the riot fairly well: "ATLANTA MOBS KILL TEN NEGROES; Maybe 25 or 30—Assaults on Women the Cause; SLAIN WHEREVER

FOUND; Cars Stopped in Streets, Victims Torn from Them; MILITIA-MEN CALLED OUT; Trolley Systems Stopped to Keep the Mob from Reaching the Negro Quarter." The *Times* reported between ten thousand and fifteen thousand rioters. Of the estimated twenty-seven killed, twenty-five were black.

The deaths of two innocent black victims were described in gruesome detail by the *Atlanta Constitution*, one of the less sensationalist and racist white papers. At the top were thick banner headlines—"ATLANTA IS SWEPT BY RAGING MOB; DUE TO ASSAULTS ON WHITE WOMEN." Under the smaller and macabrely poetic headline "CHASED NEGROES ALL THE NIGHT," the paper, which referred to blacks suspected of being criminals as "brutes," detailed what happened when two black barbers had the bad luck to be caught by a mob in their downtown barbershop where they cut wealthy white men's hair.

The two negro barbers working at their chairs made no effort to meet the mob. One man held up both his hands. A brick caught him in the face, and at the same time shots were fired. Both men fell to the floor. Still unsatisfied, the mob rushed into the barber shop, leaving the place a mass of ruins. The bodies of both barbers were first kicked and then dragged from the place. Grabbing at their clothing, this was soon torn from them, many of the crowd taking these rags of shirts and clothing home as souvenirs or waving them above their heads to invite to further riot. When dragged into the street, the faces of both barbers were terribly mutilated, while the floor of the shop was wet with puddles of blood. On and on these bodies were dragged across the street to where the new building of the electric and gas company stands. In the alleyway leading by the side of this building the bodies were thrown together and left there. At about the same time another portion of the mob busied itself with one negro caught up on the streets. He was summarily treated. Felled with a single blow, shots were fired at the body until the crowd for its own safety called for a halt on this method, and yelled, "Beat 'em up. Beat 'em up. You'll kill good white men by shooting." By way of reply, the mob began beating the body of the negro, which was already far beyond any possibility of struggle or pain. Satisfied that the negro was dead, his body was thrown by the side of the two negro barbers and left there, the pile of three making a ghastly monument to the work of the night. . . .

For two days stray mobs of armed men and boys passed by the homes of Dobbs and White. Neither had to fire a shot. But after that terrifying night, Dobbs kept loaded guns and extra ammunition in his house until he died, and White's life was changed forever. The part of White's riot story involving the gun, which he grippingly told in the opening pages of his autobiography *A Man Called White*, is dubious. It was most likely a case of a good writer knowing when to punch up and embellish a true story by fully deploying his dramatic license. But White said the experience of being hunted like an animal at age thirteen by a mob of racists with torches made him realize who and what he was. In 1948, at age fifty-five, he put down in his autobiography the thoughts and feelings he could not articulate as a teenager.

In the flickering light the mob swayed, paused, and began to flow toward us. In that instance there opened up within me a great awareness; I knew then who I was. I was a Negro, a human being with an invisible pigmentation which marked me a person to be hunted, hanged, abused, discriminated against, kept in poverty and ignorance, in order that those whose skin was white would have readily at hand a proof of their superiority, a proof patent and inclusive, accessible to the moron and the idiot as well as to the wise man and the genius. No matter how low a white man fell, he could always hold fast to the smug conviction that he was superior to two-thirds of the world's population, for those two-thirds were not white.

The race riot also changed Atlanta. Thousands of blacks left for the North. The whites in charge of the city, apparently not caring that it was ten thousand brutes of their own race who did the rioting, doubled-down on enforcing their Jim Crow laws. When the *New York World* newspaper sent a telegram to the mayor of Atlanta the next day asking for his advice on how to prevent a race riot, Mayor J. G. Woodward replied that it depended upon its cause. If the question had anything to do with "the present situation in Atlanta," his honor said, "then I would say the only remedy is to remove the cause. As long as black brutes attempt rape upon our white women, just so long will they be unceremoniously dealt with." After the riot, unnerved black businessmen moved from their locations downtown to the safety of their own segregated turf, spurring a commercial boom along Auburn Avenue that lasted decades.

Eleven years later Dobbs had another brush with disaster that the state militia and no revolver could stop. He and his growing family were living at 540 Houston Street. On the hot and breezy afternoon of May 21, 1917, a fire started in some mattresses in a warehouse not far from Auburn Avenue. With the fire department and its horse-drawn trucks busy putting out three other small fires nearby, no equipment was available to control the warehouse fire. Feeding on shanties, hundreds of black-owned frame houses, and fine white homes, driven north by a stiff southern wind, the flames raced and leapt from roof to wood-shingled roof across the densely populated Fourth Ward.

Dobbs was downtown. When he saw the smoke and heard the fire alarms he took off for home. After circling around the fire department barricades on Houston Street, he arrived to find his kids safe and wife dragging boxes of valuables and important papers into the yard. He was lucky. As it swept across three blocks of Houston Street, the wall of flames and smoke passed about five hundred feet from his wood frame house. "The Great Atlanta Fire of 1917" burned for another eight hours. It consumed fifty city blocks and two thousand buildings before it was stopped by dynamiting twenty mansions in its path. Ten thousand people, most of them black, were made homeless. Hundreds of beautiful homes were incinerated, leaving behind nothing but their blackened stone chimneys.

The disaster permanently rearranged the housing pattern of Atlanta's east side. Overnight it opened up a three-hundred-acre swath of prime urban real estate to new development and gave city hall the opportunity to practice some Jim Crow–style city planning. The day after the fire two councilmen proposed a resolution asking the mayor to appoint a five-man commission to look into establishing new municipal parks between the former black and white neighborhoods of the charred Fourth Ward. It was a chance to implement part of a "City Beautiful" plan. But more importantly, the parks were a permanent fix for a long-running problem faced by whites residing on the streets where the two neighborhoods came together. As the *Atlanta Constitution* noted in its lead front-page story about the resolution, which was approved unanimously, the wide new parks would "for all time settle the embarrassing problem" of white Fourth Warders having to live on the same streets as "negroes."

CHAPTER 8

Atlanta in Black and White

With a population of about 330,000 in 1948, Atlanta was the fourth largest city in the South after New Orleans, Houston, and Dallas. Nearly a million people—almost a third of all Georgians and a third of them black—lived in the Atlanta metropolitan region. The city was held up as one of the South's most civilized, a mecca for both whites and blacks, but it was fervently Jim Crow. During the 1930s blacks couldn't serve on juries. Interracial marriages were forbidden. Except for a park built by Booker T. Washington, blacks were not allowed in city parks. Whites and blacks had different-colored tax forms, separate tellers at banks, separate water fountains, separate entrances to theaters.

In 1947, the year John Gunther came to meet Atlanta's movers and shakers for *Inside U.S.A.*, he said it "out-ghettoes anything I ever saw in a European ghetto, even in Warsaw. What I looked at was caste and untouchability—half the time I blinked remembering that this was not India." All of the city's public and private places—schools, colleges, parks, libraries, hotels, restaurants, movie theaters, concert halls, bowling alleys, swimming pools, buses, taxis, and even elevators—were strictly segregated. So was the part of Atlanta that Ray Sprigle woke up in on Sunday morning.

The Fourth Ward was an upscale version of Pittsburgh's Hill District, only without any white people. It was where Atlanta's black elite lived and where most of them worked. Two blocks from Dobbs's house was "Sweet Auburn" Avenue, the thriving commercial, cultural, and spiritual main drag of black Atlanta that Dobbs once said was "paved with gold."

Auburn Avenue was a natural extension of Peachtree Street, the major through street in historic downtown Atlanta that Clark Gable, Vivien Leigh, and half of Hollywood took over in 1939 when they flew in to celebrate the world premiere of *Gone With the Wind*. Only a short walk from the office buildings of downtown, Auburn Avenue was pierced by trolley tracks and lined for over a mile with retail businesses, big churches, and social and financial institutions. There were grocery stores, drugstores, cafes, ice cream parlors, liquor stores, smoke shops, several movie theaters, a fish market, shoeshine stands, fried chicken restaurants, and jazz clubs that booked stars like Cab Calloway and Duke Ellington. There were also two black-owned banks and the headquarters of the Atlanta Life Insurance Company, where Walter White's brother-in-law Eugene Martin worked as a twenty-thousand-dollars-a-year vice president. Atlanta Life had been founded by entrepreneur and real estate investor Alonzo Herndon, a barber and former slave who built his fortune by cutting the hair of the city's leading white politicians and businessmen in his elegant barbershops. His door-to-door insurance company had become the city's largest black business and made him its first black millionaire.

Also throwing its shadow on Sweet Auburn was one of Atlanta's great black churches, Ebenezer Baptist Church. Martin Luther King Sr., the beloved pastor and community leader, had grown his flock from six hundred in the early 1930s to nearly four thousand. He was a friend and powerful ally of Dobbs in the constant political fight with city hall to get better black schools, more black teachers, and new bond issues. On a corner two blocks from the squared-off brick towers of King's church was the handsome headquarters of Dobbs's political and civic power, the Prince Hall Masonic Temple.

After Dobbs became grand master in the early 1930s, he started construction of the yellow-gold brick office building, but when the Masons' membership funds dried up to almost nothing during the Depression he had to wait until 1937 to finish it. Built to the edge of the sidewalk, its three stories featured elaborate brick work, classical detailing, multiple copies of the Masons' insignia, and a neon sign over the front door that left no doubt what it was. On the top floor, under arched ceilings and lighted by large windows, was the lodge where the masons held their meetings, planned their good works, and helped Grand Master Dobbs with his permanent crusade to register black voters and turn them into a political force.

Dobbs was a celebrity on Auburn Avenue long before he was declared its unofficial mayor. He patrolled its sidewalks like a rock star—like "The Grand." He patted small kids on the head. He carried a fat roll of bills and gave away money freely. He stopped in the grocery stores and barbershops where he'd enthrall people with his stories—riding the railroad and guarding the US mail, visiting Joe Louis's training camp, meeting alone with FDR at Warm Springs for forty-five minutes in 1935 to talk about masonry, traveling to backwater Georgia towns to speak at a church or Masonic lodge with his driver and armed bodyguard, Joe Phinazee.

The Grand himself had coined "Sweet Auburn." It was a reference to the opening line of "The Deserted Village," an impossibly long poem by eighteenth-century Irish poet Oliver Goldsmith that few in Georgia but Dobbs had read: "Sweet Auburn, loveliest village of the plain, Where health and plenty cheared the labouring swain." He said what made the street "sweet" was all the money that was generated by its black banks, retail businesses, and churches. *Fortune* magazine acknowledged Auburn Avenue's sweetness in 1956, calling it "the richest Negro street in the world."

Auburn Avenue was also the address of the *Atlanta Daily World*, the only daily black newspaper on the continent. It wasn't much of a paper—six or eight pages of news and local ads per edition, no paper printed on Mondays, and a circulation of twenty-five thousand. The exuberant sensationalism and bomb-throwing politics of the militant *Pittsburgh Courier* and the *Chicago Defender* put it to shame. It was nonpartisan and its owner, C. A. Scott, was a conservative Republican whose less aggressive views on politics and civil rights enabled him to attract ads from the biggest department stores in Atlanta and national companies like Coca-Cola and Sears.

Like every black paper, the *World* kept an inning-by-inning watch on Jackie Robinson—every stolen base and ankle sprain. It also faithfully reported community, church, and society news and publicized voting registration drives and community improvement efforts, including Dobbs's long fight to get black policemen for Auburn Avenue. Because it also used its presses to print as many as fifty other small black weeklies from New York State to Birmingham, at one time it had two hundred employees working three shifts in its plant.

The *World* didn't have a splashy front page and its dry editorials calling for anti-lynching laws or the end of segregation often shared the page with obituaries and classified ads. But it did its job well. Widely distributed in the South, it focused on news black Atlantans needed or wanted to read, which, if it had anything to do with segregation, lynchings, or the mistreatment of black soldiers during World War II, was usually buried deep in the city's two white dailies or not carried at all. In 1944 its Washington reporter became the first black newspaperman to be given accreditation to cover FDR's press conferences.

When Sprigle sat down to Sunday breakfast at Dobbs's house on May 9, 1948, the *World's* front page was a typical mix of local and national news and fluff. Republicans in Congress were threatening to attach civil rights legislation to a Democratic bill allowing southern states to set up segregated regional professional schools. In one Georgia county, 75 percent of the twenty-four hundred qualified registered blacks had been purged from voting rolls by white election officials. And under the headline "SEVEN NEW BISHOPS SEEN FOR AMEs" was a report on the "confusion and tumult" raging within the executive committee at the African Methodist Episcopal Church's national conference in Kansas City, Kansas.

Two photographs, both posed, floated among the dozen articles. In the smaller one, Ethel Shelley of St. Louis was reading a newspaper story about the landmark US Supreme Court decision that included her name. Earlier that week, in *Shelley v. Kraemer*, the high court ruled that all racially restrictive real estate covenants between private parties like the one attached to her property were unconstitutional. Property owners could continue to privately conspire and collude to keep blacks or Jews out of their neighborhoods, but the public written agreements that affected upwards of forty million American homes were outlawed.

The caption under the larger photo began with "Bojangles Gets Mr. Big's John Henry." It showed famed tap dancer Bill Robinson with

President Truman, who had agreed to sign an award Robinson received from the National Health Assembly for his many benefit performances. If Truman had thought the signing would get him some valuable free publicity in the black press, it worked.

Dobbs and his wife, Irene, had lived in their house on Houston Street for thirty-nine years. They had raised six smart and talented girls together, but from the start it was John Wesley Dobbs who exercised absolute parental power. Setting out to create women who were smart, sophisticated, refined, and successful, he saw to it that each daughter was prepared to become a future graduate of Spelman College, the historic black women's college some called the black Vassar. He filled his house with books and made sure his girls were at the top of their classes in high school. He advised them on everything, including sex, and encouraged them to express themselves on every topic. At the dinner table there were many lively debates that led to Dobbs reaching for the encyclopedia. Starting at age seven, each of them was required to take ten years of lessons on the big piano in the living room. They were as well dressed as they were well spoken. When they were of age, he had a chauffeur teach them how to drive.

Each daughter received heavy doses of their father's love of America and its history and his moral contempt for slavery and segregation. When he took them to New York City to see the Statue of Liberty, he made them climb the stairs to the top so they'd never forget that day. For the same reason he made them actually touch Plymouth Rock. On family trips north, he constantly pointed out to them that blacks there were much more free than they were under Jim Crow. When he drove his daughters into the Georgia countryside in one of his nice cars, he'd stop at the statues of Confederate soldiers in the centers of small towns. He'd remind his girls what the statues really memorialized: "the diabolical system of human slavery" and white power over the lives of blacks.

Out of principle Dobbs did what he could as an individual consumer to punish any business that discriminated against blacks. He subscribed to the "Don't Buy Where You Can't Work" campaign that aimed to get blacks hired at retail stores that had black customers. Long before it became an official campaign of black motorists, he followed the slogan

"Don't Buy Gas Where You Can't Use the Restroom." When he stopped at a service station, he wouldn't purchase gas until he saw that one of his daughters was allowed to use the restroom. If they were stopped, he'd drive off, often leaving the attendant standing by the pump. Dobbs never allowed his daughters to attend a segregated event or venue in Atlanta. Most important, he never let them forget that no matter what Jim Crow's rules implied or did to humiliate or demean them or their race, they were equal to anyone.

By the spring of 1948 Dobbs's parenting style had paid off. In an era when only 5 percent of women in the country had college degrees, each of his six girls, born between 1908 and 1928, had gone to Spelman College and been a star student. They were all chips off the old man's block: smart, driven, principled, proud of their race. Renie, the oldest, was the class valedictorian in 1925. In 1959 she was the first black American to receive a library card from the Atlanta Public Library. In 1973 her son Maynard—ten years old at the time of Sprigle's visit—was going to be elected Atlanta's first black mayor. Second daughter Willie graduated at the top of her class in 1931, earned her master's degree at Atlanta University and moved to Jackson, Mississippi, where she ran the language arts department at Jackson State University and had a building named after her. Millie, class of 1933, received her master's from Columbia University in speech and drama and became a professor of English and African-American literature at Spelman and several other colleges. Four years later, Josephine graduated from Spelman and earned her master's at Columbia as well. After moving to Durham, North Carolina, she would become a local activist, early civil rights leader, and chairwoman of the city school board.

Living in New York City in the spring of 1948 was daughter number five, the musically gifted Mattiwilda. Known to her family as "Geekie," she graduated first in her Spelman class in 1946 and moved to New York to get a master's in Spanish at Columbia. While she was studying Spanish, she also took vocal lessons from a renowned German opera teacher that would change her life. By the mid-1950s she was an international opera star based in Sweden. She performed at major festivals and opera houses in Europe and the United States, but because she kept her vow never to sing to a segregated audience, she didn't perform in her hometown until 1962.

The youngest Dobbs daughter, June, was not yet twenty in 1948 and set to graduate from Spelman in a month. She had already made plans to spend the summer traveling through the South to do census work for the Baptist Church with her old friend and neighbor, Martin Luther King Jr. He was nineteen and about to graduate from Morehouse College, the black men's college that shared Atlanta University's campus with Spelman. Born two blocks away on Auburn Avenue, King had been ordained a Baptist minister in a ceremony at his father's church in February and had already committed to attending Crozer Theological Seminary near Philadelphia.

The Kings and the Dobbses had known each other for years. M. L. K. Jr. and his younger brother, Alfred Daniel, known as A. D., had been buzzing around the Dobbs house, and paying special attention to Mattiwilda and June, since they were young. The King brothers used to come over and play Monopoly with the Dobbs sisters on the linoleum kitchen floor and seemed to win most of the time. Later it was learned they were arriving with their pockets stuffed with Monopoly money from their own game.

Sprigle met his first Dobbs daughter Sunday morning at breakfast. Millie Dobbs Jordan, a university instructor, and her five-year-old boy Robert were visiting from Tennessee for the weekend. Whenever Millie used the word "white" or "Negro" in her conversation she spelled it out. Robert, who would become a CBS network news correspondent and WGN-TV news reporter in Chicago for forty-plus years, didn't know there was a difference between white people and black people. He had yet to learn there were two races and that, as Sprigle angrily spun it, he was going to have to learn "how to live under the iron rule of a master race that regards him as an inferior breed" and that "for him, the Constitution and the Declaration of Independence are scraps of paper."

Millie felt it was too soon to begin explaining what all blacks in the Jim Crow South had to be taught at an early age. After Robert was chased outside, Millie—who believed she was talking to a light-skinned black man—explained further. "We try to let them have their childhood free of prejudice and confusion," she said. "But we've got to tell them before they come up against the hard facts of discrimination and prejudice for themselves. You people up North have only one set of 'the facts of life' to put before your children. Down here we've got two. And sometimes I think the racial facts of life are the most important."

Millie told Sprigle a sad but true story about a girl whose parents didn't deliver lessons in race relations until after she had started at her segregated school. When the little black girl met a little white girl on her walk home and invited her to come into her house, her parents had to do some quick thinking. The white girl was sent home, as nicely as possible, and told she should never come back. To their own child, Sprigle said later, the black parents "had to explain that she could not enter a white home except through the back door. That no white could enter a Negro's house except on business and that certainly no little white girl could ever visit a little black girl."

All day that Sunday the house on Houston Street was busy. As usual Dobbs and his wife, Irene, went to services at First Congregational Church, the preferred house of worship for Atlanta's black elite and the place they were married in 1906. It was a dignified New England–style church where the services were subdued, the sermons were serious and thoughtful, and the stained-glass windows included images of Jesus and Abraham Lincoln. It was so quiet and dull that in his later years Dobbs would fall asleep and snore so loudly his family wouldn't sit next to him.

When Millie's friends stopped by to see her on Sunday afternoon, Sprigle was introduced as Mr. James R. Crawford, a Pittsburgher who was gathering information for his friend, NAACP national secretary Walter White. Conversations naturally drifted to comparing life in the South and the North. Sprigle took notes but didn't exactly have a lot of information to impart on the subject. Dobbs's daughter and her friends schooled him in some of the indignities Jim Crow imposed on a refined southern black woman when she wanted to buy a dress or a hat in a downtown department store. Atlanta was an exception, but in most southern cities a black woman was prohibited from trying on any clothes before buying them. As Sprigle quipped, if she touched them, she had to buy them. In some hat departments, the sales clerk would pin a cloth over a black woman's head before she was allowed to try it on.

Shoe stores were as bad. Black customers had to sit on specific benches in the back of the store. Sprigle was told a famous "shoe story" that every woman in Dobbs's parlor knew well. A famous black tenor, Roland Hayes, had bought an old plantation near Rome, Georgia, where his mother had been born and had been a slave. When Hayes's wife went into town to purchase a new pair of shoes, she was ordered to sit on the benches in the back. She made a huge fuss. She had been born in New York City, where John Gunther said blacks were treated better than anywhere in the USA, but in Georgia if she wanted to buy a new pair of shoes, she had to mind Jim Crow. The moral of the story? "If it can happen to Roland Hayes in Rome," all the women agreed, "it can happen to any Negro anywhere in the South."

Simple phone conversations were also a problem at times because whites, including telephone operators, would never knowingly call a black person "Mr." or "Mrs." As Sprigle sarcastically noted, a courtesy title would not be used by any "Southern white who even pretends to be worthy of the noble traditions of the South—white supremacy—the purity of the race, the sanctity of white Southern womanhood. He'll call them 'Doctor,' 'Professor,' 'Counselor,' but he'd cheerfully burn at the stake before he'd ever so far forget his white heritage as to call one of the creatures 'Mr.' or 'Mrs.'"

One story Sprigle heard was particularly ugly, but it had a happy ending that proved to him that some progress in black-white relations was being made—in Atlanta, at least. It involved an employee of the Tuskegee Institute who dialed the long-distance operator and placed a call from Atlanta to his wife. After the black man said her name was "Mrs. Morgan," the operator demanded her first name. The man said not to worry. There was only one Mrs. Morgan at that number. "But she's a nigger ain't she," the operator said. "Do you think I'm going to say 'Mrs.' to a nigger?" The next day, as Sprigle later retold the story, the man who made the phone call "was in the office of the telephone company manager. The lily white operator was summoned and summarily fired. But the soft-hearted black man interceded and she got her job back. Negroes get normal telephone service in Atlanta today."

CHAPTER 9

On the Road to Americus

The dark green Mercury was so big and its suspension system was so soft that even at sixty mph it seemed to float over Georgia State Route 49. With Dobbs and Sprigle aboard, the spacious metal and chrome beast weighed two tons. It had a gigantic front hood and grill, fat fenders, and four "suicide doors." It was made by the Ford Motor Company, the only auto company Dobbs would buy from because it hired far more black workers than any other car maker in Detroit. Not only that, Ford gave blacks assembly-line jobs, not just janitorial or foundry jobs, and even promoted some of them to foremen and management. A Mercury was considered a luxury car, a step up in price and quality from a regular Ford. The Town Sedan model Dobbs drove cost $1,660 new. There was no air conditioning, of course, and it had a three-speed manual transmission with the shifter on the steering column. But it had a radio, a heater, a big round clock in the dashboard, and an acre of two-tone bench seats front and back. When its V-8 engine teamed with Dobbs's heavy right foot, the Mercury could reach eighty mph on a flat road with a good tail wind. It was the kind of speed he appreciated on his dashes north to see Joe Louis fight in New York or to catch Jackie Robinson and the Dodgers play in St. Louis.

The Mercury was Dobbs's second car and he used it for most of his road trips, but it was actually owned by the Prince Hall Masons. His own well-traveled family car was also a Mercury—a Zephyr. A streamlined, lower-priced luxury car, it was discontinued in the early 1940s. Dobbs loved it, but his granddaughter Juliet Dobbs Blackburn-Beamon never understood why. She was eleven in 1948. She and her mother, Willie, used to come from Jackson, Mississippi, every summer to visit her grandfather. Juliet preferred riding to church in the newer car and would often ask him why he didn't get rid of that old "rattling" Zephyr.

Having a car—or two—was especially liberating for middle-class blacks in the South. It meant being able to enjoy the basic human right to move and travel where, when, and how you wanted. But it also allowed you to completely avoid the degrading aspects of segregated public transportation. George Schuyler of the *Pittsburgh Courier* had pointed out in 1930 that "all Negroes who can do so purchase an automobile as soon as possible in order to be free of the discomfort, discrimination, segregation, and insult" they faced on trains and streetcars. Driving in a car on Jim Crow's roads alone or with your family offered black men a rare period of personal freedom and autonomy—as long as you kept going fifty miles an hour. Where you stopped to eat, sleep, or go to the bathroom was a huge practical problem. Colorblind national chain motels hadn't been invented yet. Most locally owned tourist cabins or trailer parks were white only. And few white gas stations outside large cities had "For Colored" restrooms.

Car travel in the South and elsewhere in America was such a widespread problem for blacks that in 1936 a New York mailman named Victor Green began publishing an annual booklet called *The Negro Motorist Green Book*. The travel guide, which cost seventy-five cents and was given out by some Esso gas stations, provided tips on where black vacationers and businessmen could find food, lodging, nightclubs, beauty parlors, and car repairs without incurring discrimination or embarrassment. With about fifteen thousand copies printed each year, it also warned about "sundown towns," those lovely American hamlets where nonwhites were not permitted within town limits after dusk. From Levittown, New York, to Hawthorne, California, there were thousands of places in America where blacks, Latinos, and Asians could be picked up by police after sundown and shown the city limits.

In his introductions to the *Green Book*, Mr. Green said he looked forward to a time when his publication would no longer be necessary. "There will be a day sometime in the near future when this guide will not have to be published. That is when we as a race will have equal opportunities and privileges in the United States. It will be a great day for us to suspend this publication for then we can go wherever we please, and without embarrassment." That great day came in 1964, when the Civil Rights Act was passed. Though much work, struggle, and pain lay ahead before blacks could travel with equal comfort and choice, Mr. Green kept his promise and ceased publishing his guide that year. In 1948 the *Green Book* was considered "one of the survival tools of segregated life" by many middle-class black travelers, but Dobbs racked up so much mileage and knowledge behind the wheel in the South and elsewhere that he didn't need it.

The '47 Mercury had fewer than nine thousand miles on its odometer when Dobbs and Sprigle left Atlanta on Monday morning. For two hours under a burning sun, they drove a hundred miles south into the heart of cotton and peach country. It was cotton-chopping time. In field after field, children, parents, and grandparents were swinging their hoes to chop away the Johnson grass and weeds from around the sprouting cotton plants. Monday was wash day in the South just as it was in the North. Along Georgia Route 49 and on its few dirt side roads, they could see hundreds of women boiling their family's dirty clothes in steaming iron kettles in the yards of their unpainted shacks.

The previous night Dobbs had given Sprigle the first of several refresher courses on how to behave like a black man in the South. It was something you learned in a lifetime, not a few hours. But in general, Dobbs told Sprigle, to stay out of trouble and avoid harm you had to be vigilant as well as meek, lowly, and docile. Trouble could come simply by forgetting or refusing to say "sir" to a white man. You always say "sir," Dobbs warned him, whether you or the white man starts the conversation. If a white man—drunk or sober—hits you, you never hit back. You just take it. You never argue with the white conductor of a train, bus, or streetcar or, for that matter, with any white man in a position of authority. Do what he says and shut up. You never speak disrespectfully or familiarly to a white woman. If you have the bad luck to bump into a white woman, or offend her in any way, don't reply or defend yourself if she starts insulting you. Just take off your hat, apologize, and back away.

Though he had to be prepared, Sprigle wasn't planning to bump into that many whites. He was traveling inside a parallel black world.

With his Prince Hall contacts Dobbs was going to put him in touch with middle-class black professionals and community leaders across the Deep South. He was also going to introduce him to poor country folks like ex-sharecroppers Oscar and Elizabeth Engram. The Engrams, who lived on Flint River School Road in Macon County, owned fifty-nine acres of cotton fields near the town of Montezuma.

In the late 1930s they and about a hundred other poor black share-croppers and day laborers working on plantations in their area got lucky. They were chosen to be participants in the Flint River Farms project, an experimental land reform program created by the FDR Administration's Department of Agriculture. The program, which purchased nearly two million acres of land around the United States, was designed to lift white and black sharecroppers and tenant farmers out of poverty, make them landowners, and help them become self-sustaining small farmers and entrepreneurs. The Flint River Farms project was one of two hundred locations in the country and one of thirteen all-black communities that gave families like the Engrams a chance to move out of their "shotgun shacks" and buy their own five-room homes and farmland at subsidized rates.

After dealing with local opposition from some whites who worried the project would lead to lower land values and higher wage rates if it was successful—and be a waste of money and source of disappointment if it failed—the federal government set up the Flint River Farms project. In 1937 it bought several large cotton plantations near Montezuma for $215,000 and broke eleven thousand acres into 107 homestead units. Averaging ninety-three acres of land, each unit consisted of a new wood two-bedroom home and some simple furniture, a barn, two mules, an outhouse, a chicken coop, and a smoke house. Plus there was a water well, fencing, and an electricity hookup courtesy of the Rural Electrification Administration. About ten houses were built on the Engrams' dirt street, which was surrounded by hundreds of acres of cotton and soybeans. Families like the Engrams had to sign lease-purchase agreements with the federal government. If after five years of leasing they proved they were successful at farming, they were offered forty-year mortgages at 3 percent interest to purchase their home and land.

In mid-afternoon Dobbs turned off State Route 26 east of Montezuma and stopped for a drink of well water at the Engram place. Elizabeth was "somebody," Sprigle said, after hearing her life story. He admired how she was still making a go of it as a landowner despite the tragedy that had befallen her husband four years earlier. During their first years at Flint River Farms, the Engrams worked the same way they had when they were sharecroppers on the same piece of land—they each walked behind a mule and plow from dawn to dusk. Then Oscar had a massive stroke that kept him from ever walking, using his arms, or talking again. Elizabeth "kept the mules and the plows going," Sprigle said. She raised crops for two years by herself until she was able to rent out their land to tenant farmers. Now the Engrams were bringing in enough rent to feed themselves and make their mortgage payments so that they'd own their land free and clear in thirty years.

Before her visitors from the big city could move on, Elizabeth insisted they stay for a meal. "Nothing would do but we must sit down and share supper greens and a slab of corn pone and plain water from the pump outside," Sprigle said. Elizabeth was insulted when "Mr. Crawford" of the NAACP tried to offer her some money. But Sprigle got the last word. Before he left he slid a dollar under his plate. "I wonder what she thought when she picked up my plate after we'd gone," he said later. "Bet that's the first time corn pone sold for a dollar a slice in Macon County, Georgia."

At the other corner of Route 26 and Flint River School Road, directly across from the Engrams' house, was the Flint River Farms Community Center. Along with a six-room school building, the complex had a home for the black principal, a barn, a vocational agriculture shop, and a health building. The Flint River Farms School's eight black teachers taught several hundred kids from Grade 1 to Grade 11. Boys were trained in proper farming methods, stock feeding, and poultry care. Girls learned how to can food, garden, and cook. Adults took evening classes or heard guest speakers. The Farm Security Administration boasted, without exaggeration, that the "Flint River School was better than any the county had known for Negroes before and had set new standards."

The Flint River Farms project was a New Deal dream made real. It was a rare gift from the federal government to a hundred lucky black farmers mired in the agricultural poverty of Macon County. In 1948 it was still a success. The young principal of the school, John Robinson, told Sprigle he figured half of the farmers like the Engrams were making good, about half were holding on, and only a few had given up and quit. Though Sprigle was no fan of the New Deal or government social engineering, he thought the farm project was fine. But he was also realistic. Calling it "just a drop in an ocean, a bright clear drop in a dark and bitter ocean," he said it would take ten thousand projects like it "to even make a dent in the evil sharecropping system."

In the long run Flint River Farms' goal to create a hundred self-sustaining cotton farmers using mules and the muscles of people like the Engrams was doomed. It couldn't sustain itself for a host of economic, agricultural, and sociological reasons. It slowly disappeared. By 1998 what was left of the Engrams' old street was still stranded alone on a dry plain of cotton and soybean. The community center and school at the corner of Route 26 were gone without a trace. A dozen tidy brick and mobile homes clung haphazardly to the street. The few remaining original homesteads had been remodeled—and given indoor plumbing, a feature only white-occupied government houses got when they were built. The Engram place had vanished. Like most of the original homes, it had been lifted from its foundation and moved to an empty lot somewhere in the nearby town of Montezuma. The spot where Sprigle and Dobbs shared a drink of water and a slice of corn pone with Oscar and Elizabeth was an overgrown lot with a few small piles of red brick, some junk, and a rusting hand pump.

—◆—

"If we can make Americus tonight we'll have a place to stay." It was the first thing Dobbs had said all day about where they'd be spending the night. It was nearing dinnertime. They were on empty Georgia Route 49 again, moving through a rolling pine forest at the usual speed—the Dobbs speed. He loved to drive fast as much as he loved to talk, play cards, and sip Kentucky bourbon. He got a kick out of blowing by slower white motorists. He liked to watch their faces when they realized they were being passed by a black man driving a nicer car than they had. "It was the only revenge he had for being treated badly by white people," his daughter Mattiwilda said decades later. She said her father was a good driver, but his personality changed when he got behind the wheel. He would race people, especially whites, with the whole family in the car. Her mother, Irene, would watch the speedometer in terror.

On a family trip to Boston in the 1920s, Mattiwilda said her father ran off the road into a field. Everyone screamed. Her mother fainted. No one was hurt in that accident, but in 1933 Dobbs came close to killing himself. Shortly after he became head of the state's Prince Hall Masons, he was driving at night from Macon to Atlanta with three Masonic officers in his Peerless, a high-powered luxury sedan with running boards and the spare tire on the passenger side. At sixty miles an hour he fell asleep at the wheel, hit a telephone pole, and the car ended up on the side of an embankment. The Peerless was totaled. Everyone was injured but not seriously. Dobbs was bleeding heavily from the nose, the result of a severed artery.

In an era without padded dashboards, collapsible steering columns, safety glass, and seatbelts, he was lucky to be alive. He knew it. He attributed his survival to the "good spirit" that watched over him. He took the accident as a warning, but he still didn't drop his impersonation of a race-car driver. He had what Mattiwilda called "sporting friends" who would ride with him to Washington to see black entertainers. Atlanta was a hick town compared to DC, she said, and her father and his doctor friend would drive up there to a black theater similar to the Apollo in New York. They used to brag that they could cover the 630 miles in ten hours.

Sprigle was more worried about his next meal than his next bed. He was close to starving. Except for Elizabeth Engram's corn pone he'd had nothing to eat since breakfast. There was no restaurant on the road to Americus where they could stop, but it didn't matter because they wouldn't be allowed to eat there except maybe at the back door. Suddenly Dobbs slowed down and pulled off Route 49. They drove through "a pair of great brick pillars into a woodland where monuments and row upon row of marble gravestones showed white through the dark trees." It was one of Dobbs's favorite Civil War historical sites. It was officially called Camp Sumter, but the North knew it better as the notorious Andersonville Prison. In the last year and a half of the Civil War, it was established as the South's largest military prison for captured Union soldiers. What it quickly became, however, was a squalid, overcrowded death camp. Of the forty-five thousand northern POWs held in its stockades for various lengths of time, nearly thirteen thousand died from malnutrition, scurvy, diarrhea, and dysentery.

Sprigle had told Dobbs when they first met, and several times since, that he was not interested in seeing pretty scenery, battlefield sites, parks, mansions, "or anything else that didn't concern the life of the Negro in the South." But he bit his tongue. Andersonville was special to Dobbs. "I always stop a minute here whenever I pass," Dobbs said. "Most of our people do. These men died for us." In addition to paying his respects to the 13,714 soldiers buried on the beautiful grounds, Dobbs also always took a drink from the public water fountain fed by Providence Spring. Because the site had become the property of the federal government, Jim Crow's laws did not apply. Dobbs was free to drink from the same fountain as any white man. It was a small symbolic victory he always enjoyed repeating, but it was even sweeter sharing it with Sprigle. It was the only time during his mission that Sprigle was able to drink at a water fountain that didn't have a "Colored Only" sign.

To Sprigle the laws and rituals surrounding "so simple an act as taking a drink of water" in the Deep South were yet another example of the illogic and idiocy of Jim Crow. If black lips touched a glass it was deemed to be forever "contaminated and accursed" and had to be kept separated. The easiest way to avoid that "contamination" was to prevent blacks and whites from eating or drinking in the same public places. But in drugstores, where black mothers and their kids could shop but not eat, a thirsty black child could get a drink—in a paper cup. And at gas stations, the rules were different. Blacks could drink anything they wanted as long as it was out of a bottle, which Sprigle and Dobbs jokingly agreed must have been decontaminated by "some particularly deadly acid" by the bottling companies. But they couldn't use the "Whites Only" water fountain. They had to use paper cups.

Sprigle thought the South's squeamish supremacists were going to a lot of trouble for nothing.

All of this somewhat hysterical insistence upon keeping inanimate objects such as dishes, water glasses, chairs, park benches, railroad coaches and streetcars free from contamination by Americans whose ancestors came from Africa would make better sense if there were some consistency about the thing. Do these white racial purists think that the millions of cooks and other servants in white homes never take a drink from the family glasses? Or eat off the family china? Or not infrequently thrust a black thumb into the soup? . . . . And what about those thousands and thousands of Negro nursemaids who all over the South push thousands and thousands of perambulators, each containing a small edition of the master race—what about them?

By dark the pair reached Americus, a town of eleven thousand known to the outside world for a couple of trivial things that had nothing to do with shipping cotton or peanuts to market. Shoeless Joe Jackson of the Chicago White Sox managed a local baseball team there after he was kicked out of the majors for his role in fixing the 1919 World Series. And Charles Lindbergh bought his first airplane at the local airport in 1923. The town's greatest claim to fame was born fifteen minutes away on a peanut farm in Plains. But in the spring of 1948 Jimmy Carter was just a twenty-four-year-old Navy electronics officer living in New London, Connecticut, and serving on the battleship *Mississippi*.

Through his Prince Hall connections, Dobbs took Sprigle to the home of a middle-class black family in Americus where he received a "bountiful meal" and slept in a comfortable room. Dobbs, as usual, was greeted like the visiting celebrity and leader he was. Sprigle was accepted as a visiting Negro from up North working for the NAACP, and he was given a full house tour by the proud owners. Sprigle was getting his first look at the way blacks had to travel in the South. There were hotels for black travelers in larger southern cities, though many of them were rough places not suitable for families or respectable businessmen. In small towns and rural areas, hotels were white-only or didn't exist. Calling it "another installment of the facts of life when you're black and in the South," Sprigle said blacks had been forced to create their own informal chain of free bed-and-breakfasts. "In every Southern town there are doctors, lawyers, undertakers, insurance men, who maintain open house for Negroes who are traveling. It's a kind of reciprocal affair. When they travel, they are guests at the homes of friends whom they have sheltered. There is no question of payment but it is etiquette when leaving in the morning to press upon your hostess a contribution for her church or missionary society. Or if she's an ardent member of the NAACP, then a donation to that organization."

In Americus Sprigle heard about the latest local effort of "the white man" to "roll back the rising tide of franchise that is sweeping Georgia." He said, "The courthouse gang has 'purged' the registration lists of 800 names of Negro voters. A bare 80 are left." It was a common trick by white voting officials in the South. Black voter registration rolls would be allowed to grow until near election time and then white officials would purge them for lame technicalities. The leaders of Americus's black community—i.e., Sprigle and Dobbs's hosts and their friends—formed a committee and raised six hundred dollars to go to court. The lawyer they had hired soon quit, and word came through the grapevine that the white people in charge of Sumter County were not pleased. Sprigle said the black leaders got the hint. The contributors were given back their money, and the court fight was called off. Four years earlier, thanks to a Texas case brought by the NAACP, the US Supreme Court had outlawed the white primary. Combined with poll taxes and other methods to prevent blacks from registering and voting as Republicans, the Democratic Party's white-only primary elections had effectively disenfranchised blacks and given segregationist Democrats a monopoly over politics in the South. Despite the Court's decision, Sprigle said, "the white folks of Sumter County have overruled the high tribunal. And as between the Supreme Court of the United States and the white folks, Sumter County Negroes are in no doubt as to which to obey. They'll live longer that way."

The black leaders in Americus may not have feared for their lives, as Sprigle intimated, but they knew the kind of trouble their constitutional "uppityness" could bring them. Two months earlier, 110 miles to the northeast, the local KKK franchise held a cross-burning in front of the courthouse in Wrightsville. As *Time* magazine reported in a mocking tone guaranteed to offend any practicing bigot in the South, the ceremony was intended to intimidate the four hundred Negroes who had recently registered to vote. Like the rest of the mainstream northern media, the influential news weekly paid little attention to the everyday political and economic realities of the Jim Crow South. But *Time*'s March 15, 1948, article, headlined "Sheet, Sugar Sack & Cross," painted a sharp picture of the "subtle" ways whites were able to maintain absolute political power in a state that was more than one-third black.

As *Time*'s reporter described it, as dusk fell a column of cars carrying about two hundred and fifty men and women pulled into Wrightsville's baseball park. Donning the white sheets and "sugar-sack masks" of the KKK, they marched slowly in single file into the town square, where seven hundred people waited for the show to start. The Klansmen dug a hole, planted a kerosene-soaked cross and set it ablaze. "As the flames shot up," *Time* reported, "a green-robed man—Atlanta Physician Samuel Green, Georgia's Grand Dragon—stepped into the light. Because it is hard to shout intelligibly through a sugar sack, Green wore no mask. Spectacles glinting, mustache working, he began a tirade against President Harry Truman and his espousal of civil rights legislation."

Dr. Green promised the Klan was never going to permit "the people of this country to become a mongrel race" and said there'd be blood in the street if "Yankee bayonets" tried to force equality between the races. When their leader's tirade stopped, *Time* said, the Klansmen "paraded back to the ballpark and had a barbecue." Their display of white power worked. "In the election the next day, no Negroes voted." After a considerable number of Georgia's citizens expressed their intense displeasure of the KKK's "tawdry barbarism," *Time* said, "Governor Melvin Thompson said that the Klan meetings should be outlawed. His reason: Their activities might encourage the interference of Northern 'race baiters.'"

Sprigle was nowhere close to being a Yankee race-baiter. But he was an admittedly un-objective northern journalist trying to peer into as many dirty corners of the Jim Crow South as possible in four weeks. He wanted to learn how blacks lived by living like one, but he was also deeply interested in investigating schools, crime, agriculture, and the judicial and electoral processes. Dobbs was helping Sprigle by giving him price-less access to people and places no white reporter could otherwise hope to have in 1948. And by going undercover and passing as a black man, Sprigle was seeing, hearing, and feeling things that gave his first-person journalism the depth and credibility it needed to rise beyond a stunt.

The next stop after Americus was a dilapidated Jim Crow school in the pleasant southwest Georgia village of Bluffton. In a rural town with 244 people and only a few streets, the school wasn't hard to find. Sprigle was shocked not so much by what he saw but at how absurd it was that anyone could seriously call the one-room "shanty" a school. He sneered at "the lordly white's conception of a schoolhouse for Negroes," describing it as a "sagging old shack, leaning and lop-sided as its makeshift foundations give way." Its roof leaked, its walls had fist-sized holes, there were no desks, no books to speak of, and the "blackboard" was a piece of cardboard nailed to a bare wall stud.

The school purportedly served the educational needs of thirty-eight kids in seven grades. Because it was cotton-chopping season, all the bigger boys and girls had been excused from class to help their parents in the fields. In theory every child received eight months of schooling, but only the littlest ones came anywhere close to that amount. The school had one redeeming feature—the lone dedicated teacher, a black woman Sprigle couldn't praise enough. "Tall and spare, gentle and soft spoken, earnest and intelligent," Miss Minnie Dora Lee—except for her dark skin—reminded him of "a typical New England school-marm with her sharp aquiline features." She had taught three generations of children, and it had taken twenty-seven years for her salary to reach $112 a month.

The Bluffton school was not atypical. Sprigle said he could have found many far worse and a few better, but it was Miss Lee that made her school better than most. For starters, she was actually qualified to teach. Hundreds of black schools had teachers who themselves had never gone past seventh grade. In more than one school district Sprigle had already heard about, teachers were appointed by the leading plantation owners on the basis of their cotton-picking skills. The idea that black schools were "separate but equal" was "a brazen, cynical lie and every white man knows it," he said. For proof, all anyone had to do was walk a thousand feet up the street to Bluffton's modern white school. Whereas the disintegrating black school could have been replaced for a thousand dollars, the brick white school with its six rooms, landscaped grounds, and fancy playground cost at least a hundred thousand dollars. In the little village of Bluffton, Sprigle pronounced, was "a completely accurate picture of the South's Jim Crow educational system."

Over the next several days, Dobbs and Sprigle moved around southern Georgia, staying with Prince Hall Masons who were prosperous farmers or professionals. Sprigle hadn't come south to inspect cities. He came to visit cotton country and small towns in Georgia like Americus, Colquitt, and Adel. He wanted to meet and "interview" black sharecroppers like Henry Williams.

Williams lived near Americus in a classic "shotgun-shack," so named, it is said, because you could shoot a shotgun through the front door and out the back door without hitting an interior wall. The standard housing design of the rural and urban poor from North Carolina to the Delta to Houston, it was twelve feet wide and two rooms deep. Old newspapers served as insulation. Sprigle noted that a farmer up North would think Williams's "mansion" was not fit for his cattle, and yet it was better than most shacks Sprigle had been seeing. It had two windows. That meant sunlight could enter during the dreary winters, and flies and mosquitoes couldn't get in so easily in the boiling summers. Its other relative luxury was a rickety lean-to built on the back where Mrs. Williams could cook at "a rather hopeless stove" instead of the usual open fireplace.

Sitting on a homemade stool in Williams's shack, Sprigle learned the basic economics of making a living by sharecropping cotton and peanuts from a twenty-nine-year veteran. First of all, Williams told him, you don't really make any money at sharecropping, which involved agreeing to farm someone else's land for a share of the crops that were raised on it. Sprigle had always liked crunching numbers in his big stories, and Williams gave him his humble numbers to crunch. The year before he had "made" seventeen bales of cotton and ten tons of peanuts on his landlord's plantation. He was paid two hundred dollars for each compressed bale of cotton, which weighed between four hundred and five hundred pounds, and two hundred dollars a ton for the peanuts. That meant Williams's gross income was fifty-four hundred dollars—of which "The Man" kept half.

So, in 1947, Williams earned twenty-seven hundred dollars, or the equivalent of twenty-seven thousand dollars today. That wasn't that bad, considering that Williams had no housing costs or utility bills and the median family income for the whole country was about thirty-one hundred dollars. But out of that twenty-seven hundred dollars Williams had to pay for the use of the plantation owner's tractor, plus the cost of fertilizer. He also had to pay off the debts he owed at the landowner's commissary, where he and his wife got their food and other supplies on credit all year long until the crops came in and were sold each fall.

Williams told Sprigle he figured he had ended up with a profit of seven hundred dollars from sharecropping the previous year. He thought that was a fair settlement, but he didn't really know because "The Man" did all the calculating. That was the way it was done every fall—no records, no discussion, no explanation of what the cotton or peanuts ultimately sold for at market. At the end of the season, "The Man" just handed over the money.

Williams was not a special case. All sharecroppers—black and white—were paid the same way throughout the South. Sprigle was not pleased to hear this. "Every Negro knows it and accepts it. It's a custom, a tradition, just as basic as Jim Crow. No Negro dares buck the system. Everywhere I went, and I talked with at least a score of sharecroppers, I heard the same expression: 'If you go to figure behind "The Man" you're gonna git trouble.' For that matter every Negro share-cropper I talked to admitted that he couldn't 'figure.' 'The Man jes' calls it off,' they told me, each with a wry smile."

For the next three weeks Sprigle would hear the same stories from black sharecroppers in other counties in three states. He'd also confer with black businessmen, leaders, and farm agents who knew how commonly blacks who couldn't "figure" were mistreated under the sharecropping system. He got the picture. "Not one of them but insisted that cheating a sharecropper out of his eye teeth was accepted and standard practice. Every one of them backed up his belief with instance after instance. I didn't bother taking notes. I'd talked with share-croppers myself. This share-cropping in the South is grand larceny on a grand scale. And the Negro is the victim."

The personal economics of tenant farmers, a step up from sharecroppers, were also of interest to Sprigle. In a juke joint over a couple of beers, he and Dobbs talked to the owner, a savvy tenant farmer whose name Sprigle changed in his reporting to Jared Buford. A World War II Army vet, he had bought the black bar with the profits he made from renting a piece of good farmland out of town. He knew the sharecropping game was rigged against blacks and knew he couldn't do anything about it, so he rented one hundred acres for twelve hundred dollars a year and grew and sold his own cotton and peanuts. Once he had rented the white landlord's land, Buford didn't have to have anything to do with him or any other white man. Whatever he earned—and it was $5,280 in cash—was his. Sprigle was impressed. "In every word and gesture it's plain that here is a black man who has worked out a way of life for himself. And it's plain, too, that the white man doesn't enter into that life. Here is a man, it seems to me, who has just cut himself off from white civilization. And is doing all right at it, too."

Sprigle's agricultural tour also took him to a few large farms that were owned and operated by blacks. In Miller County near Colquitt he spoke with Jordan Arline, who owned six hundred acres and grew cotton, corn, peanuts, pecans, and sugar cane and raised hogs, turkeys, and chickens. Arline used the sharecropper system, but he treated his black sharecroppers more fairly, as Sprigle learned when he crunched their numbers. The top sharecropper the previous year had made fifteen hundred dollars, less about nine hundred dollars for expenses. The trouble was, Arline said, the guy felt so rich he bought an old car, quit, and hit the road.

If that gave credence to the southern white man's charge that sharecroppers were "shiftless and undependable," Sprigle said, it was understandable. Black sharecroppers were constantly moving from plantation to plantation, looking for a better profit, an honest boss, or both. "Who can blame him if he decides he'll just quit work until he goes broke and has to find himself another boss? That was just too much money for a man who never had as much as $500 at one time in all his life before."

In Adel, a town in nearby Cook County, Dobbs took Sprigle to meet David E. Jackson, a farmer and entrepreneur whose success was legendary across the South. Twenty years earlier he had been a "penniless sharecropper." But Jackson not only owned one thousand acres of the best farmland in Georgia, he owned twenty houses and two blocks of business property downtown, ran two large produce warehouses, and also had a small trucking company. He raised, sold, and shipped huge amounts of corn, hogs, cotton, tobacco, vegetables, and watermelons as far north as Tennessee. Jackson was known as a generous man who came to the aid of white and black farmers when they needed extra hands or tractors. He never charged for his neighborliness and in return he was favored by everyone from the white county sheriff and white bankers to the white plantation owners.

Jackson, like Arline, was a Prince Hall Mason. Sprigle and Dobbs likely stayed overnight at his modern ten-room house in Adel, a carefully segregated town of twenty-seven hundred that was half white and half black (white streets were named after people; black streets were named after trees). Jackson was further proof to Sprigle that with good white neighbors, the right kind of land holdings, and a lot of hard work a black man can "do pretty well for himself in the deep South." He said Jackson had accomplished what he did because "he was fortunate enough to start in an oasis of decency and tolerance in a desert of oppression and intolerance." The trouble was that there were only a handful of exceptional black farmers like him in all of Dixie. Jackson was "one in a million," Sprigle said, or, more accurately, "one in ten million."

CHAPTER 10

An Oasis in the Desert of Injustice

His skin was barely brown. His features were clearly European. He was a white man, the only one at the big country picnic, yet everyone believed "James Crawford" was black like them. Black Americans came in all colors, as the 150 picnickers at C. D. Haslerig's dairy farm proved. But without John Wesley Dobbs vouching for him, it would have been impossible for Sprigle to pass for long as a light-skinned black man. The middle-class men and women at the picnic admired and trusted Dobbs. He wasn't just the grand master of Georgia's Prince Hall Masons. He was a local civil rights hero, a political celebrity in Atlanta who spoke on the radio and whose name and picture appeared in the *Pittsburgh Courier*. If he said Brother Crawford was a Prince Hall Mason who had come down from Pittsburgh to learn organizing tips, or if he told them he was doing research for his friend Walter White of the NAACP, there was no reason for anyone to suspect otherwise.

Mostly sunny, seventy-five degrees, low humidity—it was a perfect Saturday for an afternoon picnic in the hill country of northwest Georgia. The thinly populated ridges, valleys, and truck farms of Walker County were, as always, unhurried and peaceful. Haslerig's prosperous farm, which was also a popular weekend picnic grounds for black families on both sides of the Georgia-Tennessee border, was outside the small cotton mill town of Chickamauga, fifteen miles due south of Chattanooga.

Dobbs had driven a hundred miles from Atlanta to conduct an official district meeting at Chickamauga Masonic Lodge No. 221. He and Sprigle were staying at Haslerig's farmhouse, where Dobbs was a regular guest. The visit by "The Grand" was a good excuse for Haslerig to treat his friends and fellow Masons to an all-day social event. But before the feasting and drinking could begin, a closed-door, men-only meeting of the district's Prince Hall Masons was held at the spare, two-story wooden lodge across the road. The meeting was presided over by Grand Master Dobbs, who wore his official gold-and-silver-plated Prince Hall collar, apron, and black top hat. Sprigle didn't attend. But Chickamauga's black undertaker, black insurance man, and black dentist were there. So were the handful of black farmers who lived nearby. So were a few dozen black merchants and professionals from the strictly segregated city of Chattanooga, where nearly all of the metropolitan area's forty-five thousand Negroes lived and worked.

Rural northwest Georgia was nothing like Birmingham or south Georgia. It was nothing like Harlem or even Pittsburgh, either, but it was a relatively free and tolerant part of the Jim Crow South. Chickamauga's two thousand residents, along with the thirty-six thousand people in surrounding Walker County, were about 95 percent white. Unemployment was low for both races, but so were wages. Except for the handful of black farmers near the Haslerigs, most of Chickamauga's hundred or so blacks lived in town in their own neighborhood. They were segregated in all public spaces and subjected at all times to the local rules and "the good manners" of Jim Crow. But they didn't suffer the kind of injustice and discrimination common in southern Georgia, where blacks were usually the majority and were systematically prevented or intimidated from voting. In Chickamauga and Walker County, the black population was much too small to threaten the white power structure. They could vote all they wanted without fear—but, of course, without effect.

Echoing his description of Adel, Georgia, Sprigle described the Haslerig farm as another "little oasis in the desert of discrimination and injustice that is the black South." He also saw it as an island of productivity that proved to him that success and prosperity could be wrested out of anything by the toil of a large family. On their sixty-five acres Charles "Deedie" Haslerig, his wife, Odessa, and their kids ran a herd of prize Guernseys, grew vegetables, and raised hogs and thousands of chickens. They farmed another two hundred acres of leased land, which they planned to buy someday. Haslerig was a good farmer and a successful entrepreneur. The Haslerig Dairy, which he started and located in Chickamauga, at one time supplied all the milk to the black schools of Chattanooga and sold eggs, milk, and butter door-to-door in the city's black neighborhoods.

Besides being a successful businessman, Haslerig was a community leader and activist who wasn't afraid to stand up to white Walker County authorities. In the late 1930s he demanded—and got—new buses for black school kids. He got black drivers hired, too. Haslerig was born with a strong business gene. His father, George Washington Haslerig, who had been a slave for thirteen years, saved enough money to buy the first section of their property in the early 1900s. In 1925 someone decapitated all of C. D.'s chickens and then torched the Haslerig farmhouse. He, Odessa, and their eight kids had to flee in the middle of the night. Whoever did it was never caught. C. D. rebuilt and prospered even more.

The Haslerig family was respected by whites as well as blacks. Yet even a prominent and well-liked black family had to watch their step in northwest Georgia. If one of the Haslerigs got in trouble with the law or had a civil dispute with a white man, Sprigle said, they stood no chance of winning in court. Sprigle was as interested in the minute workings of Jim Crow's rigged judicial system as he was in the rigged electoral system and the personal finances of sharecroppers. Every black person he asked told him there was no justice for blacks in criminal or civil courts. When he asked a sharecropper why he didn't sue his landlord, Sprigle said the reply was, "If you black, you never mess with no white man in court. All you git is mo' and worse trouble."

Sprigle said a black banker told him a more polished version of the same story. When white plantation owners asked the black banker if he'd provide them with the same kind of seasonal loans he gave black farmers, the banker's reply was, "How could I ever expect to collect in court if you refused to pay me?" Black testimony and white testimony were not treated equally in Jim Crow's courts, Sprigle said, and everybody knew it. If one of their few black customers got in a wreck with a white driver, car insurance companies didn't waste their money going to court, they simply paid up. It was the same deal if an uninsured black driver had the misfortune to collide with a car owned by a white man. "There rarely is any question as to who was at fault," Sprigle said. "The Negro is told how much he is going to pay. And pays it."

~ ~

The all-day picnic at the Haslerig farm gave Sprigle a perfect way to observe and mingle with the area's middle-class blacks in an informal setting. It also gave him a chance to do one of his favorite things—eat. He investigated the food thoroughly and reported his findings like a starving man.

> Great platters of fried chicken—and listen, it's Pennsylvania Dutch fried chicken, the gooey kind—not that abomination known as southern fried chicken that I've been getting for the past two weeks. And biscuits—light, fluffy and piping hot. And here's a new wrinkle. The biscuits are baked in small pans—in the oven at a time. So when you call for a fresh one it's right out of the oven. Three or four kinds of jam; big gobs of country butter. And great pitchers of real buttermilk—what's left after you churn country butter—the first I've tasted in 20 years.

The picnic was not the end of the day's festivities. After consuming mounds of chicken and endless pans of homemade biscuits, the crowd moved nearby to the little Midway A.M.E. Zion Church. In a grove of pine trees, the ladies auxiliary of the Prince Hall Masons put on a talent show for their honored visitors from Atlanta. After the piano solos and singing came several speakers. Young and old, their essays and recitations dwelled on the issue that Sprigle said haunted the lives and thoughts of ten million southern black Americans every single day—their legal and social relations with whites.

Just before the activities at the church came to an end, C. D. Haslerig asked his houseguest "Brother Crawford" to get up and tell everyone "how the Negroes in Pittsburgh" were faring. Sprigle stood, took off his checkered cap, and bowed respectfully. He thanked Brother Haslerig for the

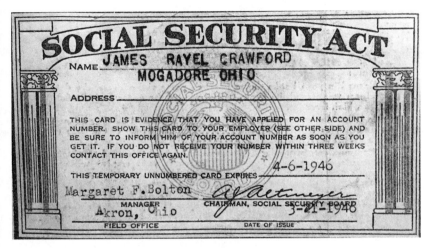

COURTESY OF SENATOR JOHN HEINZ HISTORY CENTER

opportunity to speak, but he quickly wriggled out of his assignment. He was willing to engage in a certain level of deception with the black people he was meeting and living with because his mission, if it succeeded, "may be of some slight service to them." But he said in his writings that "making speeches as the representative of the colored folk of Pittsburgh would be carrying the deception a little too far." He told the assembly a blanket truth. He said he didn't feel qualified to speak for the black people of Pittsburgh. He sat down again. The applause that followed was genuine, he said, but only because it was at the end of a long day and the audience wanted to go home.

In 1948 what went on in northwestern Georgia was of little interest and no importance to the outside world. It had been that way ever after the fall of 1863, when Confederate forces trying to retake Chattanooga defeated a Union army at the Battle of Chickamauga, the second bloodiest battle of the Civil War after Gettysburg. The big news of Sprigle's day came from the other side of a troubled planet. Overnight a new war had broken out in the Middle East—in Palestine. It was the lead story on the national radio networks, and it was bannered in large black fonts across the front page of the morning *Chattanooga Times* and nearly every daily newspaper in America. The *New York Times'* triple-decker headline tried its best to keep up with the fast-moving events: "ZIONISTS PROCLAIM NEW STATE OF ISRAEL; TRUMAN RECOGNIZES IT AND HOPES FOR PEACE; TEL AVIV IS BOMBED, EGYPT ORDERS INVASION."

A shooting war in the Holy Land was important if not unexpected news. But the men attending the Masonic meeting were probably more interested in events closer to home. In Brooklyn, a swollen knee was keeping Jackie Robinson out of the lineup in Saturday's game against the Boston Braves. The Dodgers' star infielder was playing his second season in the majors and was making a healthy salary of twelve thousand dollars a year. About $119,000 in today's dollars, it was only slightly higher than the average major league player's salary in 1948 and a pittance compared to what even mediocre major leaguers are paid today. But Robinson was already the highest paid Dodger, earning twice as much as the best white players like Duke Snider and Carl Erskine.

While the white owners of baseball crept into the twentieth century, the white people who ran the former Confederate States of America were trying to hang on to the nineteenth. The previous Saturday, eleven southern governors, all Democrats, met in Jackson, Mississippi, to discuss what to do about the liberal civil rights virus that had infected their party at the national level. About fifteen hundred delegates to the States' Rights Democratic Conference heard the fiery keynote address by South Carolina governor J. Strom Thurmond. The D-Day war hero, segregationist stalwart, secret father of a black daughter, and future Republican senator said President Truman had "stabbed" the South "in the back." He warned that unless Truman deserted his civil rights program the national Democratic Party would lose the Solid South in the coming presidential election. If a liberal civil rights plank were adopted at the party's national convention, he promised that the South's governors would meet again, form their own party, and pick their own candidates for president and vice president.

Thurmond talked tough. He famously predicted that "All the laws of Washington, and all the bayonets of the army cannot force the Negroes into their [white southern] homes, their schools, their churches and the places of recreation and amusement." The pipe dream of the states rights forces was to win enough Electoral College votes in the South to deny Truman victory and throw the 1948 election into the House of Representatives. There their segregationist congressmen could trade their votes to whichever Democratic presidential candidate promised to go easiest on old Jim Crow.

As far as Sprigle was concerned, old Jim Crow couldn't die soon enough. He wasn't enjoying being a second-class American citizen in his own country. He got the point. Whites were in charge—of everything.

Prior to his current mission, he had observed American-style apartheid on his many road trips to Arizona or Florida. And for five days in 1937 he witnessed Jim Crow at its most hateful in Birmingham, Alabama, when he was digging up KKK dirt on Hugo Black. Birmingham—even then reputed to be the most strictly segregated and racially divisive city in the USA—was still enforcing racial zoning laws that had been declared unconstitutional by the US Supreme Court in 1917. But until 1948 everything Sprigle had seen of the black world in the South was from the outside, as a white man. He had no idea what daily life was really like for blacks until he temporarily became one. Like John Gunther, when he was confronted with the reality of the Jim Crow South, he felt like he had been "dropped down on the moon"—a very oppressive moon.

— ~ —

During his weekend in Chickamauga, Sprigle was given a chamber-of-commerce tour of the Georgia-Tennessee border by one of C. D. Haslerig's sons. Willie Haslerig drove him around to see the farms and cotton fields as well as the city of Chattanooga and Chickamauga National Military Park, the country's first and largest park devoted to a Civil War battle. Willie also dropped Sprigle off in downtown Chickamauga, where for a couple of hours the reporter strolled the sidewalks by himself. Talking to the local black folk, minding his "manners" with whites, observing the scene but not daring to take notes, Sprigle checked out the segregated old stone train station and played the part of a curious northern black man without incident.

Willie Haslerig saw a lot of "Brother Crawford" that weekend. The twenty-six-year-old ex-Marine, his wife, Dorothy, and their two kids lived on his father's farm. Like his seven brothers and sisters, Willie had commuted by car to Chattanooga to go to all-black Howard High School. Late in World War II he lost his exemption for his farm work and was drafted. Assigned to the Marine Corps' newly formed all-black Montford Point unit, he became one of the first black Marines in history. He never got closer to the fighting than Hawaii, and after the war came straight home to begin what would be a long career in the family dairy business.

In 1948 he and Dorothy were used to meeting his father's overnight guests. C. D. Haslerig didn't charge for lodging or food, and visitors ate dinner with the whole family. Everything was fresh from the farm—fried chicken, green beans, corn, cornbread, apple pie. Dobbs was a cherished regular who always savored his cold buttermilk. "He was a lovely man," Dorothy recalled in 1998. "We loved him to death. He was like Martin Luther King to us. He broke barriers. He spoke up. He wasn't afraid."

She and Willie, in their mid-seventies when interviewed by this author, both remembered the weekend Dobbs and Sprigle visited. "James Crawford" was well mannered, active, but quiet too. "You enjoyed talking to him," Dorothy said. She and Willie noticed he spent a lot of time reading and writing on the porch swing. They said because the new spare bedroom in the attic wasn't finished yet, Crawford and Grand Master Dobbs had to sleep in the front guest bedroom Friday and Saturday night—in the same double bed.

Neither Willie nor Dorothy ever suspected Crawford was a white man. "He didn't really look white," Dorothy said, looking at a 1948 photo of Sprigle in a *Time* magazine for the first time. "He did a really good job of disguising himself." The Haslerig clan didn't learn of Sprigle's true identity until Dobbs revealed it to them on a visit several months later. Even if they had known all along Sprigle was a white newspaperman on a secret mission, however, it wouldn't have mattered. "If he was with Mr. Dobbs," Dorothy said, "he was all right."

In 1948, Willie and Dorothy were better off economically than most young black couples their age, but they were not untouched by Jim Crow. They didn't like to travel in south Georgia where a black man might be stopped by the county sheriff for no other reason than he was driving a nice car. "It was a lot better up here than down there," Dorothy said. Calling herself "a very country girl," she said she and Willie didn't regret what they had to put up with under Jim Crow. "It made us very strong people and we embedded that in our kids. We didn't feel deprived. It was just a way of life. Right now, we'd feel terrible about it, but that's just the way it was."

Twelve years after Sprigle's visit to their farm, Willie and Dorothy's three daughters helped change things for the better in Chattanooga before they got out of Howard High School. In the winter of 1960—unbeknownst to their parents—they joined other Howard students in sit-ins at the city's segregated lunch counters. Organized by black students to challenge a Tennessee law prohibiting blacks and whites from being served together in a public place, the sit-ins were peaceful, dignified, and morally powerful. Students sat quietly at variety store lunch counters after they were denied service and read the Bible or their school books as they were taunted by crowds of surly white adults and teenagers.

The sit-ins disrupted the city's downtown for months. They resulted in hundreds of arrests, but there was little violence and no deployment of fire hoses or police dogs. They were not as well covered by the national media as sit-ins elsewhere, but the two local segregationist newspapers, including the *Chattanooga Times* (which was owned by the Ochs-Sulzberger family that owned the *New York Times*), carried the daily twists of the sit-in story on their front pages for months. On their editorial pages they decried the breakdown in law and order and denounced the black students and their demonstrations, but to little avail. The sit-ins ultimately brought about the integration of the lunch counters and were the first steps toward desegregating all of Chattanooga's public facilities by 1963.

Before he and Dobbs returned to Atlanta, Sprigle slipped across the Tennessee border to watch a black dentist and a black doctor fix the teeth and nurse the health of white patients they couldn't sit next to at a lunch counter or on a bus. It was another example of "plain silliness" he found in what he called "the heartbreaking land of Jim Crow." In a dentist's waiting room, he and Dobbs witnessed a randomly integrated parade of people with bad or aching teeth. White farmers and their wives and children. Well-dressed city folk. Black moms with their kids.

Sprigle chatted a while with Dobbs's dentist friend, a graduate of a well-known northern university, then watched as he put "his big black fingers" and tools into the mouth of his patient, a young white woman. The popular black dentist was one of scores across the South who were making good livings touching white people in intimate ways Jim Crow did not explicitly forbid or didn't seem to notice. In a small town near Chattanooga, Sprigle and Dobbs popped in to see an older black doctor who had been delivering hundreds of black and white babies for more than three decades. Sprigle found it tragically idiotic that it was illegal in Tennessee and the rest of the South for the doctor to sit in the same rail coach as one of "his" grownup white babies. But it wasn't only harsh Jim Crow laws that demeaned and restricted the lives of blacks, he said. The few legal rights blacks did enjoy were casually, and regularly, ignored by a culture built on racism, iniquity, and ignorance.

He listed a few examples that particularly riled him: If a black man goes to a white doctor or dentist he'll most likely be served, but only at the end of the day, after all the white patients. He can't enter a white library, but if he goes to a black branch library they'll be able to get him any book he wants from the white library. Benches in town parks are assumed to be white-only unless they are marked "Colored," which few are. At bus stops benches were for whites. Blacks stood or sat on the ground. Sprigle said these examples paled next to the one that really outraged him, the one he called the "ultimate Jim Crowism." In every southern town there were two honor rolls for the Americans who had died fighting in Europe or Asia. One was for white soldiers, one for black. Sometimes they stood next to each other. Sometimes the black honor roll was "hidden in the dingy Negro" section of town. But as Sprigle said, the Jim Crow honor rolls existed for one reason—so that "No Negro is going to contaminate the white race by getting his name on the same honor roll with a white man even if he did die a hero in the service of his country."

Sprigle would have been happy to sit on the Haslerig's porch and eat gooey chicken for a week, but Dobbs had to hurry back to Atlanta for some old-fashioned, smoke-filled-room politicking. There was a fight within the state Republican Party to see which integrated faction of delegates was going to represent Georgia at the June 21 Republican National Convention in Philadelphia. After two days of meetings in the Fulton County courthouse, which Sprigle attended, Dobbs's group won. Sprigle was no stranger to such things and enjoyed watching the show. Dobbs was re-elected co-chairman of the GOP's state committee and named a delegate to the convention. Part of the selection process, however, was complicated and delayed by another of Jim Crow's silly rules: Messengers had to be used to shuttle vote totals back and forth because blacks and whites were not allowed to meet in the same courtrooms.

Between trips into the hinterlands, Sprigle stayed in one of the several guest bedrooms at Dobbs's house. He met dozens of Dobbs's middle-class friends, allies, and associates. They were the black elite of Atlanta and proudly declared their town to be the "Black Capital of America." Sprigle couldn't understand why they, Dobbs, and other similarly intelligent and successful blacks he met across the South were so fiercely patriotic about their particular cities and states. So far he hadn't seen "a square foot of the South" that he liked and swore that if he became permanently black anyone could shoot him if they "ever caught me south of the Smith and Wesson line."

The black Atlantans Sprigle met assured him that the kind of white violence blacks were regularly subjected to in less-civilized regions of the South would never happen in their liberal city. But he checked the official crime reports and Atlanta's "bloody record of Negro killings" proved them wrong. Blacks were being shot dead by trigger-happy white cops and white streetcar conductors, and they were murdering each other at a high rate. Some of the recent shootings by police Sprigle found would sound very familiar to twenty-first century readers.

There was John Mahone, black, drunk, disorderly and fighting with his wife. The cop shot and killed him. Thought he had a knife. The knife turned out to be a can opener. . . . R. D. Mance, 38, black and insane but unarmed. Cop was called to subdue a demented person. He did—with his gun. . . . Over the De Kalb county line in an Atlanta suburb, a county officer was making a search for illegal whisky. Harris Miller ran. When he refused to halt, County Officer E. C. Dailey killed him.

Sprigle was not a law-and-order man, not a cop hater, and not a racist. He counted cops and crooks and politicians among his good friends. He knew a lot about the workings of local governments and policing. But as a temporary black man, he had acquired a fresh nuance about the realities of crime and race. He acknowledged that Atlanta's police shot black men too fast and asked questions later. In their defense, however, he said, "They're usually scared stiff all the time they're on duty and a scared man shoots easily. They have good reason to be scared. In Atlanta, Birmingham, Memphis, and other southern towns with a large Negro population they're pitch-forked into a seething black maelstrom of crime. The white cop can very well find himself dead as he rounds the next corner. So his first thought when trouble looms is to grab his gun and shoot somebody quick."

He didn't look up the statistics on how many cops, if any, were gunned down annually by black men. But Sprigle said a big reason black neighborhoods in Atlanta, Birmingham, and Memphis were so crime ridden was that their all-white governments provided them with almost no law enforcement. "Decent, law-abiding Negroes, not only in these cities but in the Negro sections of smaller towns, are at the mercy of the criminals of their race because the white folks in the South don't regard it as a serious crime for a Negro to kill a Negro."

White cops generally stayed out of black neighborhoods, and in 1948 black cops in the South were rare in cities. They didn't exist in Memphis until 1949 and in Birmingham until 1966. Describing crime and policing issues that parallel those found today in cities like Chicago and Baltimore that are afflicted by gang violence, Sprigle said black criminals and killers would serve short sentences on prison gangs and then "come back to their home communities where they rule the more peaceful elements with gun and knife. Cuttings, shootings, robberies bring only fines or short jail sentences to the offender. Intelligent and adequate policing could, of course, end this chaos of crime in the Negro areas in a matter of months. But the white folks don't care and the better element of Negroes is powerless to force action."

Atlanta had a special problem that could be lethal to young black men. A 1943 city law deputized streetcar motormen as auxiliary police officers and allowed them to carry guns, which Sprigle said had led to the recent deaths of two young blacks. Both victims were shot dead at point-blank range in separate cases after having words with a white motorman. Another black man was shot dead by a civilian, a retired mailman, because he refused to put out the cigar he was smoking on the rear platform of a trolley. The judges' rulings for each of the killers was justifiable homicide. One got off by telling the judge, "I thought he was going to reach in his pocket," which Sprigle said was "the standard line of defense in the South."

Black-on-black murders in Atlanta hit one hundred in 1947 and they were keeping up that pace in 1948. Only Memphis had more homicides, putting Dobbs's hometown in second place among southern cities. Dobbs had successfully used his bloc of black votes as political leverage to get Mayor Bill Hartsfield to put eight black policemen on Auburn Avenue. Sprigle saw them patrolling the teeming sidewalks when he was there. They were stationed in the basement of the black YMCA on Butler Street where he stayed for three nights when Dobbs went out of town to give a speech. Sprigle said the black cops looked good but were largely symbols. They were poorly trained, and the only whites they could arrest were drunks and bums.

Still, the black policemen did have an immediate impact. In the first week of May, the *Atlanta Daily World* reported that of 109 arrests made by black officers, forty-eight were for drunkenness, eighteen for disorderly conduct, and thirty-four for crimes like carrying concealed weapons, selling whiskey on Sunday, and reckless driving. Sprigle knew the eight black policemen were a Band-Aid, a political PR stunt, a black-pride booster, not a real solution to controlling black crime. But he said black leaders "were powerless to institute any measures which would bring law and order to their community. First thing required, of course, is a complete overhaul of the entire police system with a proper system of training for police officers—something which most Southern cities haven't thought of. Basic reform, of course, would be a change in Southern thinking. Atlanta, and the rest of the South have got to get the idea that it's murder to kill a Negro wantonly."

While he was in Atlanta, Sprigle looked into the brutal murder of Henry Gilbert, a poor farmer from south central Georgia who was killed the previous year while in police custody. In an interview in Dobbs's parlor, Gilbert's small, bespectacled widow, Carolyn, told how the couple had started as sharecroppers, rented a piece of land for seventeen years, and saved enough to buy an 111-acre farm in Troup County near the Alabama border. They were married twenty-two years and had three daughters when Henry, forty-two, was accused of helping a young black troublemaker who had shot and killed a white man because the man was beating him with a stick. Two weeks after the incident, Henry was arrested at his home at 4:30 in the morning and charged with helping the murderer escape by letting him hide on his farm. Taken away by the county sheriff and two other policemen, he was moved around from jail to jail. Carolyn tried to keep up with his movements and heard reports that he was still alive but never saw him again. After ten days she was told to come down to a funeral parlor and claim her husband's battered body.

Carolyn told Sprigle that when she held Henry's head in her hands and kissed him she could feel "the broken pieces of bone under the skin. It was just like a sackful of little pieces of bone." He had been shot to death. The county cop who pulled the trigger, Willie H. Buchanan, said he had to shoot because during an interview in a jail cell "The nigger"—Henry Gilbert, a deacon and treasurer at his small Baptist church—"drew a chair on me." When the undertaker prepared Henry's body for burial, Sprigle said, "His skull was crushed to a pulp both in front and the rear. One leg and one arm were broken. All the ribs on one side were smashed into splinters. He was riddled by five bullets fired at close range."

A month after she buried her husband, Carolyn was arrested on the same charge of helping a murderer escape and put in the same jail where her husband was killed. She was bailed out for one thousand dollars the next day and all charges were eventually dropped, but her life—and the life Sprigle said she and Henry "had built out of toil and struggle through the years"—was finished.

The Gilberts' horror story was picked up by the black press. The *Pittsburgh Courier* carried the news of her arrest and Henry's death across the top of its front page on June 28, 1947, under the thick black headline "JAIL MOB VICTIM's WIDOW; Husband lynched in Ga. Prison." As for the killer cop, Sprigle said, Georgia-style justice let him go, ruling "justifiable homicide in self-defense." Sprigle had his own verdict: "Henry Gilbert was a victim of the mores of the white Southerner. When a Negro kills a white man and escapes, somebody has to pay. Henry Gilbert just happened to be the Negro picked for slaughter."

CHAPTER 11

Sneaking Through the Delta

And we are nothing more
Than a herd of Negroes
Driven to the field

—FROM "SHARECROPPERS"
BY LANGSTON HUGHES

Sprigle and Dobbs pushed north on Highway 61 in their big Mercury. If there hadn't been telephone wires strung along the road and Pepsi-Cola signs nailed to the fronts of the few "colored cafes" and general stores they passed, it could have been 1880. The brown fields on both sides of the two-lane highway were scattered to the horizons with ragged little columns of men, women, and children in overalls, printed cotton dresses, and wide straw hats. Sharecroppers. All of them were black. Some were in their seventies, some as young as five. Heads bowed, eyes to the ground, they mechanically worked their long hoes in short chops as they moved among the rows of baby cotton plants they'd tend until picking time in the fall.

Half a million black Americans lived in the Delta. Most were share-croppers, day laborers, and tenant farmers. They and their large families lived in unpainted shotgun shacks that were on plantations as large as twenty thousand acres or that were scattered randomly along the dirt and gravel roads. Tenant farmers who grew their own cotton on ten acres of rented land worked twelve-hour days—6:00 a.m. to 6:00 p.m. Sharecrop-pers, who paid their rent by giving their landlord about 30 percent of their crops, often worked longer—from dawn to dusk. Using tools, animals, fertilizer, seeds, and food they bought from the landlord's store on credit, the sharecroppers and tenant farmers raised cotton from seed to bale.

Like their grandparents, sharecroppers lived in shacks, walked behind one-mule plows, weeded cotton rows with hoes, and handpicked a hundred pounds of cotton bolls a day under the baking Mississippi sun. Unlike their grandparents, they were not slaves. But they were close to it. In the most advanced country on Earth, three years into the Atomic Age, they were nineteenth-century poor. They had no electricity, no running water, no property, no assets, no savings, no access to credit, no vote, no future in Jim Crow Mississippi for themselves or their children.

Fifteen miles west of Sprigle and Dobbs were the sharp bends and coils of the sleeping Mississippi River, which, along with the levees that had tamed it, formed the state's crinkled western edge. For thousands of years its floods and the floods of its equally erratic junior partner, the Yazoo, had laid down the Delta's deep alluvial plain. An oval two hundred miles tall by seventy miles wide in northwest Mississippi, the Delta stands like a teardrop between Memphis and Vicksburg. Flat as a griddle and spectacularly fertile, it's a perfect blend of climate and soil. "The richest land this side of the valley Nile!" is how plantation owner Big Daddy Pollitt described it without exaggerating in Tennessee Williams's play *Cat on a Hot Tin Roof.*

Native Americans and early white settlers were first to create the Delta's wealth. They cut down its bottomland hardwood forests, controlled the rivers with dikes, and drained the floodplain for agriculture. Since before the Civil War, thanks first to the labor of tens of thousands of slaves and later massive armies of low-paid black sharecroppers and laborers, its plantations had been growing some of the best cotton in the world. Most of the "white gold" had been produced with little more than mules, hand tools, and human muscle.

Shadowing the wandering course of the Mississippi for fourteen hundred miles, US Highway 61 stretched up the gut of America from New Orleans to Minnesota. Just ahead was the once thriving railroad town of Alligator, population 214. Twenty-five miles farther, at the crossroads of Highway 61 and Highway 49, was Clarksdale, the Delta's cultural soul. The cotton-trading town and its surrounding plantations was the region where the blues were born and raised before moving to Chicago. It's where legendary bluesman Robert Johnson sold his soul to the Devil, where Muddy Waters grew up, and why Highway 61 would someday be dubbed "The Blues Highway." It was also where Bessie Smith died in a "colored" hospital in 1937 after a violent traffic accident. The Delta's second largest city after Greenville, Clarksdale had seventeen thousand of Coahoma County's forty-nine thousand people. About 80 percent of everyone in the county was black. Except for a small middle class in the black part of town, most blacks were poor and worked on plantations in the service of "King Cotton."

From Reconstruction to World War II, not much had changed in the Delta's labor-intensive mono-economy. But in 1948 methods of mechanized cotton farming, improved and cheaper, were beginning to put thousands of sharecroppers and cotton pickers out of work. A new cotton-picking machine, one which for the first time could be mass produced, had been perfected over a number of years at a plantation outside Clarksdale. A good field hand picked twenty pounds of cotton in an hour. The new International Harvester could out-pick fifty humans—a thousand pounds of cotton in an hour, or two bales. It slashed the cost per bale from forty dollars to five dollars.

The widespread use of the mechanical cotton picker was going to quickly destroy the sharecropper system, the South's dominant rural economic institution since Reconstruction. In the next two decades, the Delta and the rest of the rural South would bleed more population, black and white. Another four million black men, women, and children would leave for the cities of the North and West in Part II of the Great Migration. As Nicholas Lemann wrote in *The Promised Land: The Great Black Migration and How It Changed America*, the chain of events set off by the coming of the mechanical cotton picker did much more than alter the economics and racial politics of the South. For the rest of the twentieth century, the migration of so many blacks affected the lives of every American. It made race and civil rights national issues, rather than just southern ones.

And liberating millions of black Americans and their descendants from dead-end "careers" in rural poverty and ignorance had a huge impact on the national economy, popular culture, presidential politics, the geography of cities and suburbs, education, urban planning, the judicial system, and federal social welfare policy.

Unaware of the cotton-picking revolution under way in their corner of the Delta, Sprigle and Dobbs sped toward their appointment with Dr. P. W. Hill. The dentist was waiting in an overgrown segregated cemetery near Clarksdale. He wanted to show them the magnificent mausoleum by the edge of the cotton fields he built to honor his dead wife and child. He wanted to tell Sprigle—aka Walter White's associate James Crawford—how they died, and why.

Dobbs and Sprigle had traveled to Mississippi from Atlanta earlier in the week. Late into the night, as Dobbs drove the '47 Mercury hard toward Jackson on narrow US Highway 80, Sprigle listened "to him recite long passages from *Macbeth* and *Hamlet*, Ingersoll's essay on Napoleon—page after page from the best in English literature." It wasn't just Dobbs's erudition and oratory skills that impressed Sprigle so much. He had fought oppression, injustice, and discrimination all his life, yet there "was no bitterness, no hatred in the man. To him, his 'southland,' as he always calls it, is the fairest country in the land. He loves his Georgia above all other states—he would live nowhere else in America."

Surviving their 413-mile sprint to Jackson, they stayed overnight with Dobbs's daughter Millie and family and then drove north toward the Delta the next day. Their game plan was to turn west toward the Mississippi River at Greenwood, go to Greenville, turn north again and run along the east side of the river on Highway 61 to Scott, Clarksdale, and Tunica. They'd exit the top of the Delta south of Memphis and angle east through northern Alabama back to Atlanta. The roundtrip was about eleven hundred miles on two-lane roads that were usually either dangerous and empty or dangerous and crowded with truck traffic.

Less than an hour after leaving Jackson they stopped in Madison County where someone Dobbs knew arranged for Sprigle to be shown one of Mississippi's many separate but brazenly unequal schools. He was quickly outraged to learn that the "lordly exemplars of white supremacy" in District No. 4 had used tax money collected from black property owners to build their kids a modern new school while black kids got stuck with the usual short end of the Jim Crow stick. The new black school sat on a back country road Sprigle said was "a desert of dust in summer and a morass of mud in winter." It was new, at least, but it was built only after many people in the state—even some white people—made a public stink about the patent unfairness of the financing arrangements.

Until the protests shamed them out of it, the whites in charge of District No. 4 were planning to have black kids remain in their two old segregated public schools. One was in a church and the other was in a lodge, private places often used for black public schools in the South. The new black school served a rural district in which blacks outnumbered whites four to one. That ratio was common in many counties across the rural South. What was uncommon was that blacks owned 90 percent of the property in the district and paid 90 percent of the tax revenue. That leverage brought little benefit to black citizens, however, as Sprigle saw.

> They haven't one single little word to say about how their tax money is spent. This new school building is just a big square box with two partitions breaking it up into four rooms. Only one of the rooms has desks. They are hammered together out of the scrap lumber left over from the building of the school. The scraps were picked up out of the mud. The mud is still on the desks. In the other three rooms there are no desks—not even muddy ones—just home-made benches and tables. There is one toilet for both boys and girls. It leans drunkenly in the wind.

The black school was a bad joke compared to the white one up the road. Designed by an architect, it had several out-buildings, a gym, a bungalow for the principal, and fifteen teachers. Sprigle mocked the idea of "separate but equal," adding that the four black teachers in "that bare box back in the country" made about fifty-five dollars a month while the minimum for white teachers in the county was $150 a month. There was a reason the black school was hidden away on a dirt road, despite an offer of free land on the main highway from a black church. The superintendent publicly admitted his district had deferred to the request of its largest white plantation owner to locate the school near his cotton gin. The planter knew a school would help him hold on to his black field hands.

Some black students in District No. 4 had to walk six miles each way to school, nothing out of the ordinary for the South. In Madison County buses were for white kids only. It was the same across most of the state. Only four or five counties in Mississippi and Georgia provided buses for black kids. "I saw groups of bright-faced, neat, little Negro children trudging the dusty or dangerous highways morning and evening to and from their tumble-down schools," Sprigle said. "From time to time the swirling clouds of dust thrown up by school buses would engulf them. The children in those buses were white. In the South white children ride to school. The black ones walk."

If Sprigle had any doubts about the absurdity of the "separate but equal" claim after seeing it with his own eyes, an education expert Dobbs hooked him up with quickly erased them with the grim facts. Mississippi paid its education budget with a 2 percent sales tax. Half the state's population was black. And though they didn't contribute 50 percent of the tax revenue because of their lower incomes, they didn't come close to getting their fair share. "Believe it or not," Sprigle said he was told, "the white masters of Mississippi pay more just to haul their white children to their schools than they spend on the entire statewide Negro school system. The figures run 3 1/2 million dollars to haul white children—only 3 1/3 million to educate the little Negroes."

It was clear to Sprigle that the black parents he met across the South were desperate to get good schools for their kids. They would suffer unfavorable working conditions or travel long distances to a plantation if it had an elementary school. But Mississippi's rulers made getting their kids an education as impossible as they could. Hundreds of schools in the Delta were open for only four months. "Discrimination against the Negro school child in Mississippi is universal and vicious," Sprigle concluded. "Many counties do not even pretend to provide school buildings for Negro children. In rich Bolivar county in the fabulous Delta country there are 121 Negro schools. Only 31 operate in school buildings. The others stumble along in churches, lodge halls and even garages." Small wonder, he said, that nearly half the state's 477,000 school-age children had never been enrolled in school. There were compulsory attendance laws in the South, just like in the North. But when it came to black kids, neither Mississippi nor any other Jim Crow state enforced them.

Within two hours of leaving Madison County, they were officially in the Mississippi Delta. Its eighteen counties and seven thousand square miles had the unhappy distinction of being one of the poorest, blackest, most racist parts of the poorest, blackest, most racist state in the Union. Sprigle and Dobbs weren't going to tour the rowdy juke joints of Clarksdale or Greenville, or spend a lazy afternoon fishing for catfish in one of the side channels of the Mississippi. They planned to squeeze as much surreptitious journalism into several days as they could without getting in trouble with "The Man."

Their first major stop was the former Mississippi River town of Greenville, the economic, cultural, and intellectual capital of the Delta. The mighty river used to flow past the foot of Main Street on the other side of the levee. But after the Great Flood of 1927 covered a million acres of the Delta with ten feet of muddy water and soaked most of Greenville up to its rooftops, the US Army Corps of Engineers straightened and redirected the channel, leaving the city's downtown next to and below manmade Lake Ferguson.

Protected by their twenty-seven-foot-high levee, Greenville's thirty thousand residents included eighteen thousand blacks. Though they were at the bottom of the economic ladder, their blues and jazz clubs, cafes, grocery stores, fish markets, barbershops, and record shops on Nelson Street were the black entertainment and commercial hub of the Delta. Atop Greenville's white middle class stood the rich, sophisticated, socially active white elite that ran the town. They owned the surrounding cotton plantations and important businesses, knew or married each other, and managed their household chores with the help of an inexhaustible supply of black servants, drivers, and yardmen.

Greenville made its living like the rest of the Delta—on cotton. But the city's best-known product was its writers. In a state famed for turning out literary giants like William Faulkner, Richard Wright, Tennessee Williams, and Eudora Welty, it could claim poet and biographer William Alexander Percy and future stars Walker Percy and Shelby Foote, the Civil War historian and principal on-camera storyteller of Ken Burns's wildly popular *Civil War* documentary series on PBS.

The city's most notable writer in 1948 was Hodding Carter, the brilliant newspaperman. As far as the rest of the country was concerned, on matters of race the editor/owner of the *Delta Democrat-Times* was the reasoned voice and enlightened liberal conscience of Mississippi, if not the entire segregated South. He had sold countless freelance articles about the South to national magazines like the *Saturday Evening Post* and *Esquire* and had profiled Mississippi's racist former governor and two-term US senator Theodore Gilmore Bilbo to the satisfaction of the *New York Times Magazine*. He made his biggest national splash in 1946 when he grabbed journalism's top honor, a Pulitzer Prize. He won for a batch of strong editorials against racial, religious, and economic intolerance and for challenging his state government to spend the money necessary to make separate schools and public facilities for blacks truly equal.

Thanks to Carter's editorial leadership, the *Delta Democrat-Times* was a superior small-town daily that made a nice profit while responsibly performing its role as the only local source of news and opinion for Greenville's white community. Carter made twelve thousand dollars a year—the equivalent of $120,000 today. Like all but the most saintly newspaper owners, he used the *DD-T* as an economic and political weapon to reward or punish his friends and enemies. He was an unabashed and enthusiastic booster of local business and the city of Greenville. He helped to raise money for the small Jewish community and for the Catholics to build a new school. To bring some high culture to his backwater town, he used the paper's money to pay the cost of importing a film series from the Museum of Modern Art in New York.

The *DD-T,* which ran the only book reviews in the state, covered the milestones and parties of Carter's elite circle, but it also printed their names when they got caught driving drunk. It stressed local news stories on the front page and faithfully reported on the 4-H Club, the sports teams, and the July 4th celebrations on the levee. On May 26, the Wednesday Sprigle and Dobbs breezed through Greenville on their way north, the *Delta Democrat-Times'* busy front page was dominated, as usual, by a chaotic mix of international and national news. The top story and banner headline was "UN Effort to Stop Palestine War Fails," but nearly twenty other items filled Page 1. The Finnish cabinet was in crisis. A new tariff bill was being fought over in Washington. Talks had resumed between Chrysler and striking United Auto Workers. Cotton sales to Europe were up. So were cotton prices.

At the bottom of the front page was a large headline of local interest—"Ambitious Civil Rights Program Appears Bogged Down Until After November Elections." It was a terse wire story about a delay in President Truman's recent request for Congress to take "immediate and decisive action to wipe out segregation and discrimination from American life." The article said "some Dixie Democratic strongholds" were in "full-fledged revolt." Filibusters were expected. Republicans had dusted off their long-pending anti-lynching, anti–poll tax, and anti–job discrimination laws. Nothing unusual. And the South's powerful congressmen, as usual, made sure nothing immediate or decisive happened.

A third of the *Delta Democrat-Times'* twelve thousand subscribers were black, but you'd have never known it from reading the ten pages of the day's paper. At the bottom of Page 1, under "News Briefs," the first item reported that county police were looking for "L.J. Rucker, 32, a Negro," who had shot "David Grant, another of his race," in the leg early Sunday morning on a local plantation. The men reportedly had been drinking. On Page 2 the tiny item, "Rites for Long-Time Negro Citizen Held," was about a Greenville man who had been a prominent citizen's chauffeur and yardman for thirty-five years. The *DD-T* was a rare southern paper because Carter capitalized the word "Negro." In a year or two he would make a more radical break, and risk resentment and obscene phone calls, by deciding to use the courtesy titles "Mr." and "Mrs." when writing about blacks.

Despite Carter's conscious efforts to give his black readers more nice news to read about themselves, those examples were the day's

only mentions of "Negroes." A tiny standing ad for the Rex Theatre—
"Mississippi's finest theatre for colored"—and three classified ads, including "Houses and lots for sale (For Colored)," were the only other clues
that blacks were the majority race in Greenville. The *DD-T*, like the white
papers in Pittsburgh, Atlanta, and other cities, ceded the black community's news and local advertising to a black paper, the weekly *Delta Leader*.
With a circulation of about six thousand, and edited by a Baptist minister who didn't approve of young people "gitterbugging," it supplied local,
national, and international news of interest to blacks and ran wire stories from the Associated Negro Press. Its editorial page pushed for black
progress in the Delta and the expansion of black rights in general, but the
Leader carefully avoided taking "radical" positions on incendiary issues
like voting rights that might bring trouble from the whites in charge of
their town.

Meanwhile, at the *DD-T*, Carter fearlessly editorialized for or against
just about everything and anyone that annoyed, infuriated, or pleased him.
He balanced serious calls for the repeal of the state's alcohol prohibition
laws, which he said only fattened the wallets of sheriffs with payoffs from
bootleggers, with lighthearted takes on Dick Tracy comic strips or the
sticky weather. If he thought he was right, he didn't care what anyone else
thought, including advertisers. One time he jumped into the middle of a
hot fight over whether the names of black veterans should be included on
the town's new World War II memorial. He argued in the paper that it
was only right that the names of all local veterans should be listed on the
honor roll, white and black. He caught hate from the usual crowd, but he
won a moral victory of sorts. Nobody's name was listed.

His editorials were hardly subversive of southern "law and customs"—the standard euphemism for Jim Crow segregation. But even his
moderation on racial matters disturbed half his readers and could easily
incite the white-supremacist demographic: "The so-called race question is
an economic one, not social. Pay the Negro good wages for his work, give
him the opportunity to demonstrate his own capacity to learn, work, and
earn, give him his Constitutional rights and you solve this distorted so-
called race problem. Only the demagogue tries to make political capital
of social equality and racial marriage."

Carter was not afraid to offend or pick fights with anyone, including the most powerful politicians in the state. Not long after he announced his own Pulitzer Prize in banner headlines across the front of his paper, in 1946, he declared war on his Mississippi home's racist icon, Senator Bilbo. Bilbo was in a Democratic Party primary race, which if he won assured him of re-election, because the Republican Party and registered black voters barely existed in Mississippi.

On the stump Bilbo was his usual bigoted self. In his canned campaign speech he vilified the North, the liberal press, black people, "kikes," "Dagoes," liberals, and communists. He called Republican congresswoman Clare Boothe Luce "the greatest nigger lover in the North except Old Lady Eleanor Roosevelt. Yep, Old Lady Roosevelt is worse . . . In Washington she forced our southern girls to use the stools and toilets of darn syphilitic nigger women. . . ." He also went after his moral antithesis and loudest nemesis, Hodding Carter. In a two-and-a-half-hour campaign speech the night before he was to come to Greenville, Bilbo called Carter a "nigger-loving communist" and liar who had betrayed the South by accepting a "Poolitzer-blitzer prize given by a bunch of nigger-loving Yankeefied communists for editorials advocating mongrelization of the race."

Not sinking to Bilbo's gutter rhetoric, Carter got in a few good editorial licks. In one he wrote that the University of Michigan Law School graduate's mind was "so soaked in the poisonous slime of his bigotry that he reminds us of nothing so much as a neglected cesspool." He also slimed the senator as "a jaundiced old man who makes his living with hate and slander as his tools." Carter and Bilbo's exchange of insults became a national media story, distributed to newspapers and radio stations by wire services like the Associated Press. Taking the high road and the long road, Carter told a newspaper reporter in a phone interview that "I have tried to love and work for my fellow man—Negro, Jews, Catholics—all of those whom Bilbo has attempted to humiliate." He said the attacks by the senator and his "jackals" weren't going to stop him from speaking out or editorializing. "In another generation the shame and evil Bilbo represents will be only an uncomfortable smudge. I am working for that generation."

Carter's dignified name-calling was no match for Bilbo's foul "pyrotechnic oratory" and the senator's popularity with both poor whites and rich Delta planters. Bilbo barely won the primary he should have lost. Carter said he won because he was able to unite voters behind him by pointing to "the outsiders"—northerners and black civil rights groups—who were openly working to defeat him or calling for federal troops to come to Mississippi to guarantee a fair election. Though Bilbo was re-elected in November without opposition, his forty-year career as a public racist was about to come to an unmerciful but just end. In the 1946 election Republicans had gained control of the US Senate for the first time since 1933. In January of 1947 they refused to allow Bilbo to retake his seat until the full body considered the findings of a senate civil rights investigation into the inflammatory and racist tactics he had used during the 1946 primary to scare black voters from registering and voting.

There was no doubt or argument about what Bilbo said. His most damning campaign quote, repeated often and broadcast over statewide radio, was a version of "I call upon every red-blooded white man to use any means to keep the nigger away from the polls. If you don't understand what that means you are just plain dumb. Mississippi is white. We got the right to keep it that way. . . . I am calling on every red-blooded American who believes in the superiority and integrity of the white race to get out and see that no nigger votes . . . and the best time to do it is the night before."

In his defense Bilbo insisted that he had always urged whites to use "any lawful means" to keep blacks away from the polls and that if he didn't use that phrase it was a slip of the tongue. After charges were heard that Bilbo had accepted "gifts" of a Cadillac and a swimming pool from federal contractors, and after some fellow segregationists filibustered the Senate on Bilbo's behalf, a Higher Being with a sense of ironic justice apparently intervened. With the decision over his Senate seat still pending, Bilbo asked if everything could be put on hold while he went back to Mississippi for medical treatment. He never returned. Eight months later he was dead of cancer of the mouth.

Bilbo, the proud KKK member, the Deep South's trademark racist, the embarrassment of the US Senate, had enough venom left in his body to crank out a self-published book, *Take Your Choice: Separation or Mongrelization*. Dedicating it "to every white man and woman, regardless of nationality, who is a bona fide citizen of the United States of America," he explained how important it was to him for the white race to stay pure. "Personally, the writer of this book would rather see his race and his civilization blotted out with the atomic bomb than to see it slowly but surely destroyed in the maelstrom of miscegenation, interbreeding, intermarriage and mongrelization. The destruction in either case would be inevitable—one in a flash and the other by the slow but certain process of sin, degradation, and mongrelization."

To the white Delta cotton planters who voted overwhelmingly for a politician as hideous as Bilbo, Hodding Carter sounded like one of those northern "communists" like Mrs. Roosevelt or Walter White. But by northern standards he wasn't close to being a liberal. Civil rights advocates in Congress and elsewhere aimed to kill Jim Crow quickly and bury his body deep. They weren't interested in putting him on life support until a couple generations of southern black kids could be properly educated in truly equal schools and twenty million whites were given introductory classes in Gunnar Myrdal's "American Creed" and the Constitution. Already caught in the shifting crossfire of the new American civil war over civil rights, Carter would always be too liberal for most of his white readers and southern friends but never liberal enough for northerners. His views on segregation would evolve with the civil rights movement during the 1950s and 1960s, and he'd get the credit he deserved for his courage and decency. But in 1948, relatively enlightened and ahead of his time though he was, he was not in favor of integrating Mississippi's public schools, swimming pools, or any other public social space. And he was adamantly opposed to the federal government using its bayonet to force anti-discrimination measures or equal rights laws of any kind on the sovereign states of the South.

❧

Hodding Carter and Ray Sprigle were star newspapermen. They played on rival teams, but it's impossible to imagine that the two Pulitzer winners hadn't heard of each other. Sprigle would have seen Carter's byline and face repeatedly in the North's major magazines and Carter had been aware of Sprigle's work for a long time. He was the thirty-one-year-old editor of the *Delta Democrat-Times* on May 3, 1938, when it ran a front-page news story announcing the winners of that year's Pulitzers. The first sentence read, "Raymond Sprigle, reporter for the *Pittsburgh Post-Gazette*, tonight was awarded the Pulitzer Prize for distinguished reporting during 1937 for his series exposing the onetime membership of Supreme Court Justice Hugo L. Black in the Ku Klux Klan." Sprigle's award-winning black-market meat series during World War II was also a huge national story Carter could not have missed.

Now, ten years later, the *Post-Gazette*'s star reporter was somewhere in Greenville. He was undercover. He wasn't wearing the trademark Stetson hat he wore in the photos that *Time*, *Life*, and other national publications ran of him as part of their coverage of the Hugo Black affair. Maybe he was over on Nelson Street reading the *Delta Democrat-Times* and eating a heavy one-dollar breakfast. Or making a $1.09 long-distance call to Pittsburgh to tell his bosses that so far the fear of him running into trouble had been unfounded. If Carter had looked out his office window on the corner of Main Street and Walnut, he might have seen Sprigle and Dobbs walking down the sidewalk toward the whites-only public library or driving out of town. While he was passing through town pretending to be a black man, Sprigle never dreamed of popping into the *Democrat Delta-Times* building to say hello to the liberal voice of the Jim Crow South. But in six months he'd meet Carter face-to-face, in Pittsburgh, as a fellow white man. Then they'd go to New York City to debate the future of segregation on a primetime network radio program heard by millions.

CHAPTER 12

America's "Last Outpost of Feudalism"

Sprigle and Dobbs had gotten lost. It wasn't hard to do on what was once the largest plantation in the United States. They were up by Scott, a few miles east of a hard S-bend of the Mississippi and just south of little Lake Bolivar, an ancient remnant of the river only five feet deep. Scott was owned by the Delta and Pine Land Company, a syndicate of British textile makers. In 1945 it had sixty-three hundred acres of cotton under cultivation and six hundred sharecropper families. Scott wasn't much of a town. It was a post office, a general store, a school, a church, and a hospital surrounded by thirty thousand flat acres of cotton fields, corn fields, and grazing lands laced with elevated dirt roads. The only landmarks were humans.

When Dobbs stopped his dusty Mercury to ask a sharecropper for directions, he broke the rule about not talking to workers walking along the road. The woman eyed them and their car suspiciously, as well she should have. What were two city slickers with Georgia plates doing driving around in the middle of a sea of baby cotton and corn? As she was telling them how to get where they needed to go, she immediately quit talking, slid down the road embankment and hustled off. A horn honked aggressively behind them. Two impatient white guys in an old car. *Uh oh*, Sprigle thought. White guys in the Delta were the enemy of blacks like him and they had been caught talking to the help. Dobbs pulled over as far as he could and the car slowly went around and drove away fast trailing dust. For the first and only time on his trip Sprigle was nervous about his health, but to Dobbs it was no big deal. He threw the big Mercury into gear, quickly caught up with the white guys, followed them to Highway 61, and turned north toward Clarksdale.

Sprigle realized his fear of suffering serious violence from the white man was rational and irrational at the same time.

Make no mistake about this. Every Negro in the south is afraid of the white man. Mathematically the chances of his being killed in any given year are only about one in 1 million—in Mississippi and Georgia he stands a somewhat better chance of winding up on an undertaker's slab. But unpleasant things, less than murder, can and do happen to him. It is an exceptional and fortunate Negro who would not be wantonly insulted periodically if he has many contacts with Southern whites. His chances of being roughed up or beaten are in direct ratio to his unwillingness to take insults and slights meekly and without protest or visible resentment.

Take just a couple of incidences out of the scores that my friends recounted. . . . They illustrate perfectly the fact that every Negro in the South, no matter what the station in life, his accomplishments, his possessions, his college degrees or his services to humanity, lives dangerously every moment of his life. Particularly is that true when he ventures outside his own community. If he is black, then he is fair game for any white man—especially if that white man wears a badge and carries a club and a gun.

～～

Sprigle didn't exert himself, but he was hard-pressed to find an upside to daily life in what he called "the last outpost of feudalism in America." The blacks who lived in the Delta's "tight little principalities" had peaceful, uneventful lives, but that was mainly because they were barely free to do anything but work. The young filled up juke joints on weekends, dancing till they closed at midnight in the city and till dawn in the rural clubs. Mississippi was a dry state, a holdout of Prohibition, but that didn't mean much in the Delta when moonshine was made everywhere, Arkansas was across the river, and the local sheriffs were corrupt.

In some cases as many as six thousand extended families lived on huge plantations. Sprigle pronounced that for all of them the landlord was "the middle justice, the high and the low. Mississippi law stops dead in its tracks at their boundaries. No sheriff, no peace officer takes a man, black or white," off a plantation "until 'The Man' tells him he may." There was a good reason you never saw headlines about lynchings or "wanton Negro murders" coming out of the Delta.

> Your Delta Negro seldom has any trouble with his white folks. Or if he does, neither the trouble nor the Negro lasts very long. Reason is that the Delta Negro lives under an iron-clad despotism so ruthless and so efficient that your ordinary share-cropper and field hand seldom comes in contact with it. In the Delta, the Negro not only "knows his place" but he keeps it faithfully from childhood to old age. Or he never lives to reach old age. It's seldom that the white folks have to kill a Delta Negro. But when they do it's done quietly and expeditiously. And there are no "political and civic" leagues as in Georgia to start raising hell about it, either. Even the remarkably efficient and almost omnipresent NAACP functions limpingly in Mississippi. The white folks see to that.

Meanwhile, white folks also saw to it that the Delta's majority population was disenfranchised. Since the end of Reconstruction, the state's oily one-party political machine had been rigged to suppress black votes and protect and preserve the power of the state's Democratic Party elite—the Delta cotton planters who thought so highly of their hero Senator Bilbo. Like nearly all of Mississippi's one million black citizens, those living in the Delta were essentially not allowed to vote. Poll taxes, literacy tests, intimidation, and other impediments were used to limit the number of black voters in the state to about ten thousand Republicans in the bigger cities, where they had no impact on election outcomes. The Democrats' white magic worked so well that the percentage of eligible blacks who were registered to vote in Mississippi was kept under 7 percent until 1964.

The black leaders Sprigle met on his trip insisted that life for blacks in the Delta was hardly better than slavery. In many ways it looked that way, and in many ways their standard of living was no better than 1860. But for one major reason Sprigle could not agree: the freedom to move. "The Negro sharecropper or field hand can pull up stakes and leave whenever he wishes. No longer do deputy sheriffs pursue fleeing sharecroppers and drag them back to the plow and hoe to work out their debts. The Federal Government broke that up 10 years ago."

City life—even in a slum—was a major improvement over sharecropping, especially for the young. Any job paid better than cotton picking, plus you had time off. In Chicago there were jobs at companies like Caterpillar making the same machines that were putting Delta sharecroppers out of work. The great blues singer and guitarist Muddy Waters got a job on the loading dock of a paper factory. Thirty years old, he had been playing for tips and living in a one-room shack on the Stovall Plantation outside Clarksdale when he and other sharecropper musicians took the Illinois Central to Chicago in 1943.

Waters revolutionized American music when he electrified the Delta blues in the late 1940s and started recording. As his Rock & Roll Hall of Fame bio says, he "transformed the soul of the rural South into the sound of the city." But before he became one of the great influences in American blues and rock, he recalled how happy he was to be working in a factory eight hours a day and able to afford to rent a four-room apartment. "I never did that before. My paycheck was fortysomething bucks or fifty-something bucks a week. You got to be kiddin', you know. Soon I put in some overtime, worked twelve hours a day and I brought a hundred and something bring-home pay. I said, 'Goodgodamighty, look at the money I got.' I have picked that cotton all year, chop cotton all year, and I didn't draw a hundred dollars."

It wasn't easy to trade the peaceful Delta for a strange, crowded, noisy, rough-and-tumble urban world when you had no money, no skills, and little education. But it had been done hundreds of thousands of times already. About 150,000 black men and women left Mississippi during the 1940s. All you needed were family or friends already in Chicago and fifteen dollars for a one-way ticket on the Illinois Central. But you had to be careful. Sprigle talked to one sharecropper who was planning his family's escape. A relative in Chicago had sent him his train tickets. He already had sent his parents there on a "visit" and was going to send his kids and wife along in a few days. As he told Sprigle, the "best way is to just leave quiet at night. That way there just can't be any trouble."

~

They may have been exploring the "backward and reactionary" Delta, as Sprigle called it, but he and Dobbs were not exactly sleeping by the side of the road on cots. They didn't stay overnight in Greenville at the black-owned Hotel Montrose or anywhere else like that. Sprigle's record of his travel expenses showed he paid three dollars for lodging at a private home. Probably somewhere between Greenville and Clarksdale, they stayed at the fine home of a former sharecropper who now had a maid, a huge mahogany table in her dining room, and enough jewelry to buy half of Bolivar County. The diamond dinner ring she wore cost $850—eighty-five hundred dollars today. The ring her husband had just picked out for her in a Memphis jewelry store was fifteen hundred dollars.

The woman and her husband had "a pleasant home, a thriving used-car business, a gasoline station and barbecue stand on the highway, an undertaking business and a small insurance company—and a fistful of diamonds." But long before the black couple had become solidly middle class, their tall, handsome hostess worked seven years as a sharecropper, chopping cotton and following a mule all day, while her entrepreneurial husband kept his used-car business afloat. In addition to working in the fields, she also borrowed money from the only "bank" available to poor blacks—"The Man." The interest rate was usurious —8 percent for three months and 32 percent a year. Plantation owners, some with as many as six thousand sharecroppers living on their land, counted on lending their money to workers each year to boost their profit margins. Though she never really needed to borrow the money, she told Sprigle she figured she'd "better fall in line."

One of the most remarkable Delta communities Sprigle couldn't afford to bypass was Mound Bayou, an all-black town founded by two ex-slaves. In 1887 Isaiah T. Montgomery and Benjamin Green bought four thousand acres of swampland and forest from the Louisville, New Orleans and Texas Railroad, began clearing the land, and incorporated a town twenty-eight miles south of Clarksdale. Next to a railroad line and promoted by Booker T. Washington as a model of thrift and self-government, the self-segregated town and surrounding farms prospered and grew. By 1907, when its population hit eight thousand, President Theodore Roosevelt visited Mississippi and called Mound Bayou "The Jewel of the Delta." It had banks, retail stores, six churches, and several public and private schools. It even had black voters—for local elections only. Seen as a showcase of black pride and economic opportunity, its church-going citizens had never built a jail because there was practically no crime.

Collapsing cotton prices after the World War I boom, the Great Migration, local political feuds, the Great Depression, and a fire that destroyed much of the business district in 1941 took their toll, however. By the time Sprigle and Dobbs arrived for their drive-by, Mound Bayou's population had sunk to twelve hundred. They met with the mayor, a Harvard Law School graduate Sprigle described as "spare, taciturn and reserved." The mayor was happy to report that his battered town—the only one in the state that did not have Jim Crow laws—was going to get a boost from the construction of a five-million-dollar Veterans Administration hospital for black war vets.

Mound Bayou already had the celebrated Taborian Hospital, a fifty-bed hospital for blacks. It had been built in 1942 by a black fraternal group, the International Order of Twelve Knights and Daughters of Tabor, that promoted "Christianity, education, morality and temperance and the art of governing, self reliance and true manhood and womanhood." Its entire staff was black. It had two operating rooms and all the modern medical marvels, including X-ray machines and incubators. Supported almost entirely with voluntary contributions, for a fee of eight dollars a year it provided free medical care to thousands of black patients each year.

Mound Bayou was off the beaten track, but one of its most prominent residents in 1948 was destined to play an important role in the future civil rights movement in Mississippi and nationally. Taborian Hospital's first chief surgeon was T. R. M. Howard, a combination doctor and entrepreneur who believed in Booker T. Washington's school of thought that black political progress would follow economic success. He owned a thousand-acre plantation, a homebuilding company, a restaurant, and an insurance company, and built a zoo for Mound Bayou as well as the first Olympic-size swimming pool for blacks in the state.

In the 1950s Howard became an important early black political foe of Jim Crow in Mississippi. When Emmett Till was murdered forty-six miles east of Mound Bayou in Money in the summer of 1955, he paid for a private investigation. He also used his lavish, heavily armed home as a safe "black command center" where journalists, black out-of-state observers, and Emmett's brave mother could stay when the trial was held in Sumner, Mississippi. A lifelong Republican and a controversial figure for his longtime pro-abortion stance, he was active in the civil rights movement into the 1970s and was a mentor to Mississippi 1960s civil rights heroes Medgar Evers and Fannie Lou Hamer. Sprigle didn't meet Dr. Howard, who spent most of his time in Washington, but he was impressed by Mound Bayou's effort to take care of "the greatest of all needs of the black folks of the Delta, education." The town's brick high school and modern elementary school were considered to be among the best black schools in the state.

On the edge of the cotton fields outside Clarksdale, in the black half of Shufordville Cemetery, Dr. P. W. Hill stood next to a gleaming tomb made of white Alabama marble. Above the wide door of the walk-in mausoleum, his name was chiseled in twelve-inch letters. The vaults inside—one containing the remains of his wife and child—were protected by a heavy iron-bar door and arranged in the walls like the drawers of a marble file cabinet. A large window of iron bars made sure the cold crypt would always be filled with moving air and morning and afternoon light. Outside by the door was a solid piece of marble carved into a bench. It was hot and sticky and mosquitoes patrolled the heavy Delta air.

Dobbs had made an appointment to meet the wealthy dentist at the cemetery so Sprigle could hear and record his awful story. The tomb was easy to find in the raggedy Jim Crow cemetery, which was just off Highway 61 near the small community of Lyon. It towered over the unmarked graves and generic headstones of its neighbors, which, leaning all over the place, were strangled and partially obscured by uncut grass and wildflowers.

After returning to Pittsburgh from the Jim Crow South in early June of 1948, Ray Sprigle donned his disguise and was photographed by a *Pittsburgh Post-Gazette* photographer. JAMES KLINGENSMITH PHOTO / COURTESY OF SENATOR JOHN HEINZ HISTORY CENTER

Sprigle without his trademark Stetson in 1940 after returning from covering the Blitz in London, and relaxing with his daughter Rae on her fourth birthday in 1939. BOTH COURTESY OF SENATOR JOHN HEINZ HISTORY CENTER

Three weeks after he guided Ray Sprigle through the South, John Wesley Dobbs was photographed by a *Life* magazine staffer as he was being given his official delegate's badge at the Republican National Convention. Dobbs, the only black person featured among *Life's* forty-some photos, was identified only as a "Georgia delegate." PHOTO BY RALPH MORSE / THE LIFE PICTURE COLLECTION / GETTY IMAGES

For three decades John Wesley Dobbs was a prominent political and civic leader in Atlanta's black community and the Grand Master of Georgia's Prince Hall Masons. In 1948, wearing his Prince Hall regalia, he met in St. Louis with educator, philanthropist, and civil rights activist Mary McLeod Bethune. COURTESY OF THE AMISTAD RESEARCH CENTER

Water fountains—like this one in North Carolina—as well as all public spaces, schools, movie theaters, taxicabs, ballfields, and elevators, were segregated by law in the Jim Crow South. SCHOMBURG CENTER FOR RESEARCH IN BLACK CULTURE, PHOTOGRAPHS AND PRINTS DIVISION, THE NEW YORK PUBLIC LIBRARY

As they toured the Deep South, Sprigle and Dobbs passed tens of thousands of black men, women, and children hoeing cotton like these Alabama tenant farmers. PHOTO BY DOROTHEA LANGE / COURTESY OF THE LIBRARY OF CONGRESS

"Separate but equal" black schools like this one located on the Mileston Plantation in the Mississippi Delta in 1939 were virtually empty during cotton-picking season. PHOTO BY MARION POST WOLCOTT / SCHOMBURG CENTER FOR RESEARCH IN BLACK CULTURE, PHOTOGRAPHS AND PRINTS DIVISION, THE NEW YORK PUBLIC LIBRARY

President Truman, Eleanor Roosevelt, and NAACP head Walter White walk to the Lincoln Memorial, where on June 28, 1947, Truman delivered a major civil rights speech to ten thousand members of the NAACP. NATIONAL ARCHIVES AND RECORDS ADMINIS-TRATION. OFFICE OF PRESIDENTIAL LIBRARIES. HARRY S. TRUMAN LIBRARY. 4/1/1985-

Scrappy, smart, segregationist Hodding Carter, the editor of the *Delta Democrat-Times* in Greenville, Mississippi, was a prolific freelance writer known in the North as the "liberal" voice of the South. COURTESY OF MITCHELL MEMORIAL LIBRARY, MISSISSIPPI STATE UNIVERSITY

Walter White, the executive secretary of the National Association for the Advancement of Colored People from 1931 to 1955, personally lobbied presidents Roosevelt and Truman for civil rights reforms. He helped Ray Sprigle find a guide for his Southern undercover mission and enthusiastically publicized his newspaper series and book. COURTESY OF SENATOR JOHN HEINZ HISTORY CENTER

Pittsburgh Courier star journalist and editorial voice for four decades, conservative satirist George Schuyler, his wife Josephine Cogdell Schuyler, and their daughter Philippa play dominoes in the mid 1940s. Philippa was a renowned child prodigy. A pianist and composer known as "the Shirley Temple of American Negroes," she became a journalist and was killed in a helicopter crash in Vietnam in 1967 at age thirty-five. SCHOMBURG CENTER FOR RESEARCH IN BLACK CULTURE, PHOTOGRAPHS AND PRINTS DIVISION, THE NEW YORK PUBLIC LIBRARY

During World War II Ray Sprigle made national news by disguising himself as a black-market meat salesman to show how easy it was to buy more than a ton of meat without using rationing stamps. COURTESY OF SENATOR JOHN HEINZ HISTORY CENTER

Wearing what he had worn during his Southern trip, Sprigle stands on the steps he built at his farmhouse in the woods west of Pittsburgh. JAMES KLINGENSMITH PHOTO / COURTESY OF SENATOR JOHN HEINZ HISTORY CENTER

Sprigle's trademark Stetson hat and corncob pipe and his under- cover exploits made him a celebrity journalist in Pittsburgh and across western Pennsylvania. COURTESY OF SENATOR JOHN HEINZ HISTORY CENTER

Willie and Dorothy Haslerig were in their mid-twenties when Ray Sprigle and John Wesley Dobbs stayed for the weekend at Willie's father's prosperous farm in Chickamauga in northwest Georgia. 1998 PHOTO BY BILL STEIGERWALD

In the spring of 1949 Ray Sprigle signed his book *In the Land of Jim Crow* in a Pittsburgh department store. COURTESY OF SENATOR JOHN HEINZ HISTORY CENTER

Less than a week after Sprigle returned to Pittsburgh, Dobbs and his wife Irene (far right) celebrated the graduation of their youngest daughter June from Spelman College. Dobbs's five older daughters, all Spelman graduates, are, from his right, Irene Dobbs Jackson, class of '29; Juliet Dobbs Blackburn, class of '31; Millicent Dobbs Jordan, class of '33; Josephine Dobbs Clement, class of '37; Mattiwilda Dobbs Janzon, class of '46; June Dobbs Butts, class of '48. SPELLMAN COLLEGE ARCHIVES

Juliet Dobbs Blackburn-Beamon stands next to the bronze sculpture of her grandfather's head in Dobbs Plaza on the corner of Auburn Avenue and Fort Street in Atlanta. 1998 PHOTO BY BILL STEIGERWALD

Though Dr. Hill had built the mausoleum only two months earlier, his wife, Marjorie, had died back in 1939. As he told "James Crawford" of the NAACP, they planned for their baby to be born at home. Everything was normal until the final hours when she began having serious complications. The local black doctors said she would die without an emergency Caesarean, something Clarksdale's twelve-bed black clinic was not capable of providing. Clarksdale had a small hospital—for whites. Like most blacks his age, Dr. Hill never even considered taking his wife there because he knew blacks were not admitted under any circumstance. Mound Bayou's modern black hospital didn't exist yet. He had no choice but to send his wife seventy-eight miles north by ambulance at midnight to a black hospital in Memphis. Shortly before dawn Marjorie and her newborn baby died on the operating table.

Dr. Hill was one of the leading middle-class black citizens of Clarksdale and a Prince Hall Mason. He was described by Sprigle as a small, scholarly, reserved man who told his story dispassionately, without bitterness, without blaming anyone or anything for his tragedy. Showing Sprigle and Dobbs through his expensive tomb, he regarded it "only as his tribute to the ones he loved." But Sprigle had already had as much of Jim Crow's rules and regulations as he could stomach. He was bitter. He said Dr. Hill had "learned his lesson well." He was "a black man in a white world." And his tomb was "a monument to the cold-blooded cruelty of the white man; to the brutal mandate of a white world that black men and women must die rather than be permitted to defile a cot or an operating table in a white hospital with their black skins."

When he pressed Dr. Hill on why he didn't even try to get the white hospital to admit his wife, Sprigle showed he still had much to learn about what it was like being black. Dobbs and the dentist both quickly set him straight. "In the South," they told him, "when you're black you don't try to fight the pattern. Hospitals are for white people. White people do not admit black folk to their hospitals. Black folk do not even ask for admission. They just die."

Sprigle thought that was one "barbarity" charged to his race that would turn out to be a myth. But when he checked later he found two recent cases of badly injured blacks being turned away from white hospitals in

Georgia and Tennessee after road accidents. Whites didn't admit blacks, and blacks knew it. It was a pattern, and it didn't make Sprigle comfortable as Dobbs rolled along through the night at seventy miles an hour. "Every time we had a close shave with another car," he said, "I could see myself riding around in a Jim Crow ambulance, hunting a Jim Crow hospital while I slowly bled to death."

Sixty-one years later, in May of 2009, Dr. Hill's tomb was hard to find and not so gleaming. (As part of a freelance feature article for the *Pittsburgh Post-Gazette*, the author went in search of Dr. Hill's marble tomb.) Shufordville Historical Cemetery was still segregated after 159 years. On one side of a dirt road white people and a half dozen Confederate soldiers were spending eternity in an orderly, fenced-in graveyard that had a big sign, mowed grass, and well-tended headstones. The remains of black people, many of them too poor to afford markers, were buried in neat rows on the other side of the road. With no formal caretaking paid for by their descendants, however, their sunken graves were hidden under a wild tangle of tall grasses, bushes, and clumps of small trees. From the road Dr. Hill's tomb was nowhere to be seen. But three hundred feet into the jungle it suddenly emerged like a Mayan ruin. Hemmed in and shaded by bushy trees, its white marble was soiled and discolored by nature and neglect. An overturned vase of weathered plastic flowers lay at the mausoleum's front step. Its heavy metal door was off its hinges and leaning against an inside wall. Inside was a marble vault carved with "Margie Hill, Born October 30, 1904; Died October 10, 1939." In another vault were the remains of Dr. P. W. Hill.

~

Though Mississippi was a dry state, booze was everywhere. Sprigle and Dobbs drank Arkansas wine every night they were in the Delta. The continued prohibition of liquor had predictable results—the creation of a thriving black market and corruption of the law. Every night, and especially in the fall after they got their seasonal cash settlements from their landlords, cotton workers rowed across the Mississippi in skiffs to buy whiskey in Arkansas river towns like Helena. Upon their return many were nabbed by county police, heavily fined, and stripped of their contraband.

While he was in the Delta, Sprigle said black folks from Greenville to Tunica were "gleefully savoring a scandal among their white lords" that had to do with smuggling booze. It involved a reform sheriff who had been elected on the promise of making his county truly dry. After the sheriff caught and fined three field hands for smuggling booze who "belonged" to one of the big plantation owners, the cotton baron showed everyone who the real boss of the county was. He roughed up the sheriff in public. Then he showed him a trunk-full of whiskey he had brought in from Arkansas for himself and told the sheriff to never bust any of his workers again. Sprigle said the point of the story, and another about a plantation owner who dragged the mayor of a small town out of his office and kicked him down the middle of Main Street, was to show how powerless blacks were. "If the Delta's cotton lords can kick the white 'Law' around in this fashion with no retribution, what chance does the lowly black man stand if he should ever be so foolhardy as to let himself come into conflict with his white masters?"

Sprigle and Dobbs weren't fans of the blues, but they dropped into enough juke joints and "colored cafes" to observe the Delta's popular gambling pastime, the "skin game." It was a simple, fast-paced card game, said to resemble the Italian favorite Ziginette, in which players bet that cards dealt from the deck will not match previously dealt cards on the table. The game was played year round but each fall, when tens of thousands of sharecroppers were suddenly flush with cash, the Delta became a huge indoor and outdoor gambling den.

Fall was "skin ball" season in the Delta. Top black gamblers and racketeers from around the country descended on towns like Clarksdale and Rosedale to run the skin game tournaments. They were held nonstop in juke joints, pool rooms, homes, sheds, or out in the open fields by campfire. For many sharecroppers skin ball season lasted about ninety seconds. That's how fast Sprigle said they could blow the five hundred dollars they made for a year of punishing field work.

Once the small fry lost their money, the visiting pros and big sharks from Memphis, Chicago, and New Orleans went to work. Stakes at a table could be as large as fifty thousand dollars. Every time anyone won a hand, 10 percent of the winnings went into "the cut box." The cut box's money was split among the owner of the juke joint, the local racketeer, and "The Law," which Sprigle said took the biggest part. In a good year, he was told, "The Law" made more from his skin-ball payoffs than from his salary. Plantation owners and their employees also got their share. "So even these famous 'skin balls' help the white folks perpetuate the Delta's way of life for the black man—don't let him get his hands on too much money at one time—and don't let him keep that little long."

Exiting the top of the Delta near Memphis, Sprigle and Dobbs crossed through northern Alabama in the night on their way back to Atlanta. Sprigle did some thinking. Though nothing violent had happened to him on his journey through the Delta, he said, "The fact remains that the black man in the South lives in fear." He had hardly spoken to a white man. But he said there had been "Too much of don't do this or that" or "Be careful" or "Don't talk to the field hands." There were towns in the Delta where Dobbs wouldn't even take him, but Sprigle didn't put up an argument. He had heard too many stories about "what had happened and what could happen to a black man in Mississippi."

A little after midnight, three hundred miles from Dr. Hill's tomb, they pulled into the black section of Huntsville, Alabama, where they could count on good food, lodging, and friends. Sprigle was unnerved—and very happy to be out of Mississippi. Only once before in his long life had he felt the same sense of relief, comfort, and safety. That was in London during the Blitz, when he was able to seek refuge from the German bombs in the air-raid shelter two stories beneath the Waldorf Hotel. He and Dobbs "unkinked" themselves from the Mercury and joined "the friendly black faces on the sidewalk." Sprigle could tell Dobbs was happy to be out of Mississippi. "I tell you there was relief in my companion's voice, too, as he turned to me with a laugh and said, 'Well, we're back safe with our people again.' And by this time they were my people, I was somewhat surprised to find. I think that was the first time I realized that I was feeling black."

CHAPTER 13

The Long Reach of "White Malice"

After three weeks and nearly three thousand hot and dusty highway miles, Ray Sprigle was looking forward to a swim in the Atlantic Ocean. His last major road trip with Dobbs, in late May, was to Savannah and Brunswick on Georgia's beautiful coast. A hundred miles of The Peach State's broad beaches were covered with white sand—and white people only. Annoyed that he had been carrying his swim trunks around the South for no reason, Sprigle called it "a Jim Crow ocean." He said there was "not a single foot where a Negro can stick a toe in salt water. North and south, South Carolina and Florida have public and private beaches reserved for us black people. Not Georgia. Georgia is going to keep her share of the Atlantic pure and undefiled—and lily white." If a black American walked into the ocean he'd be fined for trespassing. Three young girls tried to do it on a deserted beach in the mid-1940s. They were nabbed by a county policeman before they got their feet wet, and it still cost each of them half a day in jail and fifty dollars, plus costs.

Though its public beaches were closed to blacks, Brunswick and Savannah were known as the "best Negro towns in the South," Sprigle said, "better even than Atlanta." He said the historical record backed up that claim. In 215 years Savannah had never had a lynching. The closest call came during the boom years of the Klan when a mob of klansmen from a rural county came to town to lynch a black prisoner. The sheriff of Savannah, reported Sprigle with obvious delight and hyperbole, "waited on the steps of the jail with a tommy-gun across his arm and when the mob arrived he calmly shot the leader to ribbons. There was no lynching."

Savannah, population 118,000, and Brunswick, population seventeen thousand, were historic late-1700s towns. Savannah was known for its parks, magnolias, oaks, Spanish moss, and pre–Civil War architecture. Brunswick was a seaport where during World War II a hundred Liberty Ships were built and the Navy operated the world's largest base for blimps. Both cities were relatively advanced by Jim Crow standards. They each had public parks for blacks, and Savannah had a black swimming pool. Savannah also had a modern hospital for blacks, though three-fourths of its operating costs came not from the city but from private sources, much of it from the North. The city had twelve black cops on the streets, beating Atlanta to the punch by a year and becoming one of the first major integrated police forces in the Deep South. Blacks—twenty thousand of them—actually voted freely in Savannah and held the balance of power in elections of the white candidates.

Yet, Sprigle said, both towns were ruled by Jim Crow "with an iron grip. In Savannah's stately courthouse the only restrooms for Negroes are down in the janitor's quarters. Negroes may ride only in Jim Crow cabs. . . . In beautiful Forsythe Park, in Savannah, both white and black folk sit where they please. But in an adjoining extension park the tennis courts and ball diamonds are for whites only." In 1947 the state purchased Jekyll Island, the vacation playground of the Rockefellers and other millionaires, and promised to create a resort for the citizens of Georgia—the white ones.

At some point during their roundtrip drive from Atlanta to Savannah, Sprigle and Dobbs visited Sparta, a quiet historic town of nearly two thousand that Sprigle praised as "another spot of green in the desert." Once it was a thriving trading center of the pre–Civil War cotton plantation system, i.e., one whose wealth was derived from the labor of thousands of slaves. But eighty-three years later Sprigle was happy to point out that blacks and whites seemed to have figured out how to get along in public without the help of Jim Crow's ground rules.

Sparta was the biggest "city" in rolling Hancock County, which had a population of eleven thousand. About eight thousand people were black. Sparta's chief asset in 1948, as far as Sprigle was concerned, was a fine municipal baseball field. The local black team, one of the state's best, was allowed to play its home games at the town ballpark. Black fans sat in the grandstand and whites were welcome to watch from the bleachers. Another sign of Sparta's relative enlightenment was that the benches around the county courthouse in the center of town did not contain the usual "For Colored" signs. Blacks were free to sit wherever they wanted.

During the afternoon he and Dobbs spent in Sparta, Sprigle said he "got firsthand evidence that this *must* be a good town. We walked through the park. There, stretched out full length on a park bench, slept one of my black brothers. In almost any other town in Georgia he'd be on his way to the road gang so fast the soles of his shoes would be smoking. Here nobody 'pays him any mind.'" Sparta had a healthy collection of black grocers, blacksmiths, and restaurants, plus two undertakers and six taxi drivers. The most visibly successful black man in town was A. J. Washington, another "one-in-a-million" success story of the Deep South. He was a farmer/businessman/real estate mogul who grew up in Sparta and tried the big cities of Cleveland and Philadelphia as a barber before coming back home to the South he loved. He and his wife, who also had lived in Savannah and New York City, owned a large and popular general store in the black part of town. They sold everything from groceries and hardware to gasoline and catered to white and black customers.

Washington was also one of two hundred black farmers operating in the county. He owned five hundred acres and rented five hundred more, growing more cotton than anyone around and running three sharecroppers on his land who each cleared one thousand dollars in cash the previous year. Washington, who subscribed to the *Pittsburgh Courier* and the *Atlanta Daily World*, told Sprigle he did his "figuring" in the open, showing his sharecroppers exactly what he paid for seed and fertilizer and the price he got in the fall for cotton bales. Months later the globe-trotting George Schuyler of the *Courier* would come to Sparta and interview A. J. Washington and his storekeeper wife, Susie Mae, for his seven-part series, "What's So Good About the South?"

Based on his ten-thousand-mile tour of fourteen southern states, Schuyler's collection of feature stories about "average black families" living in the rural and urban South promised to find the truth under the pro and con "propaganda" about black conditions in the region. But his series had Schuyler's own upbeat agenda. It played up success stories like the Washingtons and played down the discrimination, insults, and threats of violence that blacks like A. J. and Susie Mae had to live with daily.

> The Washingtons say they have never heard of a lynching in Sparta or vicinity and that they have not been insulted or persecuted. They say they have some real good white friends. She says, "We have many good white people here who will go all the way with you. I don't have any trouble with them. It all depends on how you carry yourself. They treat me just fine. Of course you're down South and you have to act in a certain way. I think they treat Negroes pretty well around here unless Negroes give cause to be treated otherwise."

Schuyler, always the contrarian, did his best to show that the South wasn't universally horrible and that blacks could succeed in spite of Jim Crow. But the Washingtons of Sparta were among the exceptions that gave away the greater truth. Like "James Crawford," the couple didn't run into trouble with Jim Crow or white people for a very good reason. They were careful. They knew, from a lifetime of experience, how to behave.

Sprigle took part in a dozen group conversations with middle-class black businessmen and civic leaders from Jackson to Savannah. Invariably, the chief topic of the evening was race. As a white man who had received all his information about slavery from his high school history books in Akron, Sprigle was "a bit shocked by the casual way in which these Southerners refer to human bondage and the traffic in bodies of black men and women and children." At one gathering he heard blacks from Virginia and North Carolina—"Northerners"—criticizing Georgia's blacks for their lack of progress on racial matters. "By superhuman effort" he said he kept quiet and listened. He detected a superior attitude from the northerners—and so did a patriotic Georgian, who put up the argument that blacks from Virginia and North Carolina are "a softer breed."

For 250 years of slavery, the Georgian said, the slave owners in the North didn't try to handle "bad" blacks but just sold them south to

Georgia, Alabama, and Mississippi. "That left only the 'soft' slaves in the north and the slave and overseers became 'soft' too. Down here in the South a lot of those 'bad' Negroes—meaning those with too much manhood to submit to the soul-killing cruelties of slavery—died rather than break. But some were too tough to die. They survived and their children survived. But the masters and overseers became tough and hard too."

"Up north," the Georgian continued, "your people achieve 'progress' without fighting for it. The white folks hand it to you. Down here we have to fight for every inch of progress. We've been fighting for 85 years of so-called 'freedom.' That's why we've always had race trouble." Much disagreement followed, but Sprigle used the north-south debate to jump to a discussion of the ways cities and towns of the Deep South misused their judicial systems to profit from their "'bad' Negroes" as well as "their ignorant, harmless and helpless ones."

According to Sprigle, scores of cities regularly ordered their police to sweep black neighborhoods, picking up those who were genuinely disorderly as well as innocent loiterers. "Trials are a farce," he said, and "practically no prisoner with a black skin ever escapes without a fine, at least." The wholesale fining of blacks footed the bill for the local courts and part of the police budget in many towns, he said. Those who couldn't afford to pay the fine were assigned to work on road gangs, which kept highway department budgets lower for those whom Sprigle called their "white masters."

Though he learned many important things from the stories of Dobbs and his friends about the difficulties of being a southern black man, Sprigle discovered some on his own. For instance, he had traveled through the South before as a journalist and a tourist and he often noticed cars parked off to the side of lonely stretches of highway. He'd see whole black families scrambling into or out of the underbrush and never put two and two together. Naively, he had always thought it was some "eccentricity of the Southern Negro." But after his first few hours on the road with Dobbs in early May, he quickly grasped the humiliating truth that every black motorist in the South had to learn in childhood—outside the cities the only rest stops reliably open to them were the bushes.

Jim Crow bathrooms were the only ones blacks could legally use. Many of the bigger gas stations owned by national companies—Gulf and

Esso—had separate restrooms for blacks, but they were mostly in the cities. Small-town filling stations didn't provide them, either because it was too expensive or, more likely, as Sprigle said, their owners didn't "give a damn." Black gas stations were rare in the country. But because their bathrooms were for blacks only, sometimes it was desperate white guys who found themselves Jim-Crowed.

Answering Nature's persistent calls was one of the most pressing logistical problems the two old male road warriors had to deal with in their travels. Sprigle and Dobbs found themselves standing next to each other in the bushes many times. Sprigle said they also "made an exhaustive survey of the restroom situation in the Deep South from a racial standpoint. Man—we just had to." Technically, he said, in four states he and Dobbs were never turned away from a single gas station because of the color of their skin. "At nearly every filling station we stopped at—white ones, that is—we were told, 'Restroom's out of commission, we're putting in new plumbing,' or 'Restroom's closed for repairs.' At least they spared our feelings by refraining from telling us what we all knew was the simple truth: We were black." In a few cases, they were allowed to use the facilities—which meant they and the gas station owner broke the law.

Their informal restroom survey was put on hold for safety reasons when they stopped at the largest gas station in McRae, Georgia. The town of two thousand was the home base of the late four-term governor Eugene Talmadge, a demagogue and flagrant racist of the Bilbo School. It was the county seat of a rural area that was genetically inhospitable to two black gentlemen from the city in a nice new car. The previous year when Dobbs had filled up at a white gas station in McCrae, things had taken an ugly and dangerous turn.

As the black attendant began pumping, Dobbs, who was alone, casually asked the owner for permission to use the bathroom "on the off chance that he might get it." The answer came fast and clear —"No niggers." "Stop the gas," Dobbs told the attendant after thirty-seven cents worth had been pumped. He took out a fifty-cent piece and offered it to the attendant. Sprigle, quipping that "the white proprietor had sensed a threat to white supremacy and perhaps to the sanctity of Southern white womanhood," described what happened next to Dobbs.

"Nigger," he demanded, "don't you know God-damned well that no nigger can use my restrooms?"

My friend was under no illusions. This white Peckerwood was working himself up to murder.

"I know it now," he replied and started for the car.

"Nigger, you knew it God-damned well before. You knew God-damned well no God-damned nigger uses a white restroom in this part of Georgia."

"I know it now," repeated my friend. And by that time he had made the driver's seat and got out of McCrae in a cloud of dust.

It didn't take the slightest reflection to convince me that I didn't want any part of restroom research in McCrae. I guess I just didn't have that kind of guts.

The incident reminded Sprigle how close blacks always were to becoming victims of racist violence and how much abuse they had to meekly take from the lowest class of white people. Even his new black friends—men of status and substance—couldn't feel "secure and beyond the reach of white malice." Their instructions to him about how to behave—repeated over and over—betrayed to him the fear of violence they carried in their hearts every day.

Sprigle said challenging "the gauntlet of race-conscious white supremacists who rule the vital and necessitous facilities of the Southland's filling station rest rooms" wasn't the only trouble Dobbs got them into on the road. He also annoyed the heck out of black gas-station owners. Most of the black service stations they stopped at, Sprigle was sorry to report, were poorly run, dirty, and littered. Their attendants were careless and inattentive. Dobbs was a very demanding customer, no matter who was providing him service, and he was on a personal crusade to improve black gas stations. "In addition to all his other good qualities," Sprigle said, "this friend of mine" was "one of the most efficient, management-minded individuals I've ever encountered. Carelessness, negligence, uncleanliness, try his soul."

Black gas stations in four states got the full Dobbs tutorial whether they wanted it or not. "At every blasted one of them," Sprigle said, "my companion just had to put management, and help, too, through a ten- to fifteen-minute course in efficiency. He'd get out of the car, demonstrating while he lectured. 'Wash the windshield of every car that comes in,' he'd direct. 'Check the oil and water whether the customer asks it or not. See that the back window is clean too. Wipe the headlight lenses. Keep on the move. Work briskly.'" In the end, Sprigle said, they "weren't any more popular with Negro filling station entrepreneurs than we were with their white counterparts."

Unequal schools. Voting suppression. Unpunished violence against blacks by police and white civilians. During his time as an undercover journalist in the Deep South, Sprigle looked closely at those timeless issues. He also made pains to seek out the family members of victims of lynchings. To find out more about how Georgia farmer Henry Gilbert died at the hands of his local police, he interviewed his widow, Carolyn. He also looked into the murder of Maceo Yost Snipes, a returning G.I. who was killed for casting his vote in Taylor County, Georgia. And to illustrate "the pattern of Negro murder in the gentle Southland," Sprigle went to the scene of the quadruple lynching near Monroe, Georgia, that became national news and shocked the entire country.

What happened in Walton County by a bridge in daylight on July 25, 1946, was unbelievably barbaric. Two men and two women sharecroppers were pulled from a car by a mob of about twenty white men, tied up on a dirt road, and, as Sprigle described it, "shot to rags with rifles, pistols and shotguns." The slaughter of four humans like "wildlife," as one British writer would later describe it, generated thirty thousand letters to the White House and Congress. It was covered in forty-three articles in the *New York Times* and sparked massive protests in Washington and San Francisco. One of the dead men, Roger Malcolm, was a World War II veteran, which outraged President Truman so much he ordered the FBI to Georgia to investigate.

The four victims were executed because of events that had been set into motion after one of them broke the Jim Crow South's greatest and frequently ignored taboo—interracial sex. It started with the infidelity of Malcolm's wife, Dorothy. She had an affair with a white man while her husband was serving overseas. When Malcolm, twenty-seven, came home and found out who the white man was, he went after him, got into a fight, and ended up slashing him with a knife. The white man recovered quickly, and Malcolm was locked in the local jail for three weeks.

The way Sprigle retold the story, Malcolm's ultimate fate was sealed when the area was visited by Governor Gene Talmadge, "the gallus-snapping, self-styled Peckerwood" who was running for re-election. Sprigle spared no sarcasm. He said Talmadge "was traveling up and down the mud roads of Georgia preaching hatred of the Negro and pleading for votes that would restore him to the governor's chair and thus assure Georgia that white supremacy would endure and the virtue and purity of white Southern womanhood would remain unsullied."

Talmadge had a brief private talk with the sheriff of Walton County and the father of the slashed "gay young Lothario who had gotten himself all cut up for love's sweet sake." Two days later a poor white farmer named Loy Harrison came to the jail and paid the six-hundred-dollar bail for Malcolm, who worked on his land as a sharecropper. Malcolm, his wife, his friend George Dorsey, and Dorsey's wife, Mae, were riding in Harrison's old Pontiac soon after when it was blocked by a handful of vehicles at a bridge near the Walton-Oconee County line. The mob of armed and unmasked young white men quickly grabbed Malcolm and Dorsey. As they forced them down an embankment toward an oak tree, the women began to scream. When one woman recognized a member of the mob and shouted out his name, it was decided on the spot that the women also had to die. As Sprigle said, the foursome was left "sprawled in the red dust of a Georgia back road."

Nearly two years after the "Monroe Massacre," Sprigle and Dobbs spent an afternoon in Walton County interviewing locals and family members of the murdered married couples. It took Sprigle about twenty minutes to learn the names of three of the murderers. Most everyone in the county—black and white—knew who the killers were from Day One. So did the twenty FBI agents who arrived "like the Marines landing" but were able to accomplish nothing. No one talked to the G-men. No one snitched. No one would risk testifying against the killers in court and, anyway, no white jury in the state would have convicted them. Even the farmer delivering the two black couples to their doom, Harrison, was conveniently stupid and unhelpful about the details of the bloody ambush he witnessed and probably helped arrange.

Sprigle didn't believe that more than a few whites in Walton County actually condoned the "wanton and indiscriminate murder of black men and women. But as in other lynching and murder-ridden counties in the South, enough of them either approve or condone outrages upon helpless blacks to make it highly unpleasant for those whites who might be moved to protest—or even highly dangerous for those who might be moved to action—such as offering testimony on the witness stand against a Negro-killing white man."

The Monroe Massacre became the last mass lynching in the United States. By the time Sprigle was poking around the case, it was sleeping deep in the files of the FBI and the Georgia Bureau of Investigation. He was correct in predicting no one white involved in the murders would ever be convicted of committing even the smallest crime against a black person. That included the near fatal beating of an illiterate black man who had witnessed the shootings and had the poor judgment to tell a coroner's grand jury what he had seen. Sprigle had an explanation for why Roger Malcolm was allowed to sit quietly in jail for three weeks before he was lynched. It had to do with the affair his wife had with the white man he stabbed. If Malcolm had been tried in local court, the sordid details of his wife's consorting with a white man would have become public knowledge instead of a widely believed rumor.

As Sprigle noted, in 1948 black-white liaisons were no longer looked upon so favorably in the Deep South—by either race.

> Years ago a Negro woman might take a white lover without loss of too much caste among her people. No longer. Racial pride has become an outstanding characteristic of the Negro, so that the dark-skinned woman who succumbs to the wiles of a white exemplar of racial purity, whose devotion to the principle of segregation fades at the threshold of her bedroom, promptly becomes an outcast from her own people. White Southerners too have

decisively modified their three-hundred-year-old, traditional attitude on race relations. They have largely abandoned that phase of intimate racial cooperation and tolerance that has peopled the South with millions who are not quite black nor yet quite white.

In early June, the night before he left the black world of the South forever, Sprigle found himself alone at 540 Houston Street in Atlanta babysitting a five-year-old. He called him "Tommy." But it was really Dobbs's grandson, Robert Jordan, the future TV news reporter at WGN in Chicago. He was the same kid Sprigle had eaten Sunday breakfast with on his first morning at Dobbs's house, the same kid that Dobbs often took with him on his walking tours of the commercial strip on Auburn Avenue, the same kid that someday would work as a reporter with Walter Cronkite on *The CBS Evening News*. Robert—who still didn't know yet he was black—was "brown and very well-behaved." He called Sprigle "Mistuh Cwawford." After listening to him say his prayers, Sprigle had a series of fatherly duties to perform, including fetching two glasses of water.

Robert and children like him were "the actual race problem in the South," he said. His parents, grandparents, and the mass of black adults in the South were going to live the rest of their lives the way they always had. But not Robert. He and millions of other black kids were going to have a better deal. Sprigle didn't try to predict anything specific about the future of civil rights. But he said by the time Robert and his generation graduated from college—in other words, circa 1964—it was a pretty good bet that everybody in the country "will have to be doing something about those ever increasing dark millions."

Sprigle compared Robert to his thirteen-year-old daughter Rae. He said her future will be problem free. "Nobody will hate her for her color. No crack-brained 'scientists' will come up with tommyrot that she's 'biologically inferior.' Nobody will bar her from the polling place down at the crossroads. There's no better school in the county than the one she attends. She's already announced her candidacy for the presidency of these United States." Later, when Robert cried out in his sleep, Sprigle checked on him. Standing there watching the sleeping future of the South, he thought,

"It's selfish, I know. But by God I'm glad my young one is white—in this free America."

The next evening Sprigle began his escape. As he said goodbye to Dobbs, the big house on 540 Houston Street N.E. was filling up with visiting Dobbses. They were coming from Mississippi, Tennessee, and New York City to celebrate the graduation of June Dobbs from Spelman College. All of June's older sisters were in town and on June 7 "The Grand," his wife, Irene, and their college-educated daughters were going to sit on the Spelman lawn for a series of impressive photos. Six college grads of either sex from one family was newsworthy for any hometown paper in 1948. But six women grads from one black family was so unheard of the story made the front page of the white *Atlanta Journal*. Two weeks later the *Pittsburgh Courier* ran a photo of the six Dobbs daughters on the front page of its national edition.

John Wesley Dobbs had started out as Ray Sprigle's collaborator and guide. They traveled thousands of miles together in a car. They ate and drank together in colored cafes and at the back doors of white restaurants. They peed together in thickets by the roadside. They even slept in the same double bed. They would exchange an unknown number of letters over the next few months. Dobbs would read Sprigle's newspaper series when it appeared in August. He would see Sprigle written up in *Time* magazine, praised in the newspaper columns of Eleanor Roosevelt and Walter White, and criticized in the *Atlanta Daily World*. He would listen to him debate segregation with Hodding Carter on national radio. But he would never meet his friend Sprigle again.

❧

"James R. Crawford, Northern Negro" now had less than twenty-four hours to live under the rule of Jim Crow. From Dobbs's house he took a Jim Crow taxi to the Atlanta bus terminal and waited in a Jim Crow waiting room for a Jim Crow bus bound for Cincinnati. For the next six hundred miles he was on his own. He was still pretending to be a black man, albeit paler than ever. But after nearly a month of second-class citizenship it was second nature. He had become used to thinking of himself as black—and resenting the white race.

On his overnight bus ride from Atlanta through the rugged mountains of Tennessee and Kentucky, nothing dramatic or disturbing happened. He got the usual Jim Crow mistreatment. He and the other black passengers, including a minister's young son from Atlanta headed for New York City, got the least comfortable seats. They ate in "squalid cubbyholes" or didn't eat at all. The bus stations on the route were strictly segregated. The restrooms for blacks were "filthy and evil." Blacks usually ate at a counter in the corner of the kitchen. At the final stop, in Covington, Kentucky, a thousand feet across the Ohio River from the unsegregated city of Cincinnati, there were no accommodations for blacks at all. "But," Sprigle said mordantly, "we were permitted to stand outside and watch the white folks eat."

The final humiliations exacted by Jim Crow in Kentucky didn't bother him. He was just an old iron bridge away from being back in the white world. As he crossed into Ohio, he was reminded of Eliza Harris, the brave slave girl of *Uncle Tom's Cabin* who made her spectacular escape from the slave state of Kentucky in the novel's most harrowing scene. "All my life I've regarded Eliza's stunt of crossing the Ohio on the floating ice floes, with bloodhounds baying at her heels, as a pretty heroic adventure. Not any more. The night I came up out of the deep South in a Jim Crow bus, I'd have been glad to take a chance crossing on the ice if anything had happened to stall our jolting chariot on the Kentucky shore. And there'd have been no need of any bloodhounds to put me into high gear."

If he was guilty of over-stretching a famous reference from literary fiction to fit his true tale, it was defensible. He was genuinely thrilled to be back in the "safety and freedom and peace" of the North. He had suffered enough for his first-person journalism. "Again I was free with all the rights of an American citizen," he said. But he wasn't feeling quite white yet. His friends down South "had done too good a job of making me into a Negro." He had been looking forward to a big meal in a great restaurant, but he chickened out at the last minute and grabbed something at a lunch counter. Then he took a taxi to the grand Hotel Sinton. It was his first cab in four weeks that didn't have "For Colored" stenciled on its door. But again he chickened out. Instead of walking up to the front desk and registering for a room, he went around the corner and called the hotel.

Pronouncing himself as Ray Sprigle of the *Pittsburgh Post-Gazette*, he booked a room and then registered. Feeling if not looking particularly black, he "talked fast, slid past the clerk as swiftly as possible and followed the bellhop. I'll bet I know one thing that no other white man in America knows. That's how a white-skinned Southern Negro must feel when he quits his race, 'crosses over' and turns white."

CHAPTER 14

Nominating "President Dewey"

June 5, 1948

Mr. Ray Sprigle
R.F.D. #3
Coraopolis, PA.

My dear Mr. Sprigle:
    I was so glad to receive your air mail special from Cincinnati and to know that you had safely crossed the "Smith and Wesson" line.
    I am trying to get some rest after my strenuous month with you over the southland in experiences which I enjoyed very much. I know I am going to enjoy your exposure about them. . . .
    I hope you found your wife and daughter quite well. I also hope your appetite has returned to you. You saw enough down here to make you lose it.

Sincerely yours,
J.W. Dobbs

Back at his home near Pittsburgh, Sprigle got to work right away. Before his tan faded any further, and before his hair and gray moustache could grow back, he dressed up in the clothes he wore in the South and posed for a series of portraits taken at his farm. The photographer was one of the *Post-Gazette*'s best, James Klingensmith. Sprigle did some further reporting by phone and started banging out a series of articles on his typewriter. He had a great memory, but drew most of the specifics he needed from the notes he had taken while posing as an NAACP fact-gatherer. Those notes from the road didn't survive the decades, but the spiral memo book in which he documented his daily travel expenses did.

Sprigle and Dobbs had gone on three major car trips from Atlanta—down to the peach and cotton country of southern Georgia and Alabama, west into the Mississippi Delta, and out to the Atlantic Ocean and back. In the tiny notebook Sprigle kept a to-the-penny account of what he spent for food, lodging, taxis, phone calls, writing tablets, etc., plus his train trip. They added up to about two hundred dollars—two thousand dollars today. Unfortunately, his expense record revealed few clues to exactly where he was on any given day. On May 10, on the way to Americus, he wrote down that he gave former sharecropper Elizabeth Engram of the Flint River Farms project a dollar for her corn pone. On the 12th he sent a two-dollar telegram to the *Pittsburgh Post-Gazette* offices. On May 20 he paid $47.03 COD for a nice suit he apparently needed for a formal Prince Hall Mason dinner in Macon the next night. He stayed at Atlanta's black YMCA on May 22, 23, and 24 for $2.50 a night because Dobbs was out of town that weekend.

His pocket notebook also was scattered with random bits and pieces of information. Scrawled in pencil, some of the entries were place names—Lexington, Macon, Coahoma County—or parts of a sharecropper's quote—"get the mule at daylight—maybe take him back & go to bed at nine." In grocery stores, he wrote, blacks "must wait until all whites are waited on. Can't point out the steak they want—take what clerk gives them." And "alimony in negro divorce always lower . . . not to give them any notions." Some entries carefully listed the numbers of acres owned or bales of cotton raised by sharecroppers or prosperous farmers like A. J. Washington. Dr. Hill's name appeared. The word "Dobbs" appeared just once. One of the few complete thoughts in the notebook, apparently inspired by the poverty of the Mississippi Delta's landless workforce and the relative freedom enjoyed by black property owners, reflected Sprigle's conservative political beliefs, which might be described best as constitutionalist. "Complete human rights are impossible without property rights.

Property rights are human rights. The individual is not complete without property. Otherwise he is just part of the swarm."

While Sprigle was writing his series, Dobbs returned to his peripatetic "normal" life. A week after Sprigle left Atlanta he traveled to Philadelphia to attend the Republican National Convention as a delegate. Both major parties had agreed to choose Philadelphia for their 1948 presidential conventions so they could accommodate the primitive technology of network television, which was bulky, expensive, and tied to New York by heavy network coaxial cables. The GOP's convention, held from June 21 to 24, was the first in history to be fully televised and the party's last one to be held in a hall with no air-conditioning.

Philadelphia was hot, muggy, and badly short of hotel rooms. Dobbs had to be there a week early. As one of the leaders of Georgia's sixteen-man delegation, which was unanimously for Thomas Dewey, he had to beat back a credentials challenge mounted by supporters of conservative Ohio senator Robert Taft. Race was not an issue. Both contesting delegations were integrated. But Dobbs and his group favored the moderate Dewey because of his strong civil rights record as governor of New York. Dobbs's delegation successfully held on to all of its seats. The fight was so contentious and well publicized, however, that syndicated political columnist Drew Pearson wrote about it in his popular "Washington Merry Go Round" column.

Shortly after Dobbs's victory, *Life* magazine staff photographer Ralph Morse took a picture of someone from the Republican Party credentials committee pinning an official delegate badge on Dobbs. The black-and-white picture ran in *Life*'s July 5 issue, which devoted ten full pages and forty-five photos to what the cocky GOP and the rest of the country thought was essentially a pre-election victory party for Dewey.

A few of *Life*'s larger photos—particularly a double-page spread of thousands of Republicans broiling under the massive lights needed for the weak TV cameras—were spectacular. But most of the static snapshots of key political operatives and fuddy-duddy Republicans standing around in suits would have been dull in a Class of '48 high school yearbook. Everyone looked square and a hundred years old, even if they were neither. The photo of Dobbs, though small, was actually one of the better

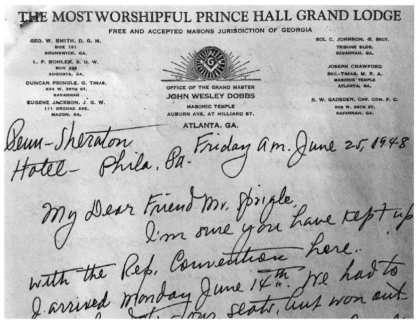

THE MOST WORSHIPFUL PRINCE HALL GRAND LODGE
FREE AND ACCEPTED MASONS JURISDICTION OF GEORGIA

GEO. W. SMITH, D. G. M.
BOX 101
BRUNSWICK, GA.

L. P. BOHLER, S. G. W.
BOX 232
AUGUSTA, GA.

DUNCAN PRINGLE, G. TREAS.
634 W. 39TH ST.
SAVANNAH

EUGENE JACKSON, J. G. W.
111 ORCHARD AVE.
MACON, GA.

SOL C. JOHNSON, G. SECY.
TRIBUNE BLDG.
SAVANNAH, GA.

JOSEPH CRAWFORD
SEC.-TREAS, M. R. A.
MASONIC TEMPLE
ATLANTA, GA.

R. W. GADSDEN, CHR. COM. F. C.
608 W. 36TH ST.
SAVANNAH, GA.

OFFICE OF THE GRAND MASTER
JOHN WESLEY DOBBS
MASONIC TEMPLE
AUBURN AVE. AT HILLIARD ST.
ATLANTA, GA.

Penn–Sheraton Hotel– Phila, Pa.– Friday a.m. June 25, 1948

My Dear Friend Mr. Sprigle,
I'm sure you have kept up with the Rep. Convention here.. I arrived Monday June 14th. We had to ... our seats, but won out

COURTESY OF SENATOR JOHN HEINZ HISTORY CENTER

ones *Life* printed. Described in the caption only as "a delegate from Georgia," he had his arms outstretched as a smiling black official pinned the badge on his broad chest. Dobbs was wearing an expensive three-piece suit and a wide triumphant grin. It was the only image of the convention *Life* printed that contained a black Republican.

On Friday, June 25, the morning after Governor Dewey was nominated on the third ballot, Dobbs whipped off a long letter from the Penn-Sheraton Hotel to "My dear friend Mr. Sprigle." Assuming Sprigle had been keeping up with events, he recounted how his delegation was forced to "battle hard" to defend their seats from Taft's people. They squeaked by on the first vote 48 to 44. Then they had to go before the omnipotent credentials committee, where Dobbs argued their case with a little rhetorical help from Sprigle.

We licked them there by 26 to 24—too close for comfort. I spoke both times. I used very effectively your expression about "the hand of Eugene Talmadge, reaching up from the grave." Well, we won out, turned down every compromise and were seated. They bluffed about taking it to the floor—but didn't. Last night I was accorded the privilege to make the announcement on the mike casting Georgia's 16 votes for Gov. Dewey. If you heard it, you will remember I said "Georgia—the Empire State of the South."

Sprigle might have heard him announce Georgia's vote for Dewey on radio, but he definitely didn't see him do it on television. He didn't own a TV and Pittsburgh didn't have a TV station yet. The Republican Convention, as well as the Democratic Convention almost three weeks later, was broadcast live by four TV networks on eighteen stations in just nine eastern cities. An estimated ten million Americans got their first televised look at gavel-to-gavel coverage of a political convention's endless speeches, floor demonstrations, and roll call votes. Consumers were buying expensive Philco and Admiral TVs as fast as they could be made, but still fewer than half a million homes in the country had television sets, and they were concentrated in New York City and Philly.

Most viewers watched the Republican Convention on small fuzzy black-and-white TV screens while sitting on a stool in their corner bar or looking through a department store display window. Television was quickly going to change the world, disrupt the news and entertainment industries, and expose the Jim Crow South to the North in ways no one could imagine. But in the summer of 1948, with the average household receiving more than one newspaper a day, the electronic upstart many in the print media were still calling "radio pictures" posed no threat to the reach, influence, or profits of the country's 1,760 daily newspapers. Pittsburgh, Atlanta, and the rest of Flyover Country were still living in the Golden Age of Radio.

Dobbs signed off his letter to Sprigle with his customary string of formalities, writing "I trust you and your family are O.K. Best wishes and kindest regards. Sincerely yours, J. W. Dobbs." Then he jumped on a train for New York City. That night at Yankee Stadium he watched his aging hero Joe Louis knock out Jersey Joe Walcott in the eleventh round of their heavyweight championship rematch. The next morning he flew home to Atlanta.

Another proud citizen of the Deep South who attended the Republican Convention kept his support for Thomas Dewey to himself. As part of the media mob covering the five thousand sweating delegates, alternates, and party operatives, he observed the Dewey-Taft delegate fight and cheered the way it ended. He kept a casual eye on the tiny, all-black Mississippi delegation and no doubt was in the convention hall Thursday evening when John Wesley Dobbs proudly announced Georgia's vote for Dewey from the floor.

But Hodding Carter was most interested in the construction of the GOP platform, specifically the civil rights plank. In addition to Republican standbys—reducing inflation, cutting federal spending, cracking down on domestic communists, containing the Soviet menace in Western Europe, and reducing the inheritance tax—the Party of Lincoln was calling for desegregating the military, a federal anti-lynching bill, and ending the poll tax.

As far as Carter was concerned, the Republicans' civil rights goals—nothing new or radical and sure to be blocked by southern Democrats in the Senate—were not as dangerous as what Truman and the northern liberal Democrats were planning. He thought Truman's aggressive civil rights program was unworkable and unnecessary and would blow up the Democratic Party by driving out its core southern wing. Though a lifelong Democrat and a New Dealer, Carter was also pragmatic and realistic. He believed the South had to have a strong and competitive Republican Party if it hoped to stop being taken for granted by the national Democratic Party or ever hoped to solve its looming civil rights crisis.

In the fall Carter and the *Delta Democrat-Times* would shock the local populace and make national news by endorsing a Republican for president. Dewey's own running mate, Governor Earl Warren of California, didn't like Dewey and once referred to him as "shifty and somewhat slimy." But Carter believed Dewey was an honest and able administrator and "the best of the candidates for the presidency." He really didn't like Truman at all. He derided him as "a game little man who tries hard; but he is also an ill-advised little man, lacking the background, training and leadership qualities that our country must increasingly require of its President." Carter wasn't alone in giving up on the president and the "stale" Democratic Party, which he said was no longer distinguishable from Republicans on all major domestic and foreign issues. Except for the *Chicago Defender*, almost every black newspaper in the country also would endorse Dewey.

It was a much more exciting time in Philadelphia when the Democrats held their convention there from July 12 to July 14. After war hero General Dwight Eisenhower made it clear he was not interested in leading the Democratic Party's insurrection to dump Harry Truman, the incumbent president had little trouble being nominated on the first ballot. As expected, there immediately was a nasty and unbridgeable North-South schism at the convention over civil rights.

Platforms are supposed to serve as honest guides to the party's intentions, but they serve mostly to attract various political, social, or racial groups, placate internal warring factions, or score symbolic public relations points with the media. Liberals in the party, black organizations like the National Negro Council, and leaders like Walter White at the NAACP were insisting that Democrats write a stronger civil rights plank—and then honestly work to enact it into law. They called for the party to drop the mushy and meaningless civil rights wordage of its New Deal past and become at least as progressive as the Republicans. White was especially adamant, insisting that "the day of reckoning" had come for the Democratic Party. The only way it could show it had the right to exist, he said, was "by adopting an unequivocal position on civil rights" and summoning the courage "to cleanse itself of the barnacles of bigotry its Southern wing has affixed to it."

Republicans had a huge advantage on civil rights. Their plank didn't have to comfort hard segregationists like Georgia's US senator Richard

Russell, who thought Truman's civil-rights baby steps were "a vicious and unwarranted attack . . . on our Southern civilization." Nor did the GOP have to dance around the issue of whether the federal government had the constitutional right to "encroach" upon a sovereign state's laws—even when those laws discriminated against some of their citizens or disenfranchised them for racist or just plain dumb reasons.

The Republicans' plank contained morally unequivocal sentences like "Lynching or any other form of mob violence anywhere is a disgrace to any civilized state, and we favor the prompt enactment of legislation to end this infamy." It affectionately paraphrased the Declaration of Independence and the Constitution, reminding everyone that one of the country's first principles "is the equality of all individuals in their right to life, liberty, and the pursuit of happiness." It not only declared that the "right of equal opportunity to work and advance in life should never be limited in any individual because of race, religion, color, or country of origin," but it also said the Republican Party favored "enactment and just enforcement of such federal legislation as may be necessary to maintain this right at all times in every part of the Republic."

Hubert Humphrey pushed the Democrats to do the right thing, even if it would mean the loss of the South's electoral votes and the party's fracturing. The young progressive mayor of Minneapolis came from a state of three million people that had only thirteen thousand blacks—less than half of 1 percent of the population. He was a principled bomb thrower and his targets were Truman and dozens of southern congressmen in his own party. Running for a US Senate seat in the fall, he was risking his future by causing trouble with his own party's leadership. But with the encouragement of other important northern liberals, including Pittsburgh mayor and party powerbroker David L. Lawrence, he delivered a historic speech to the convention.

To those who say we are rushing this issue of civil rights, I say to them we are 172 years late. To those who say that this civil rights program is an infringement on states' rights, I say this: The time has arrived in America for the Democratic Party to get out of the shadows of states' rights and walk forthrightly into the bright sunshine of human rights.

Millions saw the speech on TV or heard it on radio. It hardly seems revolutionary today. But Eleanor Roosevelt wrote in her widely syndicated daily newspaper column "My Day" that the Democratic Party "took one step toward greatness." President Truman did not agree. He wrote in his journal that it was "a crackpot amendment" to the civil rights plank voted on by "crackpots" who "hoped the South will bolt."

Bolt was exactly what the South did. Four hours after Humphrey's stronger civil rights plank was narrowly passed, all of Mississippi's delegates and half of Alabama's—including Bull Connor of Birmingham—stormed out of the convention hall. Swearing they'd never vote for a Republican, a Democrat, or any candidate that had a civil rights program like the one their party had just adopted, they attracted intense media attention. The rebels even took part in a staged event for television, gathering in a small room and, on cue, unpinning their credentials and throwing them on a desk. A few days later representatives from the southern states met in Birmingham, formed the States' Rights Party, and nominated South Carolina governor Strom Thurmond as their candidate for president. Thurmond had no prayer of winning. But the Democratic Party's Solid South was solid no more, and Truman's faint hopes for reelection grew fainter.

CHAPTER 15

Waking Up the White North

'I was scared to death.'
—Ray Sprigle
See Thursday's *Post-Gazette*.

The Ku Klux Klan never
forgot Ray Sprigle.
Neither will you!
Don't miss Monday's *Post-Gazette*.

Sprigle is digging again.
See Monday's *Post-Gazette*.

What's it like for a white man to be a Negro?
Post-Gazette reporter Ray Sprigle knows. He was a Negro for 30
days—and traveled 4,000 miles through the deep South. Now
he tells what he learned in 21 burning articles—exclusively in
the *Post-Gazette*. Don't miss a single article. It's the news story
of the year.
Starts Monday in the *Post-Gazette*

Thomas Dewey, Strom Thurmond, the print media, the Communist Party
USA, and everyone else in the country were ganging up on Harry Truman. The Olympics were under way in London. The Berlin Blockade
was a month old. The hot national issue of late summer was Soviet spies

COURTESY OF THE *PITTSBURGH POST-GAZETTE*

infiltrating the federal government. In the Senate southern Democrats were filibustering the latest anti–poll tax bill put up by Republicans. And on August 9 "I Was a Negro in the South for 30 Days" hit the front page of the *Post-Gazette* like an atomic bomb.

Ray Sprigle didn't look particularly black in the huge photo of him in his disguise, to say the least. But his heavy glasses and bald visage must have shocked tens of thousands of readers who were used to seeing his iconic Stetson, moustache, and corncob pipe. Sprigle's byline had disappeared from the *Post-Gazette* without explanation for four and a half months. In his first paragraph he summed up where he had been.

For four endless, crawling weeks I was a Negro in the Deep South. I ate, slept, traveled, lived Black. I lodged in Negro households. I ate in Negro restaurants. I slept in Negro hotels and lodging houses. I crept through the back and side doors of railroad stations.

I traveled Jim Crow in buses and trains and street cars and taxicabs. Along with 10,000,000 Negroes I endured the discrimination and oppression and cruelty of the iniquitous Jim Crow system.

It was a typical Sprigle production—a strong opening, lots of colorful writing with strong opinions, and a generous sprinkling of sarcasm and hyperbole. Objectivity was neither practiced nor feigned. Sounding a moral tone reminiscent of an old-style muckraking magazine writer, he woke up three hundred thousand *Post-Gazette* readers with the opening installment of a detailed, impassioned, and frequently bitter inside look at a part of America few of them knew or cared anything about. Along with exposing the petty workings of Jim Crow, he described what it felt like to know your "rights of citizenship ran only as far as the nearest white man said they did."

He spent Chapter One of the series explaining that his disguise, simple as it was, worked almost perfectly. He had successfully passed himself off as a light-skinned black to everyone except for two black people. One woman restaurant owner in Atlanta suspected him because he talked much too much for a black man. And a doctor he met asked Dobbs afterward why he was "carrying" a white man around with him. Dobbs silenced his doctor friend with the statement, "He says he's a Negro and that's enough for me. Have you found any way of telling who carries Negro blood and who doesn't?"

Sprigle said that during his undercover mission he had never once felt like he was under suspicion. He engaged in many long conversations with black people of all classes about everything from sharecropping and voting rights to Shakespeare. He attended a dozen political meetings in churches and elsewhere. Never did he or Dobbs have the sense that he was suspected of being anything other than a northern black man. He didn't have many prolonged contacts with white people, by design, and if he sat in the Jim Crow sections of a train or streetcar, or drank from a "For Colored" fountain, no one challenged him.

Rarely is a light or white Negro questioned in the South when he seeks Jim Crow accommodations. Now and then a conductor or policeman will remind a passenger, apparently white, in a Jim Crow coach, or a light-skinned Negro entering a "For Colored" restaurant—"That's for Negroes, you know." But the usual response of "I'm where I belong" ends the matter right there.

Though he never mentioned John Wesley Dobbs by name or provided any clues that would give away his guide's identity, Sprigle wasted no time giving him full credit. "If there is any commendation due anyone for these chronicles, surely the lion's share must go to that companion of mine. I doubt if there is a man living who knows the South, black and white, as he does. . . . If I learned anything about the life of the Negro, it is because he took me to the places, the men and the women from whom I might learn." Sprigle readily acknowledged that Walter White, the executive director of the National Association for the Advancement of Colored People, had helped him to find his guide. "If in four weeks anyone can get the actual picture of the life of the Negro in the South—then I got it. Because that friend of Walter White showed it to me."

Sprigle preemptively addressed the charges he knew were coming that he unfairly picked on the South while ignoring the North's multiple mistreatments of black people. After issuing a disclaimer that ultimately would do nothing to prevent that criticism, he explained to his readers the important difference between *de jure* and *de facto* segregation.

One last word as I begin this account of my four weeks of life as a Negro in the deep South. Don't anybody try to tell me that the North discriminates against the Negro, too, and seek to use that as a defense against the savage oppression and the brutal intolerance the black man encounters in the South. Discrimination against the Negro in the North is an annoyance and an injustice. In the South it is bloodstained tragedy.

In the North the Negro meets with rebuff and insult when he seeks service at hotels and restaurants. But, at least in states like Pennsylvania and others, he can take his case to court and he invariably wins.

But in the South he is barred BY LAW from white hotels and restaurants. He is fined and jailed, and frequently killed, if he seeks to enter a railroad station through an entrance reserved for whites, to ride in the forward end of a street car or bus, or a railway coach sacred to the white man. His children are barred from white schools and denied an adequate education in the tumbledown shacks in which little black citizens are forced to seek learning.

No Northern white can deny that there is discrimination against the Negro in the North. Prejudice against the black citizen breaks out in race riots from time to time, as witness Detroit in recent years, and Chicago and Springfield, Ill., in an earlier day. But in the North, both black and white rioters go to prison. In the South only the black ones climb the steps to a gallows or serve term in a cell.

In short, discrimination against the Negro in the North is usually in defiance of the law. In the South it is enforced and maintained by the law.

A Ray Sprigle series was a huge news event itself in Pittsburgh. He was the only media celebrity in town and his major projects could be counted on to generate higher street sales and attract new subscribers. In advance of "I was a Negro . . . ," the *Post-Gazette*'s marketing people had done their usual fine job of promoting their star reporter. A week earlier they began dropping small teasing display ads into the *P-G*'s pages. On August 2 a silhouette of Sprigle's head with his trademark hat and pipe ran in a small box at the bottom of Page 1 with the query "Has Anyone Seen This Man?" Throughout the paper in-house ads publicizing Sprigle's coming series made pitches aimed at signing up new subscribers.

On August 5 the *P-G* ran a bogus "news" article on the front page headlined "Sprigle Lives as Negro in South." Today it would be decried as an "advertorial," but in that era the high priests of good journalism didn't consider such subtle deceptions a sin. The article began with "The *Post-Gazette* is proud to present, in a series beginning next Monday, what it believes to be an outstanding journalistic achievement." It said the series would be "an account of the adventures that befell a white man who deliberately crossed the color line and lived for 30 days as a Negro in the South" and would tell readers of the "hopes, fears and aspirations" of the South's ten million blacks.

Meanwhile, a syndicated twelve-part version of Sprigle's series, bearing the less-awkward title "In the Land of Jim Crow," had been offered to 135 newspapers. It was picked up by thirteen. They were all north of the Mason-Dixon Line and included the *New York Herald Tribune*, *Hartford Courant*, *Philadelphia Inquirer*, *Scranton Times*, *Cleveland Press*, *Toledo Blade*, *Milwaukee Journal*, *St. Louis Globe-Democrat*, *Portland Oregonian*, *Seattle Times*, and the *Ottawa Journal* in Canada.

For the next twenty days, except Sundays, a new "chapter" of "I Was a Negro in the South for 30 Days" appeared prominently on the front page of the *Post-Gazette*. In his second article on August 10, Sprigle addressed the first question most readers asked: "How did you darken your skin?" He described the scary chemicals he had experimented with to colorize himself before choosing the sun. Then he said it mattered little in the end how dark or light he was.

Most of my concern over acquiring a dark skin was so much nonsense. Everywhere I went in the South I encountered scores of Negroes as white as I ever was back home in Pittsburgh. Stories of 20,000 Negroes a year "passing" to the white race are a lot of hooey.

Looks to me from where I sit, as just another light-skinned one of millions of other light-skinned Negroes, that the noble white man got hold of this racial purity thing a little late. Where does he think these millions of white, light, and brown Negroes came from?

Think the stork found 'em somewhere?

It wasn't until his third day in print that Sprigle actually began chronicling his four-thousand-mile journey through the Deep South. He spent the entire piece detailing his first fourteen hours as a rookie black man riding a Jim Crow train from Washington to Atlanta. His opening paragraph was a powerful indictment of the South's oppression of blacks. The minute he boarded that segregated streamliner in Union Station, three blocks from the US Capitol Building and a short cab ride from the Lincoln Memorial, he said, "I quit being white, and free, and an American citizen. . . . From then on, until I came up out of the South four weeks later, I was black, and in bondage—not quite slavery but not quite freedom, either. My rights of citizenship ran only as far as the nearest white man said they did."

The articles were pure Sprigle—lively, readable, edgy, and sometimes way over the top. Chapter Four described his Sunday breakfast-table meeting with Dobbs's daughter and grandson and the way black women were humiliated and disrespected by Jim Crow's racist social customs and "etiquette." Chapter Five was his heartbreaking interview with Carolyn Gilbert, the widow of Henry Gilbert, the Georgia farmer murdered in his jail cell by a county policeman. Chapter Six recounted his first road trip

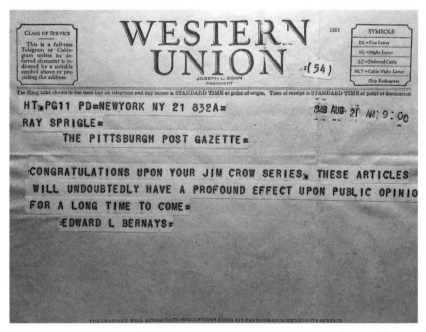

Edward Bernays, aka "The Father of Public Relations" whose clients included the NAACP, sent his praise. COURTESY OF SENATOR JOHN HEINZ HISTORY CENTER

with Dobbs from Atlanta to the cotton and peach counties of southern Georgia. It began with their visit with Oscar and Elizabeth Engram, the ex-sharecroppers included in the federal Flint River Farms project, whose names he changed to Henry and Hannah Ingram.

At NAACP headquarters in New York, Walter White couldn't have been more pleased. He had already read the entire series because Sprigle had mailed galley copies to him in July. After sending Sprigle a telegram on July 23 that read "Your articles are magnificent and we approve them heartily," White had embarked on a one-man publicity campaign on Sprigle's behalf that would last a year. One of the first people he shared the galley proofs with was his friend Eleanor Roosevelt. He also sent copies to the top editors at the Viking Press and other New York book publishers.

On August 11, with five publishers expressing interest in book rights to "In the Land of Jim Crow," White wrote a letter to the editor of the *New York Herald Tribune*. Printed in the first group of letters reacting to Sprigle's series, it said, "Mr. Sprigle's brilliant articles will do a great deal towards encouraging the growth of decent public opinion in the South, both white and Negro, which in turn will lead to the discarding of the demagogues who do such harm to the South and to America. I profoundly hope that the Pulitzer Prize committee will see fit again to honor Mr. Sprigle because of his able series."

Time and *Newsweek*, which had weekly departments that covered "The Press," each wrote favorably about Sprigle's series in their August 16 issues. *Newsweek*'s mention was merely three paragraphs long, but *Time* gave it half a page and included a photo of Sprigle in his disguise. The magazine had been sent the entire twenty-one-part series in advance and gave it nothing but praise. It told its 1.5 million subscribers that "the shrewdest reporter on the *Pittsburgh Post-Gazette*'s staff" had written "an account of man's inhumanity to man—and man's capacity for enduring it" that "made *Gentleman's Agreement* seem gentlemanly indeed." Pulling quotes from later chapters of the series that hadn't appeared in newspapers yet, *Time* wrote that "Bitter Ray Sprigle will never again feel proud to be white."

Every morning another chapter appeared on Page 1 of the *Post-Gazette*. Thanks to good promotion and marketing and the "Sprigle effect," sales of the paper were up as much as thirty thousand extra copies a day. Chapter

Eight told how ex–tenant farmer and bar-owner Jared Buford had achieved financial independence and created a happy life for himself that included no contact with white people. Chapter Nine described Sprigle's pleasant experiences at the Haslerig country picnic in Chickamauga. In Chapter Ten he jolted his readers with the story of what happened in 1946 to a returning black soldier who decided to vote in a Democratic primary in Taylor County, Georgia, a hundred miles south of Atlanta.

When they call the roll of Americans who died to make men free, add to that heroic list the name of Private Macy Yost Snipes, black man, Georgia, U. S. A.

Death missed him on a dozen bloody battlefields overseas, where he served his country well.

He came home to die in the littered door-yard of his boyhood home because he thought that freedom was for all Americans, and tried to prove it.

It wasn't that he didn't get fair warning. He knew what to expect. And he got just that.

Early in July the white folks passed the warning through the Negro countryside around the little sun-warped country hamlet of Rupert, in Taylor county, Georgia. It was brief and to the point. The first Negro to vote in Rupert would be killed, ran the word.

Macy Yost Snipes hadn't even thought of voting, so his friends told me. But when the word came that he'd die if he did—then he decided that he'd vote. He had never voted. He didn't know where or how to do it. He went to Butler, the county seat, to register. There they told him he'd have to go back to his home town of Rupert to register, and later, vote. The white folks in Rupert let him register. There were already a few Negro names on the registry lists.

Bright and early on election day Macy appeared at the polling place—and voted. Afterward Macy told a friend that the white folks on the election board appeared "sorta dazed" as he cast his ballot. "It was like they thought a dead man was voting,"

Macy said laughingly to his friend who told me the story of how a Georgia Negro died.

Private Snipes didn't know it, but the white folks were right. He was already dead when he dropped that ballot in the box. The white folks just let him walk around another week before they buried him.

Riddled With Bullets

Just a week later four white men drove up to Macy Snipes' home, called him out and after a few words riddled him with bullets and drove off.

Taking courage from the fact that the white folks had promised to kill only the first Negro who voted, another black man voted after Private Snipes. He was right. The white folks didn't kill him. They just ran him out of the county.

But even after they had murdered him, the white folks weren't finished with Private Macy Yost Snipes. The Snipes family owned a little burial plot in a Negro cemetery near Rupert. The mother and father of the dead soldier arranged with a Negro undertaker to bury their slain son in the family plot. But the day of the funeral the undertaker got word from Rupert.

"You try to bury that nigger here and you better have another grave ready for yourself." The undertaker had a plot in another cemetery at the other end of the county. That's where Macy Snipes rests.

Family Told to Get Out

But it wasn't enough to murder the returned veteran and deny his body burial because he had sought to overthrow white supremacy by dropping his ballot in the box. The white folks decided that they wanted none of Macy Snipes' family in their midst, either. The Snipes family were hard-working and respected farmers owning 150 acres which provided them with a better-than-ordinary competence. They were warned that they had better get out of the county. "Remember what happened to your son," one note read.

So the Snipes family sold their farm and fled North. They live in Ohio now.

And what about the champions of racial "purity" who murdered Macy Snipes? Well, one William Cooper proudly claimed the honor of having fired the shots that dropped the young veteran in front of his own threshold. He hunted up the coroner and explained that he and his friends were just trying to collect $10 that Macy Snipes had borrowed from him. When Snipes told him he hadn't any money he said he told Macy to go to work for his companion, a sawmill owner and the sawmill man would pay off Macy's $10 debt.

"You don't get me in no saw mill," was Macy's reply, according to Cooper. A few more heated words, said Cooper, and Macy started toward his door, saying, "I've got something in the house that'll move you fellows off."

"That's when I shot him," explains Cooper. There was no gun on Private Snipes' body but there was $40 in his pocket and all the members of the Snipes family had through the years built up a reputation for paying their debts.

"Justifiable killing in self-defense," was the verdict.

Well, what price a monument for Private Macy Yost Snipes now?

CHAPTER 16

A Civil War over Civil Rights

"In the Land of Jim Crow" was a media sensation. The series was vigorously promoted and published simultaneously for almost two weeks by fourteen large daily newspapers from Seattle to Manhattan. *Time, Newsweek,* and Eleanor Roosevelt gave it a national audience before it was halfway finished. And while no southern paper carried Sprigle's twelve-part series, papers in Atlanta, Richmond, and Savannah wrote editorials decrying it and its meddling Yankee author. Dixie's editors and columnists—especially the few liberals—were offended en masse. Segregationists all, they saw it as a one-sided mugging of their way of life by a carpet-bagging newsman engaged in stunt journalism.

To most ordinary white readers in the North, however, Sprigle's series was shocking. A real-world execution of the fictional theme of *Gentleman's Agreement,* only for southern blacks not New York Jews, his undercover mission was unprecedented. No white journalist for a major newspaper or magazine had ever made a trip like his into the black world before. For the first time northern whites were being exposed to a full and angry inside report on the poverty and mistreatment of millions of blacks under Jim Crow. Others had documented conditions in the South. But Sprigle didn't write a fat book of facts or an epic sociological study of blacks for scholars. He wrote a provocative first-person newspaper series for the average American. It was original. It was daring. It was openly biased. It was accessible. And everyone who read it could tell Sprigle was genuinely appalled by what he had seen and experienced.

"I Was a Negro in the South for 30 Days" still had two weeks to go in the *Post-Gazette*, but Sprigle had already sparked a national conversation about the future of segregation. The *Pittsburgh Courier* had acquired exclusive rights for Sprigle's series for the black newspaper market. For seven weeks it was going to deliver the series with maximum fanfare to hundreds of thousands of blacks in the North and across the South. Hodding Carter, who had been given a preview of the entire series by his editor friend at the *Providence Journal*, was busy finishing "Jim Crow's Other Side," a six-part series rebutting Sprigle that would be syndicated to many more papers than "In the Land of Jim Crow."

In New York City the popular ABC public affairs program *Town Meeting of the Air* was making plans to invite Sprigle, Walter White, and Carter to participate in a live national radio debate about segregation that millions would hear. And, on his 103-acre "ranch" in the woods west of Pittsburgh, Sprigle was writing new chapters for his future book *In the Land of Jim Crow*. Jim Crow would not get as much attention from the mainstream northern media again until the mid-1950s, when the Supreme Court's *Brown v. Board of Education* decision and the brutal murder of Emmett Till in Mississippi inaugurated a decade of intense press and TV coverage.

On August 16, as Sprigle's Page 1 article detailed the extreme poverty and pitiful finances of black sharecropper Harry Williams, the *Post-Gazette* let the first wave of letter-writers have their say. Half of the editorial page was filled with a carefully balanced sampling of "the unusually large number" of letters the paper said the series had provoked from around the country. The dozen "pro" letters were led off by legendary journalist Herbert Bayard Swope, who from World War I to the end of the Jazz Age was widely considered the greatest newspaper reporter and editor in the country.

Based in New York, energetic and influential, charming and brash, a progressive Democrat, Swope was a leading figure among intellectuals, the arts-and-entertainment elites, and wealthy Gatsby-types of Long Island. In 1917 he won the first-ever Pulitzer Prize for the dispatches he filed from inside wartime Germany for the *New York World* in 1916. As the editor of the *World* he won two more Pulitzers. In 1921, he mounted a twenty-one-part front-page assault on the then-powerful Ku Klux Klan that shined a damning light on the KKK's actions, racial and religious bigotry, sacrilegious rituals, and un-American ideology. Syndicated by thirty papers and read by five million people, the exposé got the whole country talking about the KKK and won the *World* a Pulitzer for Public Service. It's still considered one of journalism's greatest investigative works.

Swope was a high-living, flamboyant New York liberal who loafed with millionaires and celebrities and occasionally popped into the Oval Office to visit presidents. But as newspapermen he and Sprigle had much in common. Swope was also a descriptive writer, a good reporter, and staunch friend of the little man. He appreciated what Sprigle was doing with his series. He was also an innovative hardboiled newspaper editor who believed the only way to lose readers was by "trying to please everybody all the time." Facts and opinions were equally important to him.

When he took over as editor of the *World* in 1920, Swope invented the modern op-ed page, hiring such big-name political columnists as Ring Lardner, E. B. White, and Walter Lippmann. Presaging the freedom and immediacy of the political blogs of the twenty-first century, he let his all-stars spew any opinion they wanted on the page opposite the editorial page as long as it was for the next day's paper. Swope's front-page style for the *World* was said to be a model for Henry Luce's *Time* magazine, which put him on its cover in 1924. When he died in 1958, *Time* called him an "ebullient, egocentric, suave and unflaggingly dynamic" journalist who "stood splendidly apart in an era of splendid individualists."

Praise for Sprigle's series from Herbert Bayard Swope in 1948 may not have impressed the average Pittsburgher, but it was a supreme honor as far as the *Post-Gazette*'s editors were concerned. "That's a good story you're doing on 'Jim Crow,'" wrote Swope, whose photo was included with his letter. "I congratulate you. There are not many left who could have turned out as fine a job of reporting, which is rapidly becoming a lost art. For the most part, the boys want to deal in opinions these days. The sacred facts are being ignored. You mark a return to the Ancient Faith."

Other "pro" Sprigle letter-writers, including two local ministers, commended him for his public service, his "exciting writing," or for alerting the whole country to the denial of democracy in the South. Rev.

Mrs. Roosevelt Praises

Editor, the Post-Gazette:

I read Mr. Sprigle's articles with the greatest of interest. They certainly are a contribution to the understanding of a bad situation if one is able to understand anything at all.

I am afraid the real difficulty is that where there is prejudice there is no way of opening people's minds but if we go on continually trying some day we may succeed. This series of articles is a real contribution.

Mrs. Roosevelt

ELEANOR ROOSEVELT.
Hyde Park, N. Y.

Samuel Stevens, a Presbyterian minister from Pittsburgh, compared Sprigle's undercover technique to the prophet Ezekiel. Just like Ezekiel, he said, Sprigle went into "the land of captivity of his people and 'sat where they sat.'" Reverend Stevens said that method was really "the only way to completely understand the plight of an oppressed people. . . . More power to Mr. Sprigle and may he win many friends for those who are disinherited."

A Pittsburgh man congratulated Sprigle on his series but suggested that further community public service could be rendered by writing a similar one "on the life of a Negro in Pittsburgh." A reader from central Pennsylvania wrote that "I am white but I think that the Negro is getting a very dirty deal in this country. May your series do what the Civil War failed to do." Three black men from Pittsburgh, World War II vets who had trained in the South, said they felt the pain Sprigle experienced as a Negro in the South. But the trio, who called themselves "former 2nd class citizens," said their "psychological reactions were the same without the benefit of sun-tan."

The superstar of the favorable letters group was former first lady Eleanor Roosevelt. She had read the entire series in late July, when Walter White showed her the galley proofs Sprigle had sent him. She had already praised Sprigle and his work in her syndicated column. On August 12 she said Sprigle's series—which she never specifically named but clearly assumed her readers were familiar with—contained valuable lessons for white people.

I was struck by the second of a series of articles about the South, written by Ray Sprigle. I had seen his articles before publication, but rereading them in this way makes you realize how a white man really would feel who had to live as one of our Negro citizens has to live in the South today. These articles ought to add to the understanding and enlightenment of our white people. Whether they will or not depends on whether it is possible for any of us to put aside our prejudices and think objectively.

The subtle way in which this reporter's feelings changed and he began to dislike his own kind, as he identified himself more and more with the colored people, is very enlightening. That is a subtle way of telling us how every colored person feels who has had to endure segregation and discrimination.

The letter-to-the-editor in the *Post-Gazette* from Mrs. Roosevelt, printed with her headshot, wasn't punchy, graceful, well edited, or memorable, but it had great PR value. "I read Mr. Sprigle's articles with the greatest of interest," she wrote. "They certainly are a contribution to the understanding of a bad situation if one is able to understand anything at all. I am afraid that the real difficulty is that where there is prejudice there is no way of opening people's minds but if we go on continually trying someday we may succeed. This series of articles is a real contribution."

Needless to say, Mrs. Roosevelt's high opinion of Sprigle's work was not shared by everyone. The first critical letter was a lengthy one from John Temple Graves, a syndicated columnist and newspaper editor in Birmingham, Alabama. As the *Post-Gazette* pointed out, he had "long been an outstanding spokesman for the more liberal Southern viewpoint." In what actually amounted to a guest op-ed piece, Graves politely dismissed the Jim Crow series as a stunt designed mainly to win more journalism prizes and fame for Sprigle. He acknowledged that in the South black farmers were too often cheated, "some" black schools were bad, and black taxpayers "sometimes" didn't get their educational money's worth. But he assured everyone up North that such things "are on the mend now, thanks to legislation and financial aids and an increasing sense of decency and justice among Southern whites."

Graves provided a preview of what would become the standard line of defense from the South's offended newspaper corps—yes, we know there are problems, but things were getting better for blacks. And Sprigle was a biased northerner who trafficked in "false generalities" and everything he reported had been "reported many times before now without anybody having to get a sunburn and pass as a Negro." He suggested "a more truly novel and helpful story" could be had if Sprigle . . .

would come here as a white man and report on the enormity of our race problem, the impossibility of solving it in terms of places like Pennsylvania with its small Negro population, and the human nature in racial antipathy that is not going to be done away with by the distant passing of laws.

The real story is not the old one Ray Sprigle has resurrected but the present one of a genuine advance in race relations and Negro well-being in the South and how that advance is being interrupted by politicians and publicists outside the South who make capital of Southern misery with the problem.

Outsider agitators. NAACP troublemakers. Impatient Yankee do-gooders slowing down "Negro advance by turning white against black in South". . . Graves was a lapsed New Deal liberal, not a racist or a white supremacist. Yet his liberalism was conveniently selective. He was a regional minor-league version of Mississippi's prolific superstar, Hodding Carter. Like Carter and other southern liberals, Graves was against intolerance, unfairness, and inequality. But like them he was also a fervent segregationist and cafeteria constitutionalist. He was a states-rightist who didn't like Truman's civil rights rhetoric or plans and believed the question of race and "the Negro problem" should be left to the southern states to solve on their own. Actually, when Graves wrote to the *Post-Gazette* he wasn't much of a liberal anymore. He was in the process of becoming a Dixiecrat. During the 1950s he spent the decade writing and speaking out against the US Supreme Court, President Eisenhower, Martin Luther King Jr., and other advocates of integration.

The other anti-Sprigle letter-writers didn't exactly show compassion for black Americans or demonstrate a warm affinity for the ideals of Gunnar Myrdal's "American Creed." A man from Chautauqua, New York, was shocked to see the *Post-Gazette* "joining in the hue and cry to create further racial hatred and bitterness. Don't we have enough troubles with war clouds forming, inflation, and shortages without bringing up this old Jim Crow problem, better solved by those whose problem it really is, or is this the old Communistic trick to try to create Civil War in the United States? There are other and more pressing problems. Negroes are free to leave the South. No one is holding them there."

A geographically confused man from the thriving western Pennsylvania steel town of Sharon, who planned to vote for Strom Thurmond for president, said he had ordered a full-size state flag of Alabama and planned "to fly it high in the front yard on the day it arrives. I am proud of Alabama and all the other states that have the courage to stand up and fight to preserve their most treasured traditions. No spy like Ray Sprigle needs to think he can change matters." Predicting a race war if Harry Truman's federal civil rights legislation were enforced, he wrote, "I do not believe in mistreating the Negro but there definitely must be a line drawn somewhere. I've seen too many times how the majority of them get when they see they have equal rights."

A Pittsburgher confidently declared that "everything the Negro in America got, he got from whites. They have not contributed one thing to the European-American white branch of human society. God our Father created the black man, the red man, white man and yellow man. He created no equality. That 'equality' stuff is a new ideology for getting votes." With no hint of irony or sarcasm, he signed off with, "Yours for truth and justice."

Another white American who did not appreciate Sprigle's subject matter or his sympathies hailed from nearby Aliquippa, a booming but doomed Ohio River town of twenty-seven thousand people from Italy, Serbia, Greece, and other white places that produced steel and future NFL football stars like Michael Dyczko (Mike Ditka). "As a white girl born in the North and in the state of Pennsylvania," she wrote, "I have noticed that the North always pokes fun at the South. If you give the Negroes too many rights in the South they will think they are too smart. Writing stories about things like this will build up the courage of the Negroes and they will get too smart."

One local letter-writer called the Jim Crow series a poor publicity stunt that would create racial unrest. Another agreed, wondering "What earthly good does he or you expect to accomplish? Why stir up more trouble in an already troubled world?" Another said Sprigle should go back to the South, stay longer, live as a white man, and get a broader, unbiased view. A woman from Pittsburgh asked, "What is all this to-do about the Negro and his rights? What more rights does he want than the right to work and eat like the rest of us, a right he already has? . . . This is a white man's country and to my way of thinking the Negro is here on sufferance."

The *Post-Gazette*'s letters page editor let his racist writers hang themselves in public, but he didn't protect the paper's ace reporter from ad hominem attacks. "It was with disgust and annoyance that I read the first installment of the Sprigle series," wrote an angry man from Providence, Rhode Island, who added that "any jerk reporter could've done the job even better." He didn't think Sprigle spent enough time in the South to get an enlightened viewpoint. Furthermore, he said:

> The white people down there have a problem on their hands in dealing with Negroes, and I think they are doing a splendid job of it. It seems that for years blind, dumb, degenerate punks such as yourself have been stirring up trouble between the blacks and whites.
>
> I spent five years in the South in a practical capacity and have learned that you cannot treat a Negro on an even plane with the white. I suppose some sort of federal legislation will be passed which will attempt to abolish Jim Crow in the Southland. I predict that when that day comes and, if the white people there are goaded long enough, you'll see more blood spilled than your conscience can ever account for. I can see that you know little of Southern thinking. Mr. Sprigle deserves a golden Oscar for rank stupidity and ignorance.

Of the hundreds of letters he personally received, Sprigle estimated 70 percent were critical of him or his series. Most of the negative missives came from northerners, including the only threatening one from a Navy officer who promised that if Sprigle ever came to Rhode Island he'd beat him up.

～〜

Pittsburghers were used to Ray Sprigle's informal first-person reporting style and his subjective spin. They liked and expected it. But he was playing well in New York City, too. His series in the *New York Herald Tribune* was causing a buzz. After just two articles were printed, major book publishers like Dial Press started calling Walter White at his NAACP office. White and the association's top PR guy, Henry Lee Moon, had been pitching Sprigle's series as a book idea before the series started, and it was paying off. A dozen companies called White or sent telegrams or letters to him or Sprigle. A lecture bureau in New York asked White for help in signing up Sprigle. "If this keeps up," White wrote in a letter to Sprigle on August 11, "I am going to appoint myself as your combination business manager-telephone operator-office boy and general factotum. Since your series started appearing Monday, I have spent an average of two hours or more answering questions about you."

In Pittsburgh Sprigle was on vacation, putting a fresh coat of white paint on his house, helping his daughter Rae with her new horse, and finishing his book. He got a New York literary agent to negotiate his publishing deal, and on August 17 he signed with Simon and Schuster to turn his "In the Land of Jim Crow" articles into a book for publication in 1949. His advance against royalties was a respectable five thousand dollars. That same week, when Walter White learned the *Pittsburgh Courier* was planning to publish Sprigle's articles, he sent a letter to *Courier* president Ira Lewis. White reminded Lewis of the fall day in 1947 when the two of them met with Sprigle at Daisy Lampkin's house in the Hill District. "I didn't dream, did you, that the articles would turn out so sensationally," he said. "The virulence of the attacks on them, as well as the praise which the articles have received, is a revelation."

The *Herald Tribune*—like the *Post-Gazette*—encouraged letters to the editor and wasn't afraid to print their readers' criticism or counter opinions. It ran about sixty of the hundreds of letters it received, including Walter White's thank you note. Some readers thanked the *Herald Tribune* for printing Sprigle's findings. They applauded Sprigle for his courage and firmness. They also complained about his bias and his sensationalism. They disputed or quibbled with his generalities, called him a troublemaker, and said the South did not need to be coerced because it was making progress on its own. One man who said he had been in many southern train stations claimed the white and black waiting rooms were identical in size and conditions and that the ramshackle black schools Sprigle described were aberrations found only in poor communities where the white schools were just as bad.

A man from Charleston, South Carolina, who had lived in the North until the previous year, said Sprigle and others of his liberal ilk should be directing their attention "to the conditions in the black belts of the cities before indicting the white race for both injustice and stupidity in some fifteen Southern states." He said Sprigle should come back to the South as a white man "and study the problems of his own race in its relations with the Negro before endeavoring to tear down a system that, even though it was conceived by anarchy and nourished by Federal bayonets, has over the years led to a steady improvement. If those of your readers who pass through the South by train or car will realize the Negroes they see in the cotton or tobacco fields, or in the shacks along the road, are the ones who can hold the balance of political power, then will your readers appreciate the reason why 'state's Rights' [*sic*] is not an empty politician's phrase to catch votes."

Sprigle's series in the *Herald Tribune* caught the attention of Don Hollenbeck, the pioneering media watchdog at CBS radio. Hollenbeck was a top-flight newspaper and radio journalist who had risked his life covering World War II in Europe for CBS. In 1948 he was the influential host and writer of a unique fifteen-minute weekly radio show critiquing New York City's newspapers called *CBS Views the Press*. The brainchild of Edward R. Murrow, the program only lasted from 1947 to 1951. But journalism professor and Hollenbeck biographer Loren Ghiglione considers it "one of the most important radio programs in the history of American journalism."

Hollenbeck concentrated on calling out the print media in New York City for their mistakes, unfairness, sensationalism, and abuse of the vulnerable and defenseless. His targets ranged from wire services and the communist *Daily Worker* to the liberal *New York Times* and the *Journal-American*, the conservative flagship of William Randolph Hearst's newspaper empire. He was a liberal, as were most of his CBS colleagues, but he was tough on any newspaper he caught mishandling or distorting the news. He also chastised papers in the North and South for ignoring the NAACP's decade-old request to end what he called "Jim Crow journalism"—the common practice of identifying black persons in news stories and headlines as a "Negro" when it was irrelevant to do so. In the early

1950s Hollenbeck relentlessly criticized the excesses of anti-communist politicians and journalists. In turn, he was smeared as "a pinko" and a leftist traitor and hounded mercilessly in print by a powerful right-wing TV critic at the *Journal-American*. In 1954, at age forty-nine, he committed suicide. His troubled life and tragic death were portrayed by actor Ray Wise in *Good Night, and Good Luck*, the 2005 docu-movie about CBS giant Edward R. Murrow starring George Clooney.

While Hollenbeck was known and respected for his tough, insightful critiques of his fellow journalists, on August 21 he devoted most of his *CBS Views the Press* program to extolling the talents and courage of Ray Sprigle. He praised "In the Land of Jim Crow" for what it exposed about the South and how Sprigle went about exposing it. Calling Sprigle "a sort of reportorial ideal" who had previously disguised himself as a butcher, a mental patient, a coal miner, and a gambler to get to the truth, he said the series "was one of the most stimulating and thought-provoking pieces published in the American press in a long time. Many sociologists have written learnedly of the problems of race relations in America; it is safe to say that not one of them has produced one-tenth of the effect Ray Sprigle did by passing as a Negro. . . ."

Hollenbeck agreed with *Herald Tribune* letter-writers and others who said Sprigle was revealing nothing new about the plight of blacks in the South. But he said Sprigle did something new and valuable with his bold act of advocacy journalism. He put a sharp, readable, and emotional focus on an old but important issue. Hollenbeck said the Jim Crow series "illustrated vividly the fact that one story, properly dramatized and brought home to the reader as a vicarious personal experience, is worth volumes of theoretical stuff—also worth volumes of case history with which the reader can make no personal contact." He criticized the *Herald Tribune* for its wishy-washy editorial about the value of Sprigle's series, saying the paper seemed "to be half apologetic" for running it when it should have been proud to print it. If "In the Land of Jim Crow" didn't win another Pulitzer Prize for Sprigle, Hollenbeck said, the "annual awards for excellence in journalism won't have much meaning."

Chapter 17

Telling Sprigle's Story to Black America

My Dear Mr. Sprigle,

I'm here in St. Louis this week attending our Shriner's Convention. I was agreeably surprised in picking up the St. Louis Globe-Democrat to find your article No. 7. I had not seen one before that, but have read each one every day. They are certainly fine and so well written. You know I enjoyed them. Your articles are creating quite a sensation here among the people. Everybody is reading them and eagerly awaiting the next issue. . . .

You would do well to build these articles into a book. Come back again and we will get some more material along the North and South Carolina coasts. . . .

Sincerely yours,
JW Dobbs

John Wesley Dobbs was in St. Louis on August 20 with his wife and youngest daughters June and Mattiwilda. He had driven from Atlanta by way of Nashville in his beloved 1947 Mercury, which he assured Sprigle was "behaving beautifully." That morning the *Globe-Democrat* ran twenty short letters reacting to "In the Land of Jim Crow." Balanced between "Ray Sprigle Stinks" and "Splendid Job," they congratulated the paper for publishing the series and for serving "the cause of democracy." They also blasted the editors for publishing one-sided "yellow journalism" written by a biased reporter who slandered the South and was stirring up racial discontent like the communists.

Out West, where relatively few black Americans lived, Sprigle's series was carried in twelve parts by the *Seattle Daily Times* and the *Oregonian* in Portland. Both papers conspicuously promoted the coming of "In the Land of Jim Crow." In seafaring Seattle, where Caucasian supremacy was privately enforced with Jim Crow efficiency, there were sixteen thousand blacks including eight-year-old Jimi Hendrix. Until well into the 1960s the city was carefully segregated. Racial exclusions written into homeowners' property deeds and redlining by real estate agents and banks confined blacks and Asians to their own parts of town.

White communities had strict covenants similar to the one in the Magnolia neighborhood, which said "No person or persons of Asiatic, African or Negro blood, lineage or extraction shall be permitted to occupy a portion of said property, or any building thereon; except, domestic servant or servants may be actually and in good faith employed by white occupants of such premises." Blacks were refused service in many retail stores, restaurants, hotels, and even hospitals. There were neighborhoods in the city and suburbs called "sundown zones" where blacks and Asians were not permitted after dark. Black men spotted by police in the zones were regularly stopped, questioned, and told not to be seen in the neighborhood again.

The *Seattle Daily Times* started the first chapter of Sprigle's series on Page 1 with a photo of him in disguise and placed the remaining articles on its inside pages. It didn't print any of the letters it most certainly received, and its editors didn't write a commentary about what Sprigle did or said. Meanwhile, in Portland, where about ten thousand blacks also had to deal with racist housing policies, de facto segregated schools, and discrimination in employment and banking, the *Oregonian* went all out. It ran the entire first chapter and a big photo of Sprigle on Page 1 of its Sunday paper.

Over the next two weeks the *Oregonian* published six letters—four positive and two negative. It ran an editorial lauding Sprigle's series for illuminating "the exact legal restrictions under which Southern blacks live." Then a note appeared on the editorial page with the headline "Discussion Closed." It explained that the *Oregonian* had in hand twenty-six unpublished letters inspired by Sprigle's articles. Twelve approved of what Sprigle said or corroborated his testimony, the editor's note said; two were noncommittal; and twelve deplored their publication, disputed their truth, or maintained that the level of oppression and woeful conditions Sprigle described were not generally true. "Both sides have had a say," the editor decreed.

Back in Pittsburgh at the *Post-Gazette*, Sprigle's series rolled on. The eleventh chapter explained how "a terrific capacity for hard work" and decent white neighbors made it possible for south Georgia farmers David E. Jackson and A. J. Washington to prosper and become local black leaders. In Chapter Twelve he pointed out how absurd it was that black doctors and dentists in Tennessee could treat white men and women in the most intimate ways yet were forbidden to sit next to them on a bus. He also noted that blacks across the South were denied basic justice in civil courts so consistently that they didn't even bother to try to sue a white man or institution.

In subsequent chapters Sprigle visited the ramshackle black school in Bluffton, Georgia, to prove that the word "equal" in the South's pet catch phrase "separate but equal" was "a brazen, cynical lie and every white man knows it." He introduced his readers to the "iron-clad" feudalism of the Mississippi Delta, where half a million poor blacks lived like it was 1880, and told the tragedy of Dr. P. W. Hill, the dentist who built a tomb for his dead wife and child. After doing some additional reporting, he added several more examples to Dr. Hill's sad case to show that injured blacks were still being turned away from white hospitals in Tennessee.

Hundreds of letters arrived at the *Post-Gazette*, which printed another balanced batch of eighteen "For" and "Against" letters on August 25. Sprigle and the paper were praised for "publicizing the disgraceful truth" or "bringing to light one of the unpleasant aspects of our great country." One woman expertly cut down the racists who had exposed themselves the previous week.

If I hadn't looked at the names and address on most of the letters you published . . . I'd have felt that I was reading the sentiments of "racially pure" Nazis. How smug, how safe and sure these writers against Mr. Sprigle's series can be! Safe behind their white skins, and so far removed from anything so troublesome as the problems of the Negro race in the United States. Rather than suggest Mr. Sprigle return to the South in a white man's role it might be countered that they should duplicate Mr. Sprigle's role and see what their reactions are. It can safely be assumed their un-Christian, un-American, intolerant views would never permit them to make such an experiment.

Seven of the ten "For" letters came from black readers. One of three appreciative black pastors hailed from Little Rock, Arkansas. A white Pittsburgh postal worker who worked with blacks every day said he was "proud to know them" and vouched for their character and work ethic. Of the eight "Against" letters, the longest was a complaint from the editor of the *Mobile Press Register* in Alabama. Misrepresenting what Sprigle actually wrote, George Cox claimed Sprigle admitted that Walter White of the NAACP had "arranged" his "stunt" and that White's hand-picked agent had "steered" Sprigle "only to the sore spots" he wanted him to write about. A woman from rural Pennsylvania opined that "the Southern Negroes are the happiest and most care-free people in the world. Most of them don't have anything and don't want anything. Least of all they don't want the white Northerner to stir up trouble with them."

Other "Against" writers delivered barely less bigoted versions of earlier criticisms: Sprigle's series will "tend to encourage the Negro's penchant for self-pity, a habit that is fast becoming an obsession with him". . . . Blacks were ungrateful for what fifty centuries of white civilization had given them. . . . Blacks were perfectly happy with the way things were in the South. . . . We Northerners should mind our own business, and so on. A West Virginia man charged that Sprigle "no doubt" got the idea for his series from the popular book/movie *Gentleman's Agreement* and therefore deserved no "credit for originality, much less good journalism."

Someone noted, correctly, that Sprigle failed to point out that there were lots of poor white sharecroppers and they were victims of the system too. And of course one letter-writer brought up the sex angle: A man said though he and most other good white people like him believed the races should be treated equally under the law, he didn't think they should ever be allowed to mix in social situations for one important reason— "an awful lot of white people simply don't like the thought that black and white might rub elbows and get 'chummy' with each other, especially when it involves members of the opposite sex."

In her "My Day" column, Mrs. Roosevelt blessed Sprigle with another nice but awkwardly phrased national plug. She gave kudos to the *New York Herald Tribune* for publishing the Jim Crow series, saying the articles "paint for us most vividly the situation of the Negro in the South, but they should also jog our memories of his situation in every one of our communities." She said there were "some situations" in cities in which "the Mexican or the red Indian or the Chinese or the Jew live in large numbers" where "supposedly enlightened people still hold many of the prejudices accepted and practiced by our Southern citizens." To put her point more clearly, and more bluntly, she was reminding millions of northern white folks in cities like Seattle and Pittsburgh that the South didn't have a monopoly on bigotry and discrimination.

The *Pittsburgh Courier* left nothing to chance. It was the only black paper with the right to reprint Sprigle's series, and it was going to make sure fourteen million black people in America knew it was coming. On August 21 the front page of the *Courier's* national and city editions was turned into a slightly insane billboard to promote what it immodestly touted was "the most amazing, astounding, gripping and revealing story ever printed in ANY newspaper."

Across the top of the page in huge white-on-black type was written "I Was a Negro in the South for 30 Days!" Five large shoe prints in red ink—simulating the tracks of an investigative reporter hot on the trail of truth—walked diagonally across the page, tramping on the headlines of legitimate news stories like the one about "white hoodlums" throwing tomatoes at young superstar Sarah Vaughan while she sang at a jazz concert in Chicago. A six-by-eight-inch portrait of "the Nation's number one white reporter"—Ray Sprigle in his trademark Stetson—stared out at the reader. A red banner spanning the bottom of the page asked "WHAT IS IT LIKE FOR A WHITE MAN TO BE A NEGRO IN THE SOUTH? . . . Ray Sprigle, Pulitzer Prize Winner, Posed as a Negro for One Month . . . Read His Series of Exclusive Articles in The Courier Next Week."

The *Courier's* "news" article about the upcoming series broke all the rules of "objective" journalism. No misleading exaggeration was spared. It

COURTESY OF THE *NEW PITTSBURGH COURIER*

opened with "Exclusive!—The veil has been lifted! The iron curtain has been pierced!" Two paragraphs later came:

> Tearing aside the hitherto impenetrable curtain of darkness flung around the 10,000,000 Negroes in the South, Mr. Sprigle brings you a white man's graphic tale of the torments and terrors, sleepless nights of fear and trepidation, lynchings and the graphic panorama of how Negroes actually live in the South—as seen through his penetrating eyes.
>
> With one fell swoop, intrepid top-flight reporter Sprigle has ripped down the walls around the economic execution of thousands upon thousands of Negroes in the South and brought all the nefarious schemes of "white supremacy" and all its implications into the light of day. . . .
>
> Of some 2,000 daily newspapers and more than 11,000 weeklies and periodicals in the United States only twelve daily papers dared carry this graphic story . . . and only the Pittsburgh Courier—of all the Negro newspapers in the world—is presenting these historical and economically important articles.

The Sprigle promotion took up a third of the *Courier*'s front page. It shared space with real news and associate editor George Schuyler's report from Rio De Janeiro on the Brazilian military, which he said was fully integrated, tension free, and put America "to shame in the matter of democracy." In the Pittsburgh city edition, the top genuine news story of the week was the decision by A. Phillip Randolph to quit the leadership of the civil disobedience movement that was pressuring the Truman Administration to desegregate the military.

Also on Page 1 was a small item noting that Ira F. Lewis, the president of the Pittsburgh Courier Publishing Company, had suffered a serious heart attack while in New York. The sixty-four-year-old editor, businessman, and civic leader who had co-piloted the *Courier* to its greatest heights would not live to see Sprigle's series appear in his newspaper. A week later he was dead. With the presidential election two months away and the northern black vote up for grabs, President Truman and

eharry 'Plan' Blasted by Leading U.S. Doctors

Here's Ray Sprigle in Disguise

Ray Sprigle as a Negro in the South

★★★ NATIONAL EDITION of

Pittsburgh Courier

AMERICA'S BEST WEEKLY

LIVE FEATURES • Leader in Advertising, Circulation, News • CLEAN • PROGRESSIVE

TWO SECTIONS 15¢ PER COPY

VOL. XXXIX—No. 35   PITTSBURGH, PA., SATURDAY, AUGUST 28, 1948   PRICE FIFTEEN CENTS

I WAS A NEGRO
IN THE SOUTH FOR 30 DAYS

Discrimination Is Annoying in North; It's Bloodstained Tragedy in Dixie

For a month Ray Sprigle, Pulitzer prize winning reporter, roamed the South, disguised as a Negro, and was accepted as a Negro by whites and Negroes alike. He recounts his experiences in this series of articles. All of the incidents described are factual, but Mr. Sprigle has in some cases changed the names of persons and places for the protection of the individuals involved.

By RAY SPRIGLE
(Nation's No. 1 White Reporter)
(First of Seven Articles)

(Special permission for these copyrighted articles arranged through the courtesy of the Pittsburgh Post-Gazette and the New York Herald-Tribune. Reproduction forbidden.)

For four endless, crawling weeks I was a Negro in the Deep South.

I ate, slept, traveled, lived Black. I lodged in Negro households. I ate in Negro restaurants. I crept through the back and side doors of railroad stations. I traveled Jim-crow in buses and trains and street cars and taxicabs. Along with 10,000,000 Negroes I endured the discrimination and oppression and cruelty of the iniquitous jim-crow system.

It was a strange, new—and for me, uncharted world that I entered when, in disguise, I talked briefly, later turned to my Negro companion, who was leading me along the unfamiliar paths of the world of color, and demanded:

"What are you carrying that white man around with you for?" To which my friend replied:

"That friend of yours—he talks too much to be a Negro. I think he's white."

Detected No Suspicion

But in literally thousands of contacts with Negroes, from nationally known leaders of the race to share-croppers in the cotton rows I was accepted as a Negro. I sat for long hours in Negro groups where we discussed everything from Shakespeare to atomic energy and the price of cotton. Neither I nor my companion ever detected any reserve or suspicion that I wasn't just what I pretended to be, a light-skinned Negro from Pittsburgh, down South on a visit. I attended half a dozen Negro

MOB VICTIM AND ATTORNEY—Atty. Harold Boulware (left) of Columbia, S. C., prepares a complaint to the Department of Justice on charges that the Rev. Archie Ware (right), 64-year-old Baptist minister, was brutally beaten and cut by mobsters after he had cast the lone Negro vote in Calhoun Falls, S. C.

Mob Slashes, Clubs Minister at Polls

Memphis Bows To Henry Wallace

Prominent Baptist Pastor Beaten, Chased By Dixiecrats in Presence of Policemen

By JOHN M. McCRAY
(Special to The Courier)

MEMPHIS—The walls of segregation fell here this week as city officials forced to Henry Wallace by giving him the right to use Bellevue Park, Sept. 5, on his own terms. "We are telling you have your meeting on your terms," John Vosgs, chairman of the Memphis Park Commission, told Wallace representatives.

CALHOUN FALLS, S. C.—Told that white mobs planned to "finish him" for having voted in Democratic primaries Aug. 10, and just released from a hospital where a severe beating and slashing had put him, the Rev. Archie Ware, 64, pastor of four Baptist churches and moderator of the Savannah Valley Baptist Association, fled his home here last Saturday night and one week later has also fled the State.

The successful elderly pastor who cast an attractive home here in Main Street, says scenes of his imprisonment toted against elsewhere in the town and operated in his improvement room grocery, had been brutally beaten by a group of four

G.I. Sentence Reduced

NEW YORK—The former Department of the Army has been informed that had taken the sentence of the NAACP had the residence of former Pvt. Linwood Williams, for allegedly having attacked a German woman, has been reduced to thirty years.

(Continued on Page 4, Col. 1)

Ira Lewis Rallies After Heart Attack

NEW YORK — The death of Ira F. Lewis, president of Pittsburgh Courier, who suffered a heart attack here last week was definitely improved Most Mr. Lewis was stricken as preparing to return to Pittsburgh.

Jubilee Officials Mum on Negro Model

N. Y. Style Show Hits Race Sna

NEW YORK—A dress designer, a handbag designer and an actor wound up a strenuous but determined effort last week to make a Negro model—winner of the Cinderella of New York's Golden Anniversary fashion show, sponsored by the entire fashion industry of this city in connection with New York's Golden Jubilee.

Mildred Joanne Smith, who plays feature roles in "Beggar's Holiday" and "St. Louis Woman," was to have walked down the runs at Grand Central Palace to model fashion promenade. But no one seems to be sure whether or not Miss Smith's presence in the fashion show is desired.

Early in the spring when the show was being planned Mildred Joanne Smith, a Negro model, made contacts with Negro leaders in various communities, advising

MILDRED JOANNE SMITH
would like to see a Negro model in the show. Mr. Rogers is confident to have gotten no satisfactory answer from his letter. How-ever, a letter was sent Richard

in which he told that "the actresses" were being informed. He added that "one or more of performances," modeling their gowns or costumes provided this committee.

Rosetta LeNoire of "Anna Lucasta" and June White of "No Exit" and daughter of NAACP's Walter White are raised to have gotten the run of Mildred Joanne Smith who may answer from his letter. How-...

Mr. Moey called Zelda Moore dress designer, and 3 Costume Guylot, handling handbags, both designers refused to make Miss Smith's appearance possible. The Mr. Shop postponed the reduction.

STANFORD

Plans rotest; Down'

Quits s Group

Bells for Prexy

Suicide In Shrine

Schuyler:
Negroes Negligible Factor in Uruguay

By GEORGE S. SCHUYLER
(Courier Associate Editor)

MONTEVIDEO, Uruguay—Negroes and mulattoes in the southern republics of South America are few and far between, and everywhere they are a very negligible factor economically, socially, politically and intellectually.

They are not disliked, nor discriminated against in public places and all governmental facilities and services are open to them, including the

This is the seventh in a series of articles written by George S. Schuyler on democracy in the South American countries.

institutions of higher education. But they work in marginal jobs, have no businesses and to a large degree are looked upon as the lowest

tolerantly of them but always stress that these Negroes are very poor, which is simply emphasizing the obvious.

Clearly there has been much intermixture of the races through the centuries, and some undoubtedly whites will acknowledge that they possess some Negro ancestry.

"There being no open jim crow-ism, the association between the

COURTESY OF THE *NEW PITTSBURGH COURIER*

Governor Dewey each immediately wired their deepest sympathies to Lewis's family. The telegram from his friend and fellow Republican Dewey read: "Mr. Lewis was a fine American, an outstanding citizen and an influential leader. His death is a great loss not only to those of his race but to all Americans. All of us who had the pleasure of sharing his rich friendship will deeply mourn our loss."

A week later Sprigle's series took over the front page of nearly three hundred thousand copies of the *Pittsburgh Courier*. The photo of him in disguise was gigantic. The "I Was a Negro . . ." headline couldn't have been heftier if it said "World War III Declared." The subhead went right to Sprigle's main point: "Discrimination Is Annoying in North; It's Blood-stained Tragedy in Dixie." And to make sure every reader knew what a heavyweight Sprigle was, his byline was followed by "(Nation's No. 1 White Reporter)." Not much space was left on Page 1 for the news story "Mob Slashes, Clubs Minister at Polls," which told how a group of "white mobsters" in Calhoun Falls, South Carolina, almost beat a prominent elderly black minister to death because he voted in a Democratic primary. And associate editor George Schuyler, still on his inspection tour of South American democracies, had barely enough room to start his long report from faraway little Uruguay, where he found few Negroes and no Jim Crowism in its society or tiny military.

~ ~

Just as "I Was a Negro in the South for 30 Days" was making its spectacular debut in the *Courier*, the *Post-Gazette* rounded up comments from nine white newspapers that had editorialized on Sprigle's series. The North was represented by the *New York Herald Tribune*, the *Oregonian*, and the *Milwaukee Journal*, all of which ran "In the Land of Jim Crow," and a minuscule Pennsylvania paper, the *Nanty-Glo Journal*. The editors in Milwaukee gave Sprigle praise for helping northern readers understand the problems of southern blacks. They said "every thoughtful reader will profit" from reading his series. Apparently not noticing Sprigle's anger or his rhetorical embellishments, or merely agreeing with them, they added that his articles "don't rant and they don't rave. They simply describe what it would be like if you were a Negro in the South. They show what the Negro is up against."

Journalists at the South's five papers given ink by the *Post-Gazette* were unanimously displeased, for the usual reasons. The *Atlanta Constitution*, edited by the liberal and future Pulitzer Prize–winner Ralph McGill, did not appreciate Sprigle's furtive trespassing. Though McGill had joined Hodding Carter as one of the South's loudest voices of racial tolerance, he too was still a practicing segregationist. McGill wouldn't change his mind on segregation until the mid-1950s, after *Brown v. Board of Education*, when he began preaching in his daily column that it was time for the South to grow up, get real, and put an end to Jim Crow. The *Constitution*'s editorial condemned Sprigle for collaborating with the NAACP, acting as if Walter White's organization was a puppet of the Communist Party USA. It charged that Sprigle, like previous northern drive-by journalists, had depended "upon generalizations, half-truths, hearsay and innuendo" that was supplied in bulk by his "NAACP associates."

The *Richmond Times-Dispatch* mourned that northerners were accepting Sprigle's harmful "misrepresentation and sneers" as gospel. The South was faced with one of the most difficult and complex race problems in the history of the world, its editorial claimed, and "ill-advised stunts" like Sprigle's only made things worse. The *Columbia* (SC) *State*'s editorial didn't just see a stunt; it saw subversion. It said the catalogue of horrors Sprigle described was "news to Southerners, white and black." After accusing the editors of the fourteen northern papers that printed the series of being dimwitted and irresponsible journalists, it intimated that Sprigle might be soft on communism or worse. It was strange, it opined, that the northern editors didn't "recognize the diatribe as the type of divisionist propaganda for which Joe Stalin is paying good money, and that giving it credence at this time is a definite disservice to the United States of America."

The editors at the *Savannah Evening Press*—the same paper young John Wesley Dobbs delivered more than half a century earlier—challenged the accuracy of one of Sprigle's stories from their city, charging him with committing "distorted sensationalism" and accepting stories from "his Negro associates" without checking the facts. The *Savannah Morning News* urged Sprigle to disguise himself as a white man next time and report on "the illegally practiced" Jim Crowism that existed in New England, Pennsylvania, and New York. "Now when you returned to Pittsburgh, Mr. Sprigle, tell us: Did you go back to mingling with the white folk there, or did you decide, in the fullness of your super-liberal heart, to cast in your lot with your new-found colored friends? We would be fascinated to know!"

Meanwhile, "I Was a Negro . . ." came to a powerful finish in the *Post-Gazette.* The final chapters dealt with underfunded southern schools; Sprigle's trip to Savannah, and the Jim Crow Ocean; a black real estate man who outfoxed white property owners; and the deadly violence black men in Atlanta were subjected to by white police, white civilians, and their fellow blacks. In Chapter 20, after nearly three weeks of telling readers how badly blacks were treated under Jim Crow, Sprigle surprised everyone. "Strangely enough," he wrote, "the Negro in the South doesn't hate the white man." He admitted that four weeks in the Deep South might not have made him an expert, but he defended his conclusion.

Remember that I talked at length with the real leaders of the Negro—not all of them by any means—but with scores of them in Georgia, Alabama, Mississippi and Tennessee. They are the men on the firing line who are battling for Negro rights and Negro progress where it's dangerous to do it.

They are the local heads of the National Association for the Advancement of Colored People, ministers, business men, college professors, doctors, lawyers, school teachers, Negro plantation owners, men of substance and influence in their own communities among both whites and blacks.

I wasn't a white man interviewing them, remember. I was a Negro from the North, a friend of Walter White, executive secretary of the NAACP. I was a guest in their homes. We sat for hours over their dinner tables. I slept in their guest rooms. We were just a group of Negroes talking things over.

Solid Basis for Hatred

Frankly, why the Negro doesn't hate the Southern white is a mystery to me. Give me another couple of months, Jim Crowing it through the South—forever alert never to bump or jostle a white man—careful always to "sir" even the most bedraggled specimen of the Master Race—scared to death I might encounter a pistol-totin' trigger-happy drunken deputy sheriff or a hysterical white woman— and I'm pretty sure I'd be hating the whole damned white race.

It seems to me that the intelligent Southern Negro has realized that this fabric of segregation with its development of vicious discrimination; its pattern of organized brutality and oppression—all of it with its roots in slavery—has become a tyrant over both White and Black.

There are—and every Southern Negro, field hand or college president, knows it—decent, humane, tolerant white men and women in the Southland. The Negro knows too, that those white people lack courage—and it would take courage of a high order— to take a definite stand against the more vicious and unnecessary forms of discrimination. He knows they don't approve of wanton, brutal murder. They just lack courage to condemn it publicly. He knows that they lack the courage to spearhead a movement to jail, indict, try and hang the trigger-happy "nigger-killers" who are the men who actually set the pattern for race relations in the South.

Might Be Mobbed

The least that could happen to any white who so "betrayed" his race would be to be dubbed "nigger lover" and see his wife and children and his business suffer. He might easily be lashed within an inch of his life by a hooded mob.

In practically every group of Negroes of which I found myself a part, somebody was sure to say in one fashion or another:

"I'd almost be willing to quit the fight for better education for our people for five or ten years, if I could have some sort of assurance that all of these cracker whites would get a sound education. That way, the cruelty and ignorance and gullibility would be educated out of them and they'd forget their hatred and intolerance of the Negro."

Your more cynical, educated Negro has a sort of kindly contempt for most of the white race in the South. In business contacts he is accustomed to outsmarting the white—in cultural contacts he can't help realizing that quite frequently he is the superior of the white man he's dealing with.

And Nothing Will Happen

But no Negro in the South—no matter who he is and no matter how high his station—ever forgets that the white man always has the one final all-conclusive badge of superiority. The white man can kill him in his tracks, in cold blood, for fun or for no reason at all. And nothing will happen to the white man.

That's the one thing that overshadows every phase of race relations in the South. It's the terrifying specter that leers over the shoulder of every white man who talks to a Negro in the Southland. Why, I don't recall hearing a single Negro refer to the "Mason and Dixon" line. To him it's the "Smith and Wesson" line.

And despite all that, your black man in the South doesn't hate the white.

But what he does hate with all his heart is the discrimination and the oppression that dog his footsteps from the cradle to the grave. He hates most of all the fact that he is but half a citizen. He has all of the obligations of a citizen but not a single one of the rights. He fights and dies for his country, but he can't vote. He pays his taxes at a Jim Crow counter usually—but no Negro in the South has half the representation that a colonist had in 1775. The ringing sentences of the Declaration of Independence are a grim and tragic joke to him. He has no right of liberty that a Southern sheriff, court or white plantation owner is bound to respect. As witness the fact that he is killed by the score every year—and his slayers walk free.

He Wants Two Things

Those are some of the things that the Negro hates.

As for what he wants—two things. And in this order. First, the ballot. Second, proper and adequate education for his children.

At first when they'd tell me this—everywhere it was the same, Georgia, Alabama, Mississippi, Tennessee—I'd try to argue.

"Why not end murder first?" I'd demand. "Why not stop the senseless slaughter of Negroes in the South?"

One answer I got in Georgia will do for all of them—they followed the same line.

"Look," this Negro leader said, "Voters don't kill easy. Nobody's going around shooting voters just to make a record. With the vote, the Negro will have a voice in picking his officials. That's going to make it tougher for the candidate for sheriff whose only platform is the number of unarmed Negroes he killed."

Don't Want a Negro Party

No Negro I talked to expects to see an elected Negro official in the South in his lifetime. In fact many of them don't want to—not for a long, long time.

As the franchise comes slowly to the Negro in the South, notably in Georgia where close to 200,000 Negroes will be registered this fall, what Negro leaders are on the alert to oppose is anything resembling a Negro political faction, or a Negro party, or even block voting by Negroes. They realize the danger of increased racial tension if that should occur now.

In Atlanta, where some 30,000 Negroes are registered, Negro leaders carefully avoid endorsing candidates. Who am I to say that there's no quiet, under-cover proselytizing? But there are no public endorsements. For one thing, it probably would be a kiss of death for the favored candidate.

But, believe me, white candidates do diligently cultivate the Negro vote in Atlanta. They call on the Negro in home or office and solicit his vote in quite courteous fashion. How do I know? Brother, I was there.

Sprigle wasn't done yet. In his last chapter, after describing his degrading Jim Crow bus trip from Atlanta to Cincinnati, he explained why he never encountered an insult or a single "unpleasant incident" during four thousand miles of travel by train, car, and bus. It was because he was careful to never get "in the way of one of the master race. I almost wore out my cap, dragging it off my shaven poll whenever I addressed a white man. I 'sired' everybody, right and left, black, white and in between. I took no chances. I was more than careful to be a 'good nigger.'" Before ending his series with a final message to the white man of the South from "a temporary" black man, he apologized for the lack of Hollywood-worthy drama or violence.

True enough, this would be a far better story if I could show scars left by the blackjack of some Negro-hating small town deputy whom I'd failed to "sir." Or a few bullet holes, mementos of an argument with some trigger happy Atlanta motorman.

I could have gathered them all right. Just by getting "fresh" at the right time and place. But for me, no role as hero. I took my tales of brutality and oppression and murder at second hand. And was mighty glad to do so.

But if I were to become a Negro for four years or 40 years instead of a mere four weeks there's one thing to which I could never harden myself. That's the casual way in which these black friends of mine in the South refer to slavery. I have read my history, of course. I know that for 250 years slavery was a respected and respectable institution in the South. Less so for a shorter period in the North.

But to these people with whom I lived, slavery is no mere matter of history. They didn't learn about slavery from any book. They learned about human bondage and the lash and the club at their mother's knee. Most Southern Negroes, 65 or more, are the sons and daughters of slave parents.

Few former slaves are still living. They'd have to be well past 85 to know anything of it at firsthand. But sons and daughters of slaves are leaders of the Negroes in the South—and for that matter in the North, too.

Barbarism Still in Background

And when you hear a cultured, educated Negro, doctor, lawyer, educator casually remark, "My mother was sold down from Virginia to a breeding plantation in South Georgia"—Well you realize that you're not so far away from barbarism after all.

That pattern of 250 years of slavery still endures in the South. For 250 years, for instance, it was a crime, in some places, to teach a slave to read and write. And looking at some of the Negro schools in the South, it must still be a crime.

Discrimination, denial of the franchise to the black man, the South's indifference to wanton murder of a Negro—all these,

Negroes say, exist because the psychology of slavery still endures in the mind of the white South. Maybe that's what a Negro friend of mine, a $20,000-a-year executive of a big corporation, had in mind when he told me before I started on this adventure:

"You're going to learn that it's hell to be a Negro in the South."

And finally too, one last word to the white man in the South from a Negro, even though a temporary one.

Don't be concerned that the Negro seeks to rise to the stature of manhood and American citizenship.

Don't worry about him defiling either your hotels or restaurants or, above all, your race. Not one Negro did I meet who wanted to associate with white folks. True, all of them condemned segregation bitterly. But as they talked on, it developed that it was discrimination rather than mere segregation that they hated. Every man and woman I talked to, field hand or educator, betrayed the fact that he wanted as little contact with the white world as possible.

But here are a few things with which, it seems to me no decent Southerner could quarrel.

Plea for the Franchise

Quit killing us wantonly just to try out a new gun, or to teach us that it's not good for us to try to vote, or just because you "don't like a damn nigger no how."

Next, let us exercise the franchise guaranteed us by the Constitution and the Supreme Court. You'll never see a Negro party in the South. You'll find that the Negro vote, when there is one, is going to split along the same lines as the white vote.

Give our children a decent chance at a decent education—the same kind of an education that you want for your children. And give our young men and women a chance for a university education—in law, medicine, engineering. We might even be of service to you.

Surely none of that is going to destroy the way of life of the white South. It probably won't even appreciably dent white supremacy.

CHAPTER 18

Sticking Up for Old Jim Crow

"I Was a Negro in the South for 30 Days" wrapped up its run in the *Pittsburgh Post-Gazette* on September 1, but the national debate it started was hardly over. The next morning the first installment of Hodding Carter's "The Other Side of Jim Crow" appeared at the bottom of the *P-G*'s front page. Actively promoted in advance, the series bore the subhead "An Answer to Ray Sprigle" and was billed as the viewpoint of a southern liberal newspaper editor. Ten of the fifteen northern newspapers that carried Sprigle's twelve-part series also published Carter's six-part rebuttal. So did white papers across the South—none of which shared Sprigle's side of the debate with their readers. The only way a southerner—white or black—could read "I Was a Negro . . ." would be in the national edition of the *Pittsburgh Courier*.

No one was better qualified than Carter to defend the South from Sprigle's sneak attack. He was a born-and-bred son of the Old South—a "reconstructed racist," as Ann Waldron showed in her fine 1993 biography *Hodding Carter: The Reconstruction of a Racist*. Raised in a fairly wealthy and locally influential family in Hammond, Louisiana, he had stood out as a brash young southern bigot at exclusive Bowdoin College in Maine. Now he stood out as the Deep South's "most celebrated spokesman for racial justice," the liberal conscience and leading citizen of Greenville, the state's "most urbane and progressive city."

Defending, explaining, and boosting the South in the northern press was editor Carter's second career. When the publisher of the *Providence Journal*, his friend Sevellon Brown III, asked if he'd write a response to balance Sprigle's series, which he ran in his paper, Carter was quick to oblige. His Southland had been hit with a sucker punch. An outsider, a nationally famous reporter, a liberal Yankee, had parachuted in, sneaked around for a month with an agent of the NAACP, and written what Carter felt was a terribly inaccurate and unfair story for the rest of the country to read.

Carter was justified in wanting to push back at Sprigle. "I Was a Negro in the South for 30 Days" (titled "In the Land of Jim Crow" in every paper except the *Post-Gazette*) was not a work of "objective" journalism—and didn't pretend to be. It was an emotional, first-person opinion piece—essentially a powerful twenty-one-day front-page op-ed column. Sprigle admittedly had focused disproportionately on the many civil rights injustices and discriminations experienced by blacks. He was negative and bitter. But he backed up his strong opinions with a lot of solid reporting. He did the grunt work necessary for any good piece of journalism. And he'd be the first to admit that he wrote from the point of view of a pained middle-class black man, not a dispassionate newspaper reporter, and certainly not from the perspective of a segregationist newspaper owner from the Deep South who employed full-time maids, owned a thirty-two-foot yacht, and vacationed each summer in Maine.

The *Post-Gazette*'s editors bent over backwards to be evenhanded with Carter. Though the unhappy Mississippian had no intention of putting a single word of Sprigle's series in his Greenville paper, "The Other Side of Jim Crow" was promoted by the *P-G* as something any "fair-minded reader" would want to read. Carter's series and photo ran on Page 1 for six straight days. He started out his first article with a defensive disclaimer. He said he was handicapped because he was a quote-unquote "Southern liberal." That meant just about anything he said was "suspect, not only among a good many of my fellow citizens below the [Mason-Dixon] line but also among most of the professional, semi-professional and even amateur liberals of the North who demanded unqualified agreement with their goal of complete, abrupt and Federally enforced ending of the southern pattern of segregation."

Carter was a hard-nosed opinion writer. In his regular syndicated "Looking at the South" column a week earlier he had blasted Sprigle's series as "distorted, prejudiced and superficial." Echoing fellow liberal editor Ralph McGill of the *Atlanta Constitution*, he told his southern readers that Sprigle's articles were packed with "unfair generalizations, deliberate and misleading innuendo, extreme bias and direct untruths." The "unhappily significant thing," he complained, was not that he was engaged in a journalistic debate about the South with a northern reporter. It was that "the present-day South was so unknown to the non-South that the editors of thirteen [*sic*] metropolitan newspapers and two national news magazines accepted a hideously gross distortion as factual reporting."

In "The Other Side of Jim Crow," Carter employed his considerable rhetorical skills to try to discredit Sprigle, including plenty of sarcasm and a few cheap shots. He accused Sprigle of being "predisposed against the South even before he cropped his hair, acquired a deep tan and began using the entrances marked 'for colored only.'" He repeated the valid as well as the lame arguments of lesser columnists and letter-writers, only with more sophistication, without a whiff of racism and at greater length: Sprigle didn't visit long enough to see the real South. What he did was a cheap stunt. He used loaded adjectives and cherry-picked his facts and statistics. He was an outsider in the thrall of Walter White and the NAACP. He should have spent his time exposing the prejudice in his own backyard. . . .

As usual Carter was trapped in the middle. He had to admit the obvious truths—that "the Negro suffers inexcusable discriminations" and is "still subject to calculated mistreatments." He recognized that the Negro still occupied "a sub-marginal place in the South and in the nation as well" and still had "a long way to go before he gains political, economic and legal equality." But he accused Sprigle of "slanted selectivity" and "journalistic demagoguery." He said it simply was not so, as Sprigle claimed, that "it is still the established, uniform procedure to defraud the Negro sharecropper; that the Negro who wants to vote is in mortal danger of being murdered . . . that in the Delta section of Mississippi where I happen to live the planter maintains a despotic sway; that no white person dares oppose mistreatment of Negroes; and that the Negro is without hope of schools and hospitals or decent housing."

If conditions were "so fear-crazed and hopeless" for the South's blacks, he said, not taking into account the first half of the Great Migration, they long ago would have migrated "en masse." Or, he said, throwing a snide stone at the big glass house to his North, they would have "risen in bloody revolt, sporadically or in concert, so that the South would be the scene of the monstrous race riots with which the East and Midwest are so familiar."

Personally offensive to the combative Carter was Sprigle's crack about the cowardliness of the South's decent white people. It was a "gratuitous lie," he said, that good people lacked "the courage to take a definite stand against the 'more vicious and unnecessary forms of discrimination' and that they are afraid to condemn 'wanton, brutal murder' or to try to jail and punish white killers of Negroes." There were thousands of southerners who openly fought against discrimination and lawlessness in race relations and came to no harm, he said, and he was one of them.

Carter truly wanted political and economic equality for blacks. He had been writing brave editorials in favor of those goals in the *Delta Democrat-Times* for twelve years and had the hate mail, public insults, and death threats to prove it. According to one of his friends, a US congressman, he was "the moving force" behind his town becoming "an oasis in the racial strife and obsession that smothered the rest of Mississippi." But Carter cited among his fellow like-minded southern whites "other newspaper editors, churchmen, educators, judges, law officers, private citizens. The worst that has happened to any of us is being called 'nigger lovers,' particularly during political campaigns. The pressure of public opinion which such activity has aroused has been principally responsible for the dramatic reduction of lynchings and for the very real gains which the Negro has made in his quest for full citizenship in the South."

In the third article of his series, which was part history, part defense of Jim Crow, and part cultural excuse-making, Carter set out to explain why the South was such a lawless and violent region that resorted so quickly to vigilante justice. Because it was mostly rural and small town, because there was so little organized police protection, and because the average homeowner had three loaded guns within reach at all times, he said, it was "a practical necessity" that "the planter, farmer and small-town citizen" were "their own guardians against the lawless." Whites and blacks had to defend themselves equally, he said, and they did.

Carter was particularly annoyed by Sprigle's claim that blacks were being wantonly shot down by whites without punishment. To disprove it, he held up recent homicide figures for his progressive oasis of Greenville, which he pointed out was part of the impoverished so-called "Black Belt" that Sprigle had falsely characterized as "fabulous, feudal and fatal." More than half of the city's population of thirty thousand was black, as was 70 percent of surrounding Washington County's seventy-five thousand people. According to Sprigle's descriptions, Carter said, "You'd think there'd be a lot of wanton killing of Negroes."

It was true there were a lot of murdered black men in his part of the Delta every year, Carter said. But the murderers also were black. All of them. As was the pattern in America then, and still is today, in Greater Greenville blacks and whites mostly murdered members of their own race. But as is also still true today, the per capita homicide rate for blacks was much higher. In the previous year, Carter said, an average of two black men had been killed each week by another black man, "usually over gambling or women." Meanwhile, the white-on-white murder total for the year was three, while two whites were killed by blacks and no black man was killed by a white man. "There were no lynchings of Negroes," said Carter, "nor has there been one in our county in nearly 40 years."

Lynchings had declined in Mississippi and elsewhere in the South, Carter argued, not because of the NAACP and threat of a federal anti-lynching law but because "They are as abhorrent to most southerners above the poor white level today as they are to Mr. Sprigle." He acknowledged justice was still unequal and said what "the South must itself do next is to punish the white murderer of the Negro when such a crime is committed." There were white men "serving time in southern penitentiaries and penal farms for the murder of Negroes, the rape of a Negro girl and the robbery of Negroes," but he confessed that most all-white juries in the South still refused to convict white men who kill black men. Realistically, no federal anti-lynching law was going to change that sorry fact, he said, because juries in federal courts—also all-white—will still be filled with local residents. "The change must come, and is coming, in the hearts of Southerners themselves."

Before Carter's series ended, the *Post-Gazette* editorial page commented on what it called his "able, reasoned rebuttal to the findings" of Ray Sprigle. The paper continued its scrupulously fair treatment of him, saying he was "a courageous, competent journalist" who "comes to the problem of racial intolerance with clean hands, having long championed the cause of the Negro from the fastness of probably the most backward state in the South." Because he was a southern liberal, he was exposed to "the billingsgate of many in his own region as well as to the sneers of Northern reformers who want nothing less than an immediate, root-and-branch correction of generations-old abuse."

> As Ray Sprigle pleads for justice, so does Hodding Carter plead for temperateness. He emphasizes that the Negro question in the South is terribly complex—shot through with the mutual fears and distrusts that are the evil legacy of a slave economy. Above all, Mr. Carter points to the efforts of liberals like himself and the positive gains which the Negro has won in recent years. For the most part, Mr. Sprigle's and Mr. Carter's views differ in degree and not in kind. However, there is one big exception: Mr. Carter is convinced that reform must take place within the pattern of segregation. With this we do not agree. But it would be grossly unfair to judge the case of the Southern liberal until his arguments were heard and studied. That is why we earnestly recommend Mr. Carter's essays to thoughtful readers in this district.

Though Carter had only lived in Greenville for twelve years, he loved the Delta like a native. In Chapter Four of "The Other Side of Jim Crow," he unspun his version of its history for northern readers. It was a "fabulous area" built by the tenacity of settlers willing to suffer floods, yellow fever, the Civil War, and the misrule of Yankee outsiders during Reconstruction. On top of that, the North continued to abuse the South's agrarian economy with unfair federal economic policies. Cotton was forced to compete in the open world market, while Republican politicians protected the Northeast's manufacturing interests with high tariffs that forced everyone in the South to pay more for practically every product, tool, or piece of equipment they needed.

Carter, the son of a prominent Louisiana farmer and local politician, explained how the sharecropper system was born. It developed out of necessity in an agrarian economy that had been left in ruins and chaos by the Civil War and the sudden emancipation of four million slaves. He also explained how tough it still was in 1948 for even the biggest cotton plantation owners to earn a living and avoid bankruptcy, much less get rich. In his sad tale of the white man's heroic struggle to survive and thrive in the Delta, he forgot to mention the contribution made to its wealth by the free or cheap labor of several hundred thousand slaves and their descendants.

Putting on his well-worn chamber of commerce hat, Carter said much progress and economic diversity had come recently to the Delta and more change was on its way. With its fruit farms, stockyards, and timber farming, it was no longer a mono-economy that lived and died with the price of cotton. Sprigle hadn't noticed it, he said, or cared to mention it, but the Delta's large-scale cotton plantations were no longer run like feudal baronies. The modern planter was looking for smart, skilled tenants who knew how to operate the tractors, cotton pickers, and flame cultivators that were transforming cotton farming and uprooting a majority of the Delta's labor force. The Delta was "symbolic of a newer South," Carter said. The poorest state in the union in 1948 would still be the poorest seven decades later, but he said Mississippi was making progress. Its agricultural diversification and industrialization were bringing higher incomes to people and generating tax dollars that were increasingly being used to build new schools for both races and the state's first public hospital for blacks.

In Chapter Five Carter landed a blow below the belt and did some prophesizing. He claimed blacks and whites whose major goal was immediately desegregating the public spaces of the South were the liberal equivalents of the KKK and hardcore racists like his dead enemy Senator Bilbo. He complained that certain "well organized and uncompromising Negro and white groups outside the South" like the NAACP would be satisfied only when every form of legalized segregation in the South is wiped out by the federal government. He warned that the struggle between these liberal "extremists"—i.e., those who sought immediate freedom, equal rights, and dignity for ten million black American citizens—and the South's racists would be disastrous to blacks. It would enflame "the sub-marginal poor" whites who he said hated blacks and were in economic competition with them. It would also disaffect "the white Southerners who recognize, willingly or grudgingly, the validity of every Negro goal except the ending of general segregation."

Like Sprigle, Carter was well aware of "the ironic aspects, the contradictions and the individual humiliation and tragedies of segregation." He admitted the "separate but equal" public facilities of the South were "rarely equal in fact." He believed the good people of the white South were slowly moving toward his enlightened position on equality for blacks. But they, like him, would insist on the permanence of segregation "regardless of any Federal legislation aimed at its discontinuance."

> I cannot emphasize one point too strongly. The white South is as united as 30,000,000 people can be in its insistence upon segregation. Federal action cannot change them. It will be tragic for the South, the Negro and the nation itself if the Government should enact and attempt to enforce any laws or Supreme Court decisions that would open the South's public schools and public gathering places to the Negro.

In his final article, Carter cooled down a little. He suggested he may have been too tough on Sprigle for failing to perceive that the Deep South was not "the static, stagnant and hopeless" region that he portrayed. The things Sprigle condemned were exceptions, not the rule, he said. Turning the tables on Sprigle, who had addressed white southerners as a "temporary black man" at the end of his series, Carter made a plea to "the politicians and to non-Southerners who aren't running for the Presidency or for Congress and who aren't dues-paying members of organizations that flourish on the South's misdeeds."

How about giving some recognition to the good things that are happening in the South? How about admitting that we've come a long way and that, moreover, there is both a historical and a psychological explanation for the way we were and are? How about putting yourselves in our shoes?

Next, why don't you clean up your own sewers? I've been in Harlem and Chicago's South Side. Have you?

Why don't your political spokesmen and you yourselves admit that humanity's evil predisposition toward discrimination isn't limited, even in the United States, to the South? Why don't you be honest about the anti-Protestant, the anti-Catholic, the anti-Semitic, the anti-Oriental and the anti-Negro biases that flourish in different non-Southern areas to a degree at least equal with Southern prejudices? . . .

Why don't you wake up to the fact that within the next 15 or 20 years and maybe sooner the thing you call the Southern problem will become a national problem because of the accelerating departure of the Negro from the South? . . .

The Negro is decreasingly vital to the South's agricultural economy, because of mechanical displacement. There is little likelihood that he will be absorbed by Southern industrialization or that a comprehensive program for his rehabilitation as a small farm owner will be adopted. It is far more probable that he will become a tragic migrant, crowding into the industrial areas of the North. I wish I could believe that he will find security, contentment and equal treatment there. . . .

Addressing the leaders of the Republican and Democratic parties, Carter asked them not to use their identical civil rights programs to punish the South for political gain. Showing his conservative states-rights colors, he explained why he did not see the need for federal action on the poll tax, which he didn't like but was going away, or the proposed anti-lynching bill, which was unnecessary because the crime of lynching had decreased almost "to the vanishing point." As for a federal fair employment law to ban racial discrimination in hiring, he contended it would be as unenforceable as Prohibition was.

Carter proved he was still a card-carrying New Deal Democrat by running down a list of federal social programs he claimed would fix up the South and help blacks far better than any planned civil rights program. They included more federal aid for education, a broader national health program, intensified soil conservation, a resettlement program, and "a national slum clearance and housing program" that "would raise the Negro's living standards and his self-respect far more quickly than would the abolition of segregation." While he was at it, he threw in a plea for the northern politicians in Washington to end the economic discriminations "against an entire region that are inherent in Federal taxes on oleomargarine, for instance, and the freight rate and tariff structures."

His final kick at the North was aimed at Sprigle. Carter's fundamental argument was that the worst of what Sprigle said was wrong with the Jim Crow South was no longer true in 1948. "Calculated mistreatments" remained, yes. But he said the South was rising above "its traditional and tragic racial attitudes" and punitive, unbalanced articles like Sprigle's only slowed that evolution. The Yankee's troublemaking journalism and alleged distortions had raised a national ruckus in the media and disturbed the peaceful equilibrium of the South's system of apartheid. Carter was annoyed, to say the least. "I know it's easier to jaunt through the South in disguise than it is to understand the reasons why things are as they are," he concluded. "It's easier to endorse scattershot, politically profitable legislation whose cost in dollars and cents is small than to enact a broad-gauged, expensive program for the benefit of sub-marginal Americans, North and South, white and black. But how about being a little more two-sided and a little less two-faced?"

The *Post-Gazette* ran a handful of letters responding to Carter's series. One complained that he used too many fancy words. Another said he presented "a mighty poor defense for the South" and said his arguments reminded him of a thief brought to trial who complained that the cop who arrested him was prejudiced against thieves. One letter praised Carter's articles as representing "the white light of truth." Another said white southern liberals like Carter say the right things but then "whitewash" the racist acts of violence after they occur. A black pastor from Pittsburgh, born in the South, said, "Every Negro with any kind of intelligence knows that the treatment of the Negro in Northern states is as far from that of the South as heaven is from hell."

Tireless Walter White had the last word in the *Post-Gazette* and elsewhere in his syndicated column. Responding to what he called Carter's "disappointing" series, he called him an able and courageous writer for remaining in the South to "do battle there against ignorance and bigotry." But he was disappointed with Carter's "dishonest" complaint that Sprigle should clean up "his own sewers" before outing the South's downsides. White said it was true there were terrible slums in Chicago and Harlem and racist violence in the North. But people were working to wipe out those slums and when a black was killed by a white in the North the murderer was brought to justice, not automatically acquitted by juries of their white neighbors.

While agreeing that things had "measurably and progressively improved" for blacks in the South, White dismissed Carter's claim that pressure from the NAACP and other liberal groups in the North had nothing to do with it. To see how much work still needed to be done in the Southland, he said, all Carter needed to do was look around and read the latest news reports of blacks being discriminated against, intimidated, or victimized by violence. Or he could just read the recent speech in favor of "white supremacy" by John Rankin, the long-serving openly racist, anti-Semitic US congressman from his own state of Mississippi. "Unhappily for the liberal South," said White, after quoting both Lincoln and Bilbo in his column, "Mr. Carter's 'reply' to Mr. Sprigle is in some respects as damning as Mr. Sprigle's articles."

Carter's litany of carps, excuses, and pleas for understanding and leniency for the South was duly noted by *Time* magazine. On September 6 it efficiently summarized "Jim Crow's Other Side" and said it was the answer to Sprigle's "admittedly one-sided" series of "stories of segregation, discrimination and degradation." Without comment or spin, the magazine let Carter snipe at the NAACP and reprinted a few paragraphs' worth of his juicier complaints about Ray Sprigle's "slanted selectivity" and "punitive spirit."

Time treated Carter respectfully but showed zero sympathy for his pain or his segregationist point of view. It noted dryly that while no paper in the South had enough room to run Sprigle's "Land of Jim Crow" series, many ran Carter's rebuttal and also "found space to print a Northern Negro publisher's account of his own untroubled tour" of Jim Crow's eastern seacoast.

> Negro Publisher Davis Lee of the Newark weekly *Telegram* (circ. 110,000) found a Negro's life below the Mason-Dixon line more tolerable than north of it. In an editorial Lee wrote: "When I am in Virginia or North Carolina I don't wonder if I will be served if I walk into a white restaurant. I know the score. However, I have walked into several right here in New Jersey . . . and have been refused service . . . New Jersey today boasts of more civil rights legislation than any other state in the union, and the state government itself practices more discrimination than Virginia, North Carolina, South Carolina or Georgia. . . ."

In Lee's column, which appeared in small white papers in the South like the *Dothan Eagle* of Dothan, Alabama, he argued that the legal separation of whites and blacks had been "the economic salvation of the Negroes in the South." Whereas in New Jersey blacks owned and controlled almost no businesses, he said, in southern cities like Atlanta blacks "controlled millions of dollars worth of businesses."

Based on his many trips through the South, Lee said that blacks had far more economic opportunity there. In the North, for example, where transportation was strictly regulated by state or local laws to protect existing bus or cab companies from competition, no black (or anyone white, either) would be allowed to start a bus company. But the South had black bus lines and cab companies in every city. In the South he claimed blacks and whites got "along much better than Northern agitators would have you believe." He said racial trouble stemmed "from dumb ignorant whites and Negroes, not from the intelligent, better-class element of the two races."

Sounding like Hodding Carter, Lee had sympathy for southern whites. "No section of the country has made more progress in finding a workable solution to the Negro problem than the South. Naturally southerners are resentful when the North attempts to ram a civil rights program down their throats." He said their racist attitude toward blacks was "a natural psychological reaction and aftermath of the Civil War. . . . The whole economy of the South was built around slavery. The South was forced by bloodshed and much harm to its pride, to give up slavery. Overnight these slaves became full-fledged American citizens enjoying the same rights as their former masters. Certainly you couldn't expect the South to forget this in 75 or even 150 years."

Lee also sounded like super-conservative George Schuyler of the *Pittsburgh Courier* when he criticized blacks for taking what he believed was the wrong approach to achieving equality. Blacks were wasting too much energy and money trying to "convince white people that we are as good as they are, that we are an equal," Lee wrote. Black Americans should take a lesson from Joe Louis as an example of how it should be done. Louis proved to the whole world that he was the greatest fighter of all time, black or white, not by using propaganda or agitation, but by demonstrating it. Never saying a word about the importance of integration or the need for civil rights legislation, Lee concluded:

> Our fight for recognition, justice, civil rights, and equality should be carried on within the race. Let us demonstrate to the world by our living standards, our conduct, our ability and our intelligence that we are the equal of any man, and when we shall have done this the entire world including the South will accept us on our terms. Our present program of threats and agitation makes enemies of our friends.

While Hodding Carter, *Time*, and Mr. Lee reacted to "I Was a Negro in the South for 30 Days," its author was growing his hair back and sticking to a doctor-supervised low-salt, low-sugar diet. Sprigle's career as a big eater was over. Along with his chronic bronchial asthma, he had developed a mild case of Type 2 diabetes. The grandfatherly paunch that had sometimes pushed his weight to 220 was no more, and he was visibly thinner, but his iconic moustache, tan Stetson, and corncob pipe were back. He had signed his book deal with Simon and Schuster quickly in mid-August, disappointing half a dozen major New York publishers like Prentice-Hall, Random House, and Houghton Mifflin. He would be finished polishing and adding new material to *In the Land of Jim Crow* in late November, and the book would be published in the spring of 1949.

On September 14 Sprigle received a letter from John Wesley Dobbs containing a few clippings from southern papers that had criticized his series. "You still have them 'squaking [*sic*],'" Dobbs was happy to report from Atlanta. He said he was going to speak in Detroit later in the week and then he'd "return and be ready for the campaign call to duty. Looks like Dewey-Warren to me." (Dobbs's letter—one of a handful kept by Sprigle—was the last known written contact between the two friends. If Sprigle sent letters to Dobbs, they were not preserved with his papers at the Amistad Research Center at Tulane University in New Orleans.) Dobbs's roomy house at 540 Houston Street was quieter than usual, because his youngest daughter, June, had left for graduate school at Columbia University in New York City. Her friend Martin Luther King Jr. had also gone north to the Philadelphia area. Only nineteen, he was settled in at Crozer Theological Seminary near Chester, Pennsylvania, where he was one of eleven blacks in a student body of ninety and hitting the books a lot harder than he had when he was at Morehouse College in Atlanta.

In mid-September the *Post-Gazette* began aggressively peddling a fifty-six-page booklet containing Sprigle's series and Carter's six-part answer. It cost twenty cents and carried an illustration of Sprigle's face, hat, and pipe on the cover. It was destined to sell 9,937 copies in twenty-eight states and Canada. Sprigle had started back to work at the *Post-Gazette*, but he was doing more public speaking than writing. His first article since before his trip in early spring, appearing on September 25, was a short, light feature story about the career of the chancellor of the University of Pittsburgh. He wouldn't write anything else until late November. To promote himself and the paper, he was doing radio interviews and hitting the local lecture circuit, giving a dozen talks on his

"I WAS A NEGRO in the South for 30 days"

By Ray Sprigle

and including

"THE OTHER SIDE OF JIM CROW"

Hodding Carter's Reply to Mr. Sprigle

reprinted from the

Pittsburgh Post-Gazette

southern trip at Kiwanis clubs, churches, and women's club lunches. At the end of the month, he'd be the main draw at a packed public meeting of the Pittsburgh branch of the NAACP, whose posters billed him as "America's No. 1 White Reporter" and author of "I Was a Negro in the South for 30 Days."

By the end of September, Sprigle, Hodding Carter, and Walter White had accepted invitations from *America's Town Meeting of the Air* to go to New York City and continue their fight face-to-face on national radio. On November 9, exactly a week after Election Day, they were scheduled to appear on the ABC Radio Network's immensely popular weekly public affairs program. With a fourth man, liberal editor Harry Ashmore of the *Arkansas Gazette*, they were going to debate the future of Jim Crow. Several million Americans, North and South, black and white, would be listening.

CHAPTER 19

Truman's November Surprise

As President Harry Truman and Governor Tom Dewey rode their whistle-stop campaign trains around the country in search of votes, Walter White set sail for Paris. For the next five weeks he would serve as a consultant to the US delegation at a meeting of the United Nations General Assembly, which tried to get a human rights resolution passed but was repeatedly blocked by the Soviet Union. Because of his bad heart, the NAACP's national secretary and "demon lobbyist" for his race was given a year's leave of absence on September 25. A week later his autobiography, *A Man Called White*, was published by Viking Press. It was favorably reviewed by the *New York Times* and *Saturday Review*, which commented that it was "a book to make a white man hang his head in shame—provided he has enough moral maturity to recognize what is shameful."

Down in the Mississippi Delta, where it was time to start harvesting cotton, Hodding Carter was back at his office in downtown Greenville. As the society page of the *Delta Democrat-Times* briefly noted, he and Mrs. Carter and their three sons had just returned from summering at their seaside home in Rockport, Maine. It probably didn't strike Carter as ironic that he had written his "Jim Crow's Other Side" series while vacationing in one of the whitest, most northerly states in the Union. Maine's 911,000 citizens included twelve hundred blacks, about .1 percent of the population, while Mississippi's one million blacks made up 45 percent of its people.

Carter's answer to "I Was a Negro in the South for 30 Days" had already run its course in his newspaper, jumping off the front page for six straight days. Each time it was preceded by an editor's note explaining it was a response to a series of articles by Ray Sprigle of Pittsburgh that were "one-sided, non-factual in considerable part and gave a completely unfavorable and derogatory account of the South." Unlike the editors of the *Post-Gazette*, editor Carter didn't play fair or balanced. He had no interest in presenting both sides to his readers. He never published a word of Sprigle's series in his paper or when it reprinted his "Jim Crow's Other Side" in a booklet. During September more than three thousand letters generated by his series found their way to Carter from around the country. Many were long and thoughtful and about 80 percent were favorable.

Though their battle of words in the papers was over, Carter was still sniping at Sprigle. Both were strong anti-Communists. But on September 13, the front page of the *Delta Democrat-Times* carried a short, snarky news item intimating that Sprigle was an unwitting tool of the Soviet Union. "Carter's Articles on South to be Beamed Abroad by Voice of America" didn't come from a wire service and carried no byline, but it had Carter's dirty fingerprints all over it. The Voice of America was the "official" overseas radio voice of the US government. Prepared under contract for the State Department by CBS and NBC radio at the time, and broadcast in dozens of languages, the VOA's music, news, and commentary was beamed around the world via shortwave radio. In 1947 it also began lobbing anti-Communist propaganda over the Iron Curtain into Soviet-occupied Eastern Europe, the U.S.S.R., and Asia.

Pandering to America's anti-Communist zeitgeist, the *DD-T* article stated that Carter's "Jim Crow's Other Side" was being used by the VOA to answer what a State Department official said was "Russian radio propaganda which grossly exaggerates racial tensions and injustices in America." After reminding everyone in the Delta for the umpteenth time that Sprigle "posed as a Negro on a Southern tour and wrote a series of condemnatory articles about the South," the not-so-subtle smear job quoted a government spokesman saying Carter's series "will be used to put the picture into correct focus." The State Department said it was unable to determine whether Sprigle's articles were actually being used by Communist broadcasters "to paint a bloody picture of social conditions" in the South. But that didn't matter to editor Carter. The innuendo was made.

Sprigle's troublemaking was not just hurting the South, it was also help-ing the Reds.

The *Pittsburgh Courier* spent September banging the drum for Gover-nor Dewey and delivering Sprigle's entire twenty-one-part series into the hands of hundreds of thousands of black Americans. For six straight weeks the headline "I Was a Negro in the South for 30 Days" blared from the front page of every edition. Pullman porters on streamlined passenger trains carried bundles of the paper to cities from coast to coast and into every corner of the South. A. J. Washington read it in Sparta. David Jack-son read it in Adel. Dobbs and his daughters read it in Atlanta, Jackson, and Durham.

In Miami, where there were 245 uniformed black police officers, more than any southern city, the *Courier* reported that white policemen using "Gestapo-like tactics" selectively tore down posters and placards advertising Sprigle's series while ignoring hundreds of other signs. Police also arrested the paper's distributor for violating the city's rarely enforced ordinance against posting bills, releasing him the next day. The *Courier*'s Pittsburgh office filed a formal complaint with the mayor's office, which promised to look into the case and later promised it wouldn't happen again.

By that time, the *Courier*'s peripatetic associate editor and columnist George Schuyler had returned from his inspection tour of Negro popu-lations in the countries of South America. As he had done for almost twenty-five years, no matter what continent he was on or what special project he was doing, every week he cranked out the *Courier*'s unsigned editorials and his two personal columns. What he wrote was sophisti-cated, politely contentious, simultaneously conservative and radical, irrev-erent, contrarian, and politically incorrect—then and now. No subject or person was too small or too big to be spared Schuyler's unique sting.

He called Dixiecrat presidential candidate Strom Thurmond a big-ger liar than Joe Stalin. In a column about the ideological fight over anti-Communism between two black leaders—Truman Administration cheerleader/adviser Walter White and Soviet Union fellow-traveler/ scholar W. E. B. Du Bois—he referred to the differently hued rivals as

"Blondie" and "Darkwater." He complained about the United Nations' cynical plan to return Italy's former African colonies of Libya, Somaliland, and Eritrea to the "craven, back-stabbing" former Axis dictatorship. Italy would be given the territories in "trusteeship," which he said was "a nice euphemism for imperialism."

In other editorials that spoke for the *Courier*'s owners, Schuyler showed he was a federalist who defended states rights as much as any Dixiecrat—just for different reasons. He supported the governor of Illinois who promised to resist the idea coming from Washington to merge his state National Guard units with the regular US Army and Navy. He praised the University of Arkansas for deciding—without being coerced—to admit its first black medical student to go along with the first black law school student it admitted the previous year. He gave New York State a hearty, extended pat on the back for quietly, successfully, and peacefully integrating the military training for one of its New York Guard units—and then asked why the secretary of the army couldn't "try the same thing."

On September 25 the *Courier* shocked no one by declaring its full support for Thomas Dewey for president on Page 1. Though happy that President Truman, Dewey, and Henry Wallace were all talking about the importance of passing civil rights legislation, the *Courier*'s president and treasurer, Mrs. Robert L. Vann, stressed that as a governor Dewey had done much more than talk. She said he "has achieved in New York, for Negroes, most of the objectives and has enacted most of the laws which President Truman and Mr. Wallace have advocated for the nation as a whole." The *Courier* believed that with Dewey's election "the Negro people would have the best chance of winning 'equal citizenship status' and of having their national interests protected."

It's not clear whether George Schuyler wrote Mrs. Vann's enthusiastic endorsement of Governor Dewey. But there's no question he produced the lead editorial that day, "The Non-Existent Negro Vote." Schuyler was living proof of the obvious but often forgotten truth that black Americans—like any racial or ethnic group—were unique individuals and not monolithic in their thinking or voting habits. It was true that since 1932 blacks had been voting solidly for Democrats by nearly 80 to 20 percent. But he berated "political partisans, white and colored," who "continue to insult the colored people of this country by asserting that there is such a thing as a Negro vote: i.e., that colored people vote in a racial bloc which can be captured by one or another political group solely by racial appeals."

> There is the same diversity of thought and interests among colored Americans as will be found among all other Americans. To imply that all Negroes are the same in their thinking, tastes and interests is to accept the fallacy of racism, and of course the corollary fiction that all white Americans, all East Indians and all Chinese are the same, and that their actions can be predicted accurately on that basis.

Though there's no evidence Schuyler and Sprigle knew each other, they agreed on many important political matters. As old-school conservatives, they were natural enemies of socialism and big central governments and defenders of the individual, the Constitution, and the little guy. Sprigle was a loyal Republican. Schuyler leaned Republican, but his libertarian streak created wide differences between him and Sprigle—and between him and nearly everyone else. For example, unlike about 99 percent of Americans, including his fellow journalists, Schuyler immediately condemned the internment of 120,000 Japanese Americans after Pearl Harbor. He charged that it was done for racist reasons that "placed our democracy on a par with dictatorial European and Asiatic countries."

Later, in 1943, he said the US government should pay Japanese Americans reparations for the land, homes, and furnishings it stole from them. For good measure, he suggested, satirically or not, Washington also should pay reparations to American Indians for "the destruction of their societies and the wanton slaughter of their people" and to "the colored gentry for 250 years of slave labor and 75 years of peonage." He may not have been entirely joking when he added it would "only be fair if Negroes received several billions of dollars in gold for the barefaced robbery of their music, the filching of their folk songs, the taking of their art forms, the appropriation of their dancing, and the stealing of their wit, humor and exuberance which together have made their white brethren outstanding in the Caucasian world."

Sprigle and Schuyler also were poles apart when it came to assessing the social, political, and economic conditions of blacks in the South. Based on his many southern travels over the decades, Schuyler was more in agreement with Hodding Carter and his fellow "liberal" segregationists. He didn't think southern blacks were as oppressed as their leaders and northern liberals claimed. He didn't think they needed the federal government to intervene on their behalf with civil rights legislation. He emphasized—correctly—that on their own they were gradually improving their living conditions in the South and North.

On his southern trip Sprigle found conditions for blacks to be as bloody awful as the NAACP had been saying they were. Yet his month as a black man had made him Schuyler's soul brother on at least one major position—the irrelevancy of a person's race. Sprigle told an interviewer that his trip had taught him "there is no difference between a white man and a colored one. If you want to put it this way, a Negro is a white man without white skin. But it's going to take a long time for people to realize it."

<hr style="width:10%" />

During the final weeks of October, the Truman-Dewey election hurtled toward its rendezvous with history. The big newspapers, important magazines, pollsters, famed pundits, and anonymous political wise guys were unanimous—Truman was toast and Dewey was an Electoral College shoo-in. The *Nation, Business Week*, and the *Wall Street Journal* thought so. So did the *New York Times* and the *Chicago Tribune*. *Time* expected Dewey to win twenty-nine states and 350 electoral votes. *Life* ran a big photo of Dewey—"the Next President." Illustrious radio columnist Walter Winchell gave the odds of Dewey losing at 15 to 1. The last nine Gallup polls showed Truman losing, though by shrinking margins, and when Gallup asked voters who they *thought* would win, only 9 percent said Truman.

After first declaring "the outcome is as much of a foregone conclusion as ever before in our history," on October 14 the *Pittsburgh Post-Gazette* joined the *Courier* and the majority of white and black newspapers by heartily endorsing Dewey for president. A week later Hodding Carter made national news and shocked his fellow Democrats across the South when his *Delta Democrat-Times* came out for the Yankee Republican candidate. About two-thirds of the country's 771 (white) daily papers backed Governor Dewey while 15 percent endorsed Truman. Schuyler and everyone at the *Courier*, which ran pro-Dewey stories on Page 1 and a full-page "Elect Dewey" campaign ad each week of October, also had written off President Truman. On October 30, three days before Election Day, the headline above the article filed by the paper's Washington correspondent Lem Graves read, "Lem Graves Sees Dewey's Electoral Vote Doubling Truman's; Victory Certain."

Everyone was wrong about Truman, of course. It turned out that overconfident Tom Dewey had been slowly losing voter support all fall while "Give 'em Hell" Harry was slowly gaining it. On November 2, Truman won fairly handily, winning the popular vote twenty-four million to twenty-two million and the electoral vote 303 to 189. He took twenty-eight states to Dewey's sixteen while Strom Thurmond and the Dixiecrats carved away four traditionally Democratic states—Mississippi, South Carolina, Alabama, and Louisiana. Despite Dobbs's hard work for the state's undersized Republican Party, Georgia went to Truman and the lily-white Democratic Party, in a landslide as usual. Republicans came in a distant third. Both the US Senate and House of Representatives flipped from Republican to Democratic control, with young congressmen Richard Nixon and John Kennedy each winning re-election easily.

Dewey won the industrial Northeast but got wiped out in the West, South, and most of the Midwest. He lost for many good reasons. He was competent and smart, but he was a dull, cautious, cardboard candidate. Farmers didn't vote for him. The Republican Party didn't spend enough money. Voter turnout was the lowest since 1924. Despite the near unanimous support of the black press for Dewey, nearly eight in ten blacks chose Truman. That percentage was only slightly higher than in 1944, when 77 percent of blacks voted for FDR. But as Walter White had argued to the president in 1947, and as NAACP staffer Henry Lee Moon had predicted, black voters in the North held the margin of victory in some key states. Truman narrowly won Ohio, Illinois, and California. He carried Ohio, where 130,000 blacks voted for him, by just seven thousand votes. In Illinois and California black vote totals for him also far exceeded his margins of victory. Truman proved Democrats could win the White House without the Solid South. But if he had lost those three close states, he wouldn't have won enough Electoral College votes to be elected and Strom Thurmond's pipe dream of throwing the election into the House of Representatives would have come true.

On the Friday after Election Day, Hodding Carter flew from upstate New York to Pittsburgh, where he would meet his nemesis-in-print Ray Sprigle for the first time. The "fighting editor and famed spokesman for the South," as Carter was called in the *Rochester Democrat and Chronicle*, had given a speech to Rochester's Ad Club the night before on the topic "Is the South That Bad?" Giving the same speech Friday morning in Pittsburgh to several hundred members of the Allegheny County League of Women Voters, he defended the Southland and blasted newspapers in the North for their "distortions."

Carter didn't name Sprigle or single out the *Pittsburgh Post-Gazette*. But as reported by the *Pittsburgh Press* that afternoon, "the scrappy little Southern editor" said the South's ability to solve its racial problems was being hurt by northern papers that emphasized "sensational as well as violent news" and gave "only one side of the South." In addition to the arguments he had made in his series "Jim Crow's Other Side," he added that the failure of the northern press to present an accurate view of the South was helping the Communists in their propaganda campaign against America. That same night, south of Pittsburgh, Sprigle appeared in a crowded black church and spoke to the Washington County branch of the NAACP about his series "I Was a Negro in the South for 30 Days."

Sprigle and Carter didn't meet each other until Monday morning, when Carter delivered his "Is the South That Bad?" speech to a suburban women's club meeting in a downtown Pittsburgh hotel. The *Post-Gazette* ran a large photo of the two Pulitzer Prize winners sitting next to each other at a luncheon. Though they were looking at each other and smiling, they were ideological enemies in the early moments of America's escalating civil war over segregation. The next evening they'd be in New York City's Town Hall dueling in a national radio debate. It would be a

COME HEAR

Washington County Branch
N. A. A. C. P.

Presents

Ray Sprigle

Author of

"I WAS A NEGRO FOR 30 DAYS"

FRIDAY, NOV. 5 at 8:15 P. M.

Presentation of Charter
Atty. Paul Jones

St. Paul A. M. E. Church

West Wheeling Street   **Washington, Pa.**

fight between equals. But Carter had cooked up something of an ambush for his northern rival. Over the weekend in the *Pittsburgh Courier* he had read George Schuyler's provocative description of what life was really like for black people under Jim Crow. "The South's fighting editor" planned to use what Schuyler wrote to discredit "America's No. 1 White Reporter" on *America's Town Meeting of the Air*.

CHAPTER 20

The Great Radio Debate

The makeup man had extra work to do. The problem was Hodding Carter's color. His hair and eyes were black, his skin dark and swarthy. Walter White's skin was noticeably whiter. Plus his hair was gray-blond, his eyes were blue, and he looked European. Tens of thousands of people in New York City and Philadelphia watching at home on their small, fuzzy TV screens would be hopelessly confused. The face of the white editor from Mississippi who was defending Jim Crow segregation would look darker than the face of the black man from the NAACP who wanted to outlaw it. To help the black-and-white TV images coming from Town Hall's stage accurately reflect reality, the makeup man for *America's Town Meeting of the Air* made White's pink skin darker and Carter's brown skin lighter.

Ray Sprigle's skin color was just fine. He, Carter, White, and the last-minute replacement, editor Harry Ashmore of the *Arkansas Gazette*, were in New York to debate the present and future of legal segregation. *America's Town Meeting of the Air* was the most popular and most influential of a half-dozen public affairs programs on radio. Broadcast live by ABC Radio from Town Hall on Tuesday nights in front of an audience of fifteen hundred, its hour-long discussions on politics, culture, war and world peace, free speech, Social Security, communism, immigration, the Constitution, the economics of the South, and race relations reached about ten million people each week. In addition to broadcasting on its coast-to-coast network of 252 radio stations, ABC had recently begun televising the program on its two infant TV stations, WJZ in New York and WFIL in Philadelphia.

NOW ON TELEVISION

WJZ-TV NEW YORK   WFIL-TV PHILADELPHIA

NOVEMBER 9, 1948

Town Meeting

BULLETIN OF AMERICA'S TOWN MEETING OF THE AIR

BROADCAST BY STATIONS OF THE AMERICAN BROADCASTING CO.

Reg. U.S. Pat. Off.

THE TOWN HALL

Reg. U.S. Pat. Off.

What Should We Do About Race Segregation?

Moderator, GEORGE V. DENNY, JR.

Speakers

RAYMOND SPRIGLE   HODDING CARTER

WALTER WHITE   HARRY ASHMORE

(See also page 12)

COMING

——November 16, 1948——

What Should the Administration Do About the High Cost of Living?

——November 23, 1948——

Should There Be Stricter Government Control of Lobbies?

Published by THE TOWN HALL, Inc., New York 18, N.Y.

VOLUME 14, NUMBER 28 $4.50 A YEAR: 10c A COPY

America's Town Meeting of the Air was created in 1935 by George V. Denny Jr. to imitate the town meetings of old New England. Denny, an ex-professor of drama production, was the associate director of the League for Political Education, a group originally founded by suffragettes to educate people on important political issues. Worried about the health of democracy and the ability of everyday people to defend it, he wanted to educate the American public by presenting lively, balanced, and reasoned radio debates on serious subjects between the smartest or most important people he could get. The first program—"Which Way America: Fascism, Communism, Socialism or Democracy?"—set the high tone. So did such timeless topics as "Personal Liberty and the Modern State" and, after World War II, "Should the U.S. Open Its Doors to Displaced Persons Now?"

A marketing whiz far ahead of his time, Denny built *Town Meeting* into the country's first interactive talk show. As the producer and on-air moderator, he sought as many ways as possible to involve the audience at home and in Town Hall. The program went on the road six months of the year, encouraged letters and comments from listeners, offered study guides, and sent debate transcripts to schools. It spawned nearly a thousand listening clubs around the country and printed 250,000 little magazines that for ten cents a copy or $4.50 a year provided subscribers with a complete transcript of each program. Half the program topics came from listener requests. During broadcasts unscreened questions were taken from the Town Hall audience, who got their tickets for free and were expected to be part of the action. Though "Moderator Denny" orchestrated the flow of the show and strictly enforced civility, applauding, cheering, booing, and even heckling panelists was tolerated, within reason, as long as there were no personal insults.

Town Hall was the perfect venue for debating important public issues. It had been built in 1921 by the League for Political Education and was already historic by 1948. It had become an important political meeting space for liberals, their causes, their speakers, and their debates. It was also a superior performance space, thanks to its acoustics and the progressive values and artistic tastes of its management. In addition to booking classical musicians like Rachmaninoff and Paderewski, it was especially welcoming to blacks. The great opera singer Marian Anderson made her New York debut there in 1935 after being turned away at other locations because of her race. Jazz stars Charlie Parker and Dizzy Gillespie had early bop concerts at Town Hall. Billie Holiday made her solo concert debut there in 1946. And in 1954, John Wesley Dobbs's second-youngest daughter, Mattiwilda, on her way to becoming an opera star in Europe and the rest of the world, had her New York City debut on Town Hall's stage.

Though *Town Meeting* had discussed aspects of America's "race issue" in a few previous programs, the November 9 debate was the first time it had dared to directly address the explosive subject of segregation. Walter White had appeared on the program in 1947 with author and former Republican congresswoman Clare Boothe Luce, when the not-very-edgy topic was "What Can We Do to Improve Race and Religious Relationships in America?"

In 1944 poet, author, and activist Langston Hughes provided the spark for a far more spirited discussion titled "Let's Face the Race Question." Moderator Denny introduced that 1944 program with a warning to listeners across America that its subject matter was so dangerous it might shock timid souls. Hughes proved him right by bashing the segregation of the armed forces, the poor training given to black soldiers, and the South's "profound fear" of intermarriage. The hundreds of letters to *Town Meeting* from the show's listeners were mostly approving. They included one from a group of Spelman College girls in Atlanta who said they had huddled around radios in their dormitories and cheered Hughes for "so frankly and beautifully" speaking "the truth on the 'race question.'"

According to University of Pennsylvania professor Barbara Dianne Savage, author of *Broadcasting Freedom: Radio, War, and the Politics of Race, 1938–1948*, President Truman's open support for civil rights reforms in 1947 had liberated national programs like NBC's *University of Chicago Round Table* and ABC's *Town Meeting* from their cowardly self-censorship on race. The shifting political wind, accelerated by Truman's executive order to finally integrate the armed forces in the summer of 1948, allowed the public affairs shows to drop any pretense of neutrality on civil rights and address the "dangerous" issue of black inequality in America more directly and substantively. In *Town Meeting's* case, Professor Savage said, the program was "emboldened to finally confront the question that had remained politically untouchable on the air: 'What should we do about race segregation?'"

— ❦ —

Sprigle and Carter had jumped at the chance to defend their polarized positions on *America's Town Meeting of the Air*. It was not just priceless national publicity for two newspapermen who liked getting it. They each were getting paid two hundred dollars for being on the radio program. Plus the next morning they'd get another two hundred dollars for their one-on-one debate in front of a paying audience in Town Hall's sold-out Wednesday lecture series. Walter White was in Paris when he was invited to join the radio show, but he would have dog-paddled back to take part in it for free. He was a savvy media man, the go-to spokesman for his race. He knew radio's power and how to use it to advance his causes and his prestige.

Newspaperman Harry Ashmore had been recruited to replace Prentice Cooper, the former segregationist governor of Tennessee who had to bow out at the last minute for medical reasons. Ashmore turned out to be a prescient choice. The executive editor of the *Arkansas Gazette* in Little Rock was then a liberal segregationist like his friend Carter. But he'd soon evolve into an integrationist and win a Pulitzer for his forceful editorials denouncing the racist mobs that tried to stop the desegregation of Little Rock Central High School in 1957.

Though producer Denny pointedly avoided stuffiness on *Town Meeting*, he left little to chance. Each sixty-minute program was carefully constructed and timed for maximum fairness and efficiency. Each participant was allotted a three-and-one-half minute opening statement—two typewritten pages, double-spaced. As usual, Denny had instructed the panelists to send their statements to him in advance so he could share them with other debaters, so there'd be no duplication of material or unfair surprises.

Town Hall was famous for not having a bad seat in the house, and on November 9 the house was overflowing. Extra lighting for the hulking TV cameras warmed the panelists sitting in their chairs behind the podium. Like every episode of the show, the 533rd broadcast of *Town Meeting* opened with a New England town crier ringing a bell and shouting "Town Meeting Tonight! Town Meeting Tonight!" Then Denny went to work. Speaking to the millions listening, he began with, "Good evening, neighbors. What do you think we should do about race segregation?"

He framed the issue like a teacher, seeking information without betraying his position. Reminding everyone that segregation of some kind existed to some degree or other in every part of the country, he asked if President Truman's re-election was a mandate to Congress to pass his proposed civil rights legislation. "Mr. Walter White and Mr. Ray Sprigle think that it is," Denny said. "Mr. Hodding Carter and Mr. Harry Ashmore do not agree. All four gentlemen have reasoned arguments for their views, and we, the people, throughout this great land of ours, must attempt to find the right answer or answers to this great problem."

Sprigle was first. He didn't beat around the bush or dial back his "I Was a Negro in the South for 30 Days" rhetoric.

Mr. Denny, ladies and gentlemen. I'd like to get one thing clear at the start, Mr. Denny. When I talk about race segregation, I insist upon doing so from the standpoint of the southern Negro leaders who welcomed me into their homes and with whom I lived and traveled for four weeks as a Negro myself. To the southern Negro, segregation is not merely the enforced separation of the races in hotels and restaurants and the like, it is the whole vicious and evil fabric of discrimination, oppression, cruelty, exploitation, denial of simple justice, denial of the rights to full citizenship and the right to an education, which the white South imposes upon the Negro.

Sprigle denounced murder—"wanton, inexcusable, capricious murder" that walked "the streets and highways of the Southland, dogging the heels of ten million black men—women, too—and pouncing whimsically, with or without provocation." Then he argued for equal voting rights for blacks.

What about the right of franchise? Either the Negro—that means all Negroes—is a citizen of the United States or he isn't. The Constitution and the Supreme Court say that he is. Thousands of heroic Negro dead—sown broadcast over the seven seas in the far corners of the world, who died in the uniforms of the armies and fleets of the Republic, and lie with their bodies wrapped in the flag for which they died—these dead men say the Negro is a citizen.

Including Denny, Sprigle was the only northern native on the program. He said he'd leave the details of the progress the South was making in black voting-participation rates to Carter and Ashmore. But he added, "If a few Negroes are going to vote in the South, why not [let] all of them vote? 'Wait just a few more years,' some southerners tell us. The southern Negro has been waiting for eighty years for his first fundamental right of citizenship. How much longer must he wait? Why not tomorrow morning?" Then he took a shot at one of his favorite targets—the South's "criminally inferior" black schools, for which he said "no fair-minded southerner can offer excuse or explanation." He decried "the despicable denial of the right of little black citizens to a decent education" and charged that "the white South—white southern educators—are willfully cheating the Negro out of the education to which he is entitled."

Next up was Hodding Carter. Ignoring the text of the opening statement he had sent to Denny in advance, he surprised everyone on stage by immediately quoting George Schuyler of the *Pittsburgh Courier*. Carter explained to the audience that when he was in Pittsburgh the previous weekend he had read the first installment of Schuyler's series "What's Good About the South?" Billed by the *Courier* as an "objective" account of black life in the South, the collection of feature stories about "average black families" living in the rural and urban South from Virginia to Mississippi was ballyhooed as "an exclusive, sensational series which digs into the hearts and minds of Dixie's people, with the brilliant George S. Schuyler telling the true inside story."

There was nothing "objective" about the motives of Schuyler's series, which ran for seven weeks and included thirty detailed articles about black people's personal lives, jobs, incomes, and interracial relations. It was his deliberate effort to balance the grim and harrowing picture of the South that Sprigle's series recently had painted across the *Courier*'s front pages. In his weekly "Views and Reviews" column, Schuyler summarized the encouraging conditions and trends he had found on his ten-thousand-mile "flying trip" to fourteen southern states.

The South was prospering. Blacks could buy homes and farms. Most cities had black policemen. Opposition to blacks voting wasn't as strong as it once was. And while there were a few highly publicized murders connected with blacks voting, Schuyler said that violence against blacks was rare and there "was little or no evidence that blacks anywhere in the South were terrorized." As he had been on many previous southerly excursions, he said he was treated courteously and "as well as anywhere else by both white and colored people. True, there are jim-crow laws, the existence of which I deplore, but I obey them, and their existence (which irks me) does not blind me to the opportunities Negroes have there."

Schuyler wasn't naïve. He didn't live in an ivory tower on some quiet college campus. He lived in the best black neighborhood in New York City, Sugar Hill, where his neighbors were Walter White, Duke Ellington, and other prominent black professionals, political leaders, artists, musicians, and writers. The editor of the *Courier*'s New York edition, he had visited and reported on the conditions of black people living all over the world. He knew blacks in the Jim Crow South suffered discrimination and were third-class citizens. He knew they disliked being barred from public places and deeply resented being discriminated against because of their color. But he said "they are not hopeless and despairing, any more than the Negroes in most of the area outside the South who are subjected to racial proscription." Though black schools were inferior, he said, "any honest observer who has visited Dixie periodically can see and must admit that there has been vast improvement in physical plants and teachers' quality and pay. Swarms of Negroes are graduating from high schools and colleges."

Pointing to entrepreneurial blacks like the Washingtons of Sparta, Georgia, who had prospered despite the odds, he said it was his "sincere opinion" that if more Southern Negroes applied themselves to the economic fundamentals it would be easier for them to solve their "socio-political problems." "The tolerance on display in the South today is little short of amazing," he wrote. "Moreover, most Southern white people of prominence in every state are apologetic about these shortcomings and the less timid are sincerely trying to better conditions. For this they should get more credit than professional propagandists are wont to give them...."

Schuyler had observed the Jim Crow South and its black population through the filter of his conservative, contrarian, rose-tinted glasses. His positive spin wouldn't have been out of place in a Hodding Carter column—which is why the crafty Mississippian used it to discredit Sprigle. Carter laid on the sarcasm and aimed it right at Sprigle: Schuyler "had just returned from a tour of fourteen southern states," he said, "not three. He wasn't disguised as a Negro, Mr. Sprigle, because he is a Negro." To make his case that the South was not nearly as bad for blacks as Messrs. Sprigle and White claimed it was, and was getting better all the time, Carter fired off a burst of killer quotes he had pulled at random from Schuyler's "Views and Reviews" column.

"After the tour, it strikes me that the biggest handicap the Negroes are encountering is themselves.... Most of what is being said about the South is untrue.... Today it is not a place of terror and persecution, nor has it been in many decades ... Nowhere is there studied insult or discourtesy within the social framework of the section, and everywhere Negroes tell me the persecution and police brutality are rarely encountered, and they should know."

I'm still quoting. "For all the faults of the South, it must be admitted that colored people are better off there than any other minority elsewhere with comparable background, and I believe I have more information," says Mr. Schuyler, "about the position of minorities in other countries than most people."

...So much for what a militant, northern Negro newspaper-man says. It should carry more weight than anything Mr. Sprigle discovered in four weeks, or that I might assert after forty years.

After using the country's most prominent black journalist to under-mine Sprigle, Carter repeated the basic arguments he had made in his series "Jim Crow's Other Side." He said, "Segregation is one aspect of our folkways" and "Folkways cannot be ended by abrupt federal action." And he said that education and economic advancement, and lots of fed-eral help for both, must come before the "so-called civil rights program." Carter closed with more sarcasm. He said he didn't mind the North taking an interest in Mississippi's shortcomings, which he admitted to. But "on the other hand Mississippians have a right also to imitate the North's utter perfection in race relations, in crime reduction, in the end-ing of segregation, in slum riddance, equality of job opportunities and enlightened politics."

Next it was Walter White's turn to deliver his opening statement. Before White spoke, Denny tried to head off any racial confusion. He pointed out that "Mr. White is a Negro but those of you who are witness-ing this program on television tonight, as well as those here in Town Hall, will not recognize him as such." White was his usual sharp, persuasive self, arguing that segregation was inherently unequal and support for Tru-man's civil rights program proved that "decent Americans want segrega-tion abolished and they want it abolished now."

Ashmore weakly challenged some of Sprigle and White's points, using the long history of segregation in human affairs in his rote defense of the South's racial policies. He agreed with Sprigle that the South had a race problem but, as he saw it, the biggest problem "is not what to do about segregation but what to do about those injustices and inequalities that have accompanied it." He accused Sprigle and White of letting their zealous crusade to quickly end the institution of segregation cloud their ability to see and weigh the facts. Progress was being made, he said. "In eighty years, only a moment in the sweep of history, the Negro has moved within the sight of his traditional goal of proper civil rights."

There were no commercial breaks, but the hour flew. When Ashmore finished his opening remarks, Denny asked Sprigle for a comment. While the others had been talking, Sprigle had scribbled out a handful of sentences in pencil on the back of a piece of paper. Ignoring Hodding Carter's "Schuyler surprise," he said:

> Certainly I will agree that the problem of racial relations in the South has shown a constant trend for the better. I don't want to be smug about it, but there was only one way for the problem to go. Here, as I see it, are some of the immediate racial problems for the South and the Nation to solve: How long is the South going to continue the wanton murder of Negroes? How long is most of the South going to deny the Negro the ballot, either by fiat or subterfuge? How long will the South deny adequate education to little children because they are not white?

Ashmore and Carter answered Sprigle's questions in turn. Ashmore thought it was an impressive sign that in his home state of Arkansas—which was 30 percent black—more than 10 percent of qualified blacks had voted in the most recent election. Carter was predictable—prickly and cutting. He said Mississippi will stop its murders when the State of New York stopped "having more murders, interracial and otherwise, in one month than we have done there in a year." As for the equal education angle, he said, if the North was so concerned about educational opportunities in Mississippi, why "don't you put your money where your hearts are and help us out on that problem?"

White, Carter, and Ashmore briefly exchanged arguments over what was wrong and what was right about the South and who was responsible for both. To prove white-on-black violence was still a valid concern, White pointed out an example of a Georgia man, Isiah Nixon, who had been lynched a few days earlier for voting and urging other blacks to vote. Ashmore, though not a tenth as combative as Carter, nevertheless defended the Southland and its white people, who he said needed to be shown tolerance as they worked to fix the flaws of segregation. Contrary to what Walter White intimated, he said, the South's whites were not all "depraved," "ignorant," and "living a life of ease" based on the exploitation of "our colored brethren."

❧

Soon it was time for Moderator Denny to take questions from the audience. The questions were intelligent, challenging, and noticeably tilted to the North. To Ashmore—"Why should the southern states not be subjected to federal civil rights legislation?" To White—"What practical things can whites in the North and South do to hasten the end of segregation?" Sprigle was asked by a man in the crowd if he thought passing civil rights laws would "antagonize the people of the South and cause them to become even more hostile towards Negroes." Wouldn't education be a better way?

"Well, how long is this education supposed to go on?" Sprigle replied. Only a minority of southerners were against alleviating the condition of blacks, he said, and the important civil rights laws could "be enforced without any great resistance in the South because they are inevitable, and I think even the South recognizes that." Sprigle also was asked if he thought America's "race segregation" was an international problem that should be brought to the United Nations. He said no. The thing to do was for Americans "to keep plugging away and work it out right here."

Another man asked Walter White if he thought "the Gandhian solution" of passive resistance could "be useful in removing racial segregation from the United States?" White, who was smart but didn't have the benefit of a crystal ball, said he didn't think so for two reasons. Gandhi's tactics had worked in India because the odds were in his favor—four hundred million Indians to only one hundred thousand white Europeans. Also, he said, "nonviolence, passive resistance, requires great discipline. I think in the Hindu religion there is a great deal of that kind of discipline which we do not find in the Christian religion, whose typical song, in my opinion, is 'Onward Christian Soldiers.'"

A New York public school teacher, who joked he was "a refugee from the South," asked Hodding Carter why Mississippi's laws limiting the rights of Negroes were not an example of what John Stuart Mill defined as the "tyranny of the majority." Mill, the brilliant British philosopher, was a seminal champion of individual freedom and limited government, an abolitionist, and author of "On Liberty." But he was born in 1805 and had zero influence on the framers of the American Constitution or federalism. Carter, uncharacteristically confused or maybe just faking it, made a mess of his answer. "You might recall that John Stuart Mill was also the spokesman of 'the least government, the best government' and, therefore, the first spokesman which this country seized upon in setting up its initial doctrine of states rights. I can see no relationship between the Constitution of Mississippi and Mill's doctrine of tyranny. Our Constitution reads no differently from any other Constitution save in this one insistence upon segregation."

When Denny asked the foursome to briefly sum up their arguments, Harry Ashmore apologized for "the unfortunate weakness" of his newspaper profession to sensationalize the news and over-publicize "the loud and the intemperate" few. Then he said with God's help and a few wise politicians his region might solve its racial problems on its own and be "brought back into the Union."

Walter White simply quoted a speech Lincoln made in 1858 during the Lincoln-Douglas debates at Edwardsville, Illinois—"And when by all these means you have succeeded in dehumanizing the Negro, when you have placed him where the ray of hope is blown out as in the darkness of the damned, are you quite sure that the demon you have aroused will not turn and rend you? . . . Familiarize yourselves with the chains of bondage and you prepare your own limbs to wear them. Accustomed to trample on the rights of others, you have lost the genius of your own independence and become the fit subject of the first cunning tyrant who arises among you."

Hodding Carter summed up by indirectly quoting but not naming his new conservative friend, George Schuyler. He said the *Courier*'s associate editor, "a Negro, himself," had pointed out that it was the leadership of blacks and whites in the South "that will jointly and primarily direct our destinies down there, all federal activity to the contrary. The professional propagandist, the sensational reporter, and the federal sleuth may irritate us or disturb our progress," Carter said, taking his final swings at White and Sprigle, "but only education, economic well-being, and a reduction in numerical pressures can hasten it."

The final word went to Ray Sprigle, whose undercover trip into the Jim Crow South in search of a good newspaper story had started a four-month national fistfight in the media about ending segregation. Ignoring Carter's crack about "sensational reporters," he stuck to the high road. "I think I can very briefly summarize my end of this discussion, and that is this: that it seems to me to require some effrontery to discuss when and how you are going to apply the Constitution of the United States to a segment of the population. I think that many of your problems of seg-regation would be solved by the simple recognition of the Negro in the South as a citizen of the United States, subject to the rights granted him and every other citizen by the Constitution."

CHAPTER 21

A Mission Forgotten by History

As many as ten million Americans tuned into *America's Town Meeting of the Air* each week. How many millions listened to Ray Sprigle, Hodding Carter, Walter White, and Harry Ashmore debate the fate of Jim Crow is anyone's guess. From Harlem to Los Angeles to Atlanta, thousands of blacks had listened in their homes, at their local NAACP branches, or at private listening parties. Dobbs and most of his scattered family heard it. So did Walter White's brother-in-law Eugene Martin, the rich Atlanta insurance executive who told Sprigle nine months earlier that if he wanted to pass as a black man he should just get a good tan. Uncounted thousands of New Yorkers and Philadelphians who weren't interested in watching the *Milton Berle Show* on NBC also saw the debate live on ABC's two TV stations. With only about six hundred thousand television sets in the entire USA, and no television station operating yet in Pittsburgh, Rae Jean Sprigle and her mother, Agnes, had to listen on the radio.

Network radio's first intensive discussion of race segregation in the South didn't get much coverage in the print media. The *Post-Gazette* wrote a brief item about their star reporter the next morning with the headline "Make Negro 'Citizen,' Says Sprigle on Air." The debate wasn't mentioned at all in either the *New York Times* or *Time*, neither of which paid close attention to *Town Meeting of the Air* over the years.

Public reaction to the *Town Meeting* broadcast was generally positive. Though Memphis radio station WMPS reported receiving complaints from fifty callers, the program on segregation was the most popular of the season so far. It drew 2,580 letters from listeners—the highest total in several years. The majority of writers were pleased that segregation was chosen for discussion, according to a nine-page typed summary prepared by a *Town Meeting* staffer. About 13 percent of the responses were described as critical. The woman who read through the correspondence and wrote the report concluded that "the most striking manifestation in this week's mail" was "an apparent change in the attitude of Southerners. Much of the deep hatred seems to be diminishing and making way for a new view."

Based on just one person's sunny and unscientific impressions, the report didn't quantify or seriously analyze the readers' comments. But it gave the sense that while most southerners wanted to help blacks, they were not keen on ending segregation any time soon. Intermarriage and socializing between the races were common fears. The report included excerpts from fifteen letters. Like the tsunami of letters that reacted to Sprigle's newspaper series, they proved that some Americans were racists, some were saints, and most fell somewhere in between.

A more sordid falsehood never polluted the air. . . . One would think the South used Negroes for target practice.
—P. V. Mathews of Shreveport, Louisiana

I am pretty sick and tired of hearing the South reviled and attacked. I notice when you damn yankees [*sic*] want a vacation, you head first for the South, expect our hospitality, and then depart to revile and insult us. . . . I'll never listen again to your dreadful programs of hate.
—Harriet Landon Smith of Tucson, Arizona

What should we do about race segregation? Eliminate it entirely by recognizing and promulgating the scientific, logical fact that there is one, only one race, viz., the human race!
—T. Isidore Flynn of Sarasota, Florida

To me race segregation is just one of those things which ought not be found in a democracy. I believe it ought to be the privilege of every citizen to work at any vocation he is capable of . . . I only oppose marriage between the races.

—Dora Carnahan of Auburn, Indiana

I do not believe you realize the harm that has been done by such programs, and I really feel that such men as Ray Sprigle and Walter White should be kept off the air entirely. Those of us who live in the South feel we are doing pretty well with the Negro question and that we are really giving them very much more than they are justly entitled to. . . .

—H. W. Brooks of Memphis

I'm just a housewife (white) living in a small town of narrow, intolerant people who will not open their hearts to the injustice done here to the defenseless Negro. I am ashamed to live in the South since there is nothing I can do—but talk.

—Mrs. Ralph W. Taylor of Doyle, Tennessee

Ray Sprigle saved a few of the telegrams and letters he received after the *Town Meeting* debate but never said how many there were or what they contained. Walter White received 250 personal letters, telegrams, and phone calls, with all but five agreeing with what he and Sprigle had said on the radio. Lucille Randolph, the wife of powerful black leader A. Phillip Randolph, sent a spirited telegram: "Walter you were superb. You certainly gave those Southern crackers everything that was coming to them. More power to you." From Pittsburgh White's friend and NAACP colleague Daisy Lampkin wired, "You were magnificent tonight on Town Hall. Your knowledge of facts and conditions made the opposing side sound weak and unconvincing." Mary McLeod Bethune, the educator, civil rights activist, and adviser to three American presidents, sent White a letter, telling him, "You represented us in a way that made me so proud of you. I prayed that God would give you wisdom and strength on that occasion. You did a marvelous job."

In a reply to a woman who wrote to tell him she was boycotting the *Pittsburgh Courier* because of what George Schuyler had written in his column, White wrote, "I am sorry you are boycotting the *Courier.* . . . I can well understand your emotion upon hearing Hodding Carter make the use he did make of Mr. Schuyler's article." White said he and everyone else on the program was blindsided when Carter began quoting Schuyler's opinions about the conditions of blacks in the South. But while he and George Schuyler had often disagreed, White told the woman, he said he believed "in the statement attributed to Voltaire: 'I disagree with everything you say but I will fight to the death for your right to say it.'"

There had been no clear winner in the *Town Meeting* debate. It resolved nothing. It only proved how far apart the North and South were on an issue that would bring trouble and shame to America for decades. In his letter White told the woman he "felt sorry for Messrs. Carter and Ashmore. Both men, especially the latter, are able and honest men. But they are sorely handicapped by having to defend a system which deep in their hearts they do not believe either just or workable."

White repeated those kind sentiments about the good souls of Carter and Ashmore in his syndicated newspaper column in the *Chicago Defender* on November 20. Under the headline "That Controversial Town Hall Meeting," he also said he was encouraged by what happened during the radio debate. Always the optimist, he said there were "as yet imperceptible but very significant signs" that the steady water drops of protest were "wearing away the stone of resistance to the abolition of segregation."

The event marked a new stage in the continuing struggle against segregation. Unlike almost any other controversial issue which might be discussed on such a forum, there was not a single question which indicated anything but the most unequivocal opposition to segregation. This was especially noticeable among some of the white questioners whose accents showed they were from the deep South. And the flood of comments demonstrated that the tide of intelligence is apparently running more swiftly and deeply than seems at times true. Those who favor second-class citizenship for

Negroes or who are afraid to move forward to face it are increasingly being put on the defensive and that is all to the good.

～～

For the *Pittsburgh Courier*, which never missed a chance to toot its own horn, Hodding Carter's acclaim for George Schuyler on *Town Meeting* was pure public relations gold. In its November 20 edition, the paper went all in. "What did Schuyler *really* say?" was bannered across the top of Page 1 between oversized headshots of Schuyler and Carter. Did Carter deliberately misquote Schuyler? Were the good things Schuyler said about the South correct? "These questions ricocheted around the Nation last Wednesday morning," the *Courier* reported proudly. So that hundreds of thousands of its readers could judge for themselves, the *Courier* printed the transcript of what Carter said on *Town Meeting* next to a reprint of Schuyler's original column. Both articles started on the front page under the headline "Nation All Ears as Geo. Schuyler Is Quoted on Air." The *Courier*'s editors presented all the evidence—and also decided the case: Carter had been unfair to Schuyler and was guilty of taking his quotes out of context, which he only slightly did.

The *Courier* exploited Carter's journalistic misdemeanor as an excuse to praise their star iconoclast and itself to the heavens. In an editorial titled "Mr. George S. Schuyler," the paper declared there was no "Negro in America today who is better fitted to investigate and evaluate the South than our associate editor, George S. Schuyler. Author, traveler, sociopsychologist student and analyst, and for many years a field investigator for the NAACP even while writing for the *Courier* prior to 1924, Mr. Schuyler knows his field." But the *Courier* made it very clear that Schuyler's contrarian opinions were entirely his own and that, like most large newspapers, its editorial positions were set collectively by a board of editors after discussion and deliberation. The *Courier* reassured everyone that its editors did not agree with Schuyler's sanguine assessment of the South and promised to carry on its forty-year crusade for full social, economic, and political equality for all black Americans.

Not surprisingly, Schuyler didn't agree with his own paper. In his "Views and Reviews" column, he wouldn't criticize Hodding Carter for quoting him out of context on the radio. He wrote that what Carter had said about the improving interracial situation in the South was the truth, even if he was a segregationist. "Conditions in the South are vastly better than they were twenty years ago," insisted Schuyler, "and nobody who actually knows the score down there will deny it." He stuck to his favorite conservative guns. He repeated that it was up to blacks in the South to improve their own economic and political lives and upgrade their culture "through their own efforts and the help of friendly whites." Finishing with his usual unflinching confidence, he said, "Of course it is unpopular to say such things, but popularity must ever be sacrificed to truth by honest men with no axes to grind. By this time we Negroes should have matured sufficiently to face and accept the truth."

The special one-on-one debate between Sprigle and Carter the morning after the *Town Meeting* broadcast received no media attention. Part of Town Hall's popular Wednesday lecture series, and costing $1.80 per ticket, the sold-out event was titled "The Negro in the South." Sprigle typed out a fresh six-page opening statement, rephrasing the same arguments he had made the night before. He began with the theme that "the life, liberty, welfare and happiness" of the South's ten million black-American citizens was a national problem the South alone could not be trusted to solve. Washington's politicians were going to have to do their part by dropping the "hypocrisy and chicanery" that he said had marked the handling of racial relations and voting rights for sixty years. He admitted it wouldn't be possible "to blackjack the South into reversing completely its traditions and mores as regards relations between the races." But again he asked Carter the question no liberal segregationist wanted to answer in 1948: How long was the South going to keep blacks "in bondage that was not quite freedom, nor yet quite slavery?"

After graphically describing one of the decrepit black schools he visited in what he derided as the deliberately "starved" Jim Crow educational system, Sprigle turned and praised his younger opponent. "And just to keep the record straight let me say here that there is no more valiant fighter in all the Southland against these school conditions than Hodding

Carter. Hodding Carter and thousands of Southerners like him are all right—in my book—on most of these racial evils. Trouble is that there are too many in the South who are all wrong."

Sprigle respected Carter as a writer and journalist. He tipped his hat to him later in the debate, calling him a representative of the "new rising South." He told the audience of fifteen hundred "any Southern town that would put up with Hodding Carter and his paper must be a good town." Carter never returned Sprigle's respect or publicly complimented him in the slightest way. More than anyone he was aware of how much trouble and bad publicity one northern newsman had brought his morally flawed Southland. When it came to Sprigle, the "South's fighting editor" never seemed to find himself in a forgiving mood.

In his Sunday column in the *Delta Democrat-Times*, Carter told the homefolks how he had used the findings of a northern Negro writer named George Schuyler to counteract Sprigle's distortions about the South. Carter paid tribute to Schuyler, saying he was impressed with his "evident intention to show the good with the bad to accent the encouraging and the normal." After padding his column with the same quotes from Schuyler he had used in the radio debate, Carter wrote that it was too bad "this Negro newspaperman's" reasoned series about the South was never going to receive the national attention "that was accorded the fantastic stories by another Pittsburgh reporter. . . . If the millions who read white Ray Sprigle's venomous distortions could also read Negro George Schuyler's fairer story, much of the earlier harm could be undone."

Carter wasn't done throwing jabs at Sprigle. A year later he made fun of him and his Jim Crow series in a *Look* magazine parody titled "A Southerner Tells What's Wrong with the North." It featured a crusading southern journalist, known to his staff as "Ol' Fearless," who disguised himself as a pale, left-wing, drug-taking New Yorker so he could expose the many injustices and depravities of the North. To make sure there was no doubt whom Carter had in mind, the investigative newspaper series that Ol' Fearless was going to write was called "In the Land of Grim Snow."

A year later the dogged defender of the South wrote *Southern Legacy*, a non-satirical first-person book in which he explained, excused, and criticized his region's culture and politics. Though never identifying Ray

Sprigle or his paper by name, Carter said he belonged to the "hit-and-run school" of shallow reporters from the North who regularly took advantage of the "imperfect condition of the South" to write "superficial and punitive appraisals." He repeated his complaint that Sprigle had either "deliberately or by direction" produced "as venomously one-sided, exaggerated, and pugnacious an interpretation of a region and its sins as has ever been published in American newspapers." Aside from the "personal emoluments gained by the disguised Pennsylvanian" and any circulation gains made by his paper, Carter said, "only harm resulted from the stunt. A great many people, North and South, were embittered for contradictory reasons. There was already bitterness enough and to spare."

Despite the stubborn enmity of segregationist southern editors like Carter and the lavish praise his series generally got from the northern media, Ray Sprigle was forgotten almost entirely by chroniclers of the pre–civil rights era. In 1994 John Egerton wrote *Speak Now Against the Day*, a massive award-winning account of the southerners, white and black, who challenged the South's race laws before the civil rights movement arrived in the mid-1950s. Sprigle was mentioned once in 627 pages—briefly and erroneously. Egerton, a Tennessee native, wrote that "the white Pittsburgh reporter named Ray Sprigle" was "a self-righteous Yankee liberal."

In her 1999 book *Broadcasting Freedom: Radio, War, and the Politics of Race, 1938–1948*, professor Barbara Dianne Savage apparently didn't do a thorough background check on Sprigle, either. In her long treatment of the *Town Meeting* radio broadcast and its significance to civil rights history, she unfairly declared that Sprigle—at the time a sixty-one-year-old nationally famous newspaperman—had gone undercover as a black man to "make a name for himself."

Sprigle was treated more accurately and with greater respect by two fellow newspapermen in the 2006 book *The Race Beat: The Press, the Civil Rights Struggle, and the Awakening of a Nation*. All-star journalists Gene Roberts and Hank Klibanoff won a Pulitzer Prize for their sweeping history of the white and black reporters, photographers, and TV cameramen who covered the civil rights movement in the South during the 1950s and 1960s.

Both superior reporters and veteran big-city editors with experience in the North and South, they proudly pointed to the courage of the northern journalists who penetrated "the South to see firsthand—and, more importantly, to show—the raw grip of white supremacy on an entire region of the country." They said the stories those reporters filed starting in about 1955 "emboldened national leaders—presidents, congresses, religious figures, corporate executives and, especially, black civil rights leaders—to press for change."

Sprigle was given credit in *The Race Beat* for writing a series that "described in raw detail the daily degradation of being Negro in the South." Identifying him as "an old-style white reporter for the *Pittsburgh Post-Gazette*," Roberts and Klibanoff extolled him for being one of the first mainstream journalists to go into the Deep South and show that the phrase "separate but equal" was a total fraud. They vaguely noted, almost in passing, that his series got "widespread attention." That was certainly true, but it didn't begin to do justice to the enormous impact Sprigle and "In the Land of Jim Crow" had on the mainstream white media.

In the late summer of 1948, Sprigle's syndicated exposé had singlehandedly started an intense three-month-long public argument in America about racial segregation—the first one ever. Overnight his dramatic account of his travels as a black man in the Deep South appeared simultaneously on the front pages of fourteen major northern newspapers. Every day for almost two weeks Sprigle introduced millions of white people from Manhattan to Seattle to the inequalities, discriminations, and humiliations faced by black Americans in the Jim Crow South. After that, for seven straight weeks as many as a million blacks above and below the Mason-Dixon Line read the longer version in the *Pittsburgh Courier*.

The reaction to Sprigle's passionate exposé had been intense. Hundreds of editorials, columns, and letters were published around the country. He and "In the Land of Jim Crow" were publicly praised or criticized by Eleanor Roosevelt, the bosses at the NAACP, white and black newspapers in the North and South, the national news magazines, George Schuyler of the *Courier*, the top editors of major New York book publishers, and other members of the New York media elite. The multi-media frenzy Sprigle stirred up didn't end until November, when *Town Meeting's* radio debate was heard by millions of Americans.

Sprigle's newspaper series had exploded on to the scene long before civil rights became a daily national news story. It came six years before the US Supreme Court's landmark *Brown v. Board of Education* took away the constitutional authority of Jim Crow to enforce white supremacy. It came seven years before Rosa Parks refused to give up her seat on a bus to a white man in Montgomery, Alabama, which broke a Jim Crow law, got her arrested, and marked the start of the modern civil rights movement. And it came seven summers before the entire country was stunned and sickened by the murder and mutilation of teenager Emmett Till in the Mississippi Delta town of Money.

In *The Race Beat*, Roberts and Klibanoff identified the torture killing of Till, who was slain while visiting from Chicago, as the first news event to bring "white reporters into the Deep South in unprecedented numbers to cover a racial story." *Jet*, "The Negro Weekly News Magazine," broke the story first to its readers in September of 1955. Its horrifying photos of Till's disfigured face and head created a national sensation in the white press. The full-blown media coverage of Till's murder, his mother's decision to have an open casket in Chicago, and the trial in Mississippi that acquitted his killers "had exactly the impact that Gunnar Myrdal had predicted more than a decade before," Roberts and Klibanoff said. "Northerners were shocked and shaken by what they read."

"In the Land of Jim Crow" had a similar effect in 1948, albeit briefly. Powered by Sprigle's engaging writing and moral fury, it created the kind of sympathetic publicity among hundreds of thousands of good white people in the North that Myrdal said in 1944 would be needed if the South's blacks were to ever gain equality and full citizenship.

Sprigle's "stunt" journalism clearly affected public opinion. It shocked the white North, enraged the white South, and delighted blacks everywhere. Unfortunately, Sprigle turned out to be his profession's lone civil rights pioneer. The front-page mugging he and the owners of the *Post-Gazette* gave Jim Crow wasn't repeated by other northern reporters or influential newspapers like the *New York Times*. Civil rights in the South didn't suddenly become a hot newsbeat for *Time, Newsweek*, or anyone else. In 1948 it was still too soon for the northern white press to practice civil rights journalism. It was too soon politically and socially. And newspapers, like most of the country's major institutions, seemed visionless when it came to recognizing the immorality of inequality and discrimination in the South and North.

There's no evidence Sprigle's series dramatically changed history or radically influenced the people who were shaping it in 1948. President Truman didn't read "In the Land of Jim Crow" and run out and give a speech calling for Congress to immediately outlaw America's apartheid. Young Martin Luther King Jr. didn't watch the *Town Meeting of the Air* debate on TV in Philadelphia and resolve then and there to become an American Gandhi. But by exposing the cold heart and soul of Jim Crow to the entire country, Sprigle provided a priceless contribution to the embryonic civil rights movement. He'll go down in history as the first journalist—white or black—to strike a serious blow against segregation in the mainstream media. But he and the trouble he caused were quickly forgotten by history, swept away in the national flood of newspaper and television coverage of segregation in the South that began in 1955.

It would take the power of television to arouse the North's conscience for good. And it would still take many years. But black-and-white news footage of ugly mobs taunting schoolchildren and local governments using clubs, police dogs, and fire hoses on peaceful American citizens were ultimately more persuasive than the colorful words of "America's No. 1 White Reporter." Ray Sprigle always had plenty of strong opinions and was never shy about sharing them with his readers. But at heart he was always a reporter, a troublemaker, a friend of the underdog, not a preacher or propagandist. When he set out on his southern expedition in the spring of 1948, he wasn't looking to punish the Jim Crow South or start a crusade. As he confessed later, all he "saw was the possibility of a darned good newspaper story."

❧

When Sprigle expanded his Jim Crow series into a book for Simon and Schuster, he didn't reveal that John Wesley Dobbs had served as his trusted guide, mentor, and host. That secret wasn't made known to the general public until a 1998 article by the author in the *Post-Gazette*, four decades after he and Dobbs had died. But at the end of the first chapter of his book *In the Land of Jim Crow*, which was published to mixed reviews in the spring of 1949, Sprigle added a new paragraph. It admitted some things he had not shared with readers of his newspaper series—or perpetually angry Hodding Carter.

> Let me make clear at the start . . . that this is no complete and impartial survey of the race problem in the South. This is the story of a newspaper man who lived as a Negro in the South and didn't like it. I deliberately sought out the worst that the South could show me in the way of discrimination and oppression of the Negro. I spent most of my time in Georgia, Mississippi and Alabama. I ignored Virginia and North Carolina, where the greatest progress in development of civilized race relations has been recorded. How can you correct evil until you find it? I deliberately sought the evil and the barbarous aspects of the white South's treatment of the Negro. It is of that only that I write.

Sprigle's newspaper series obviously was not objective—no journalism written by a human being truly can be. That should have been obvious to anyone after reading its opening paragraphs. Though he and the editors at Simon and Schuster tempered and smoothed away some of the series' more sensational edges, the book version remained a blistering indictment of the evils of Jim Crow.

Black Like Me is the book most people think of when they first hear about Sprigle's undercover mission to the Jim Crow South. But John Howard Griffin's blockbuster about how he dyed his skin black to see what daily life was like for a Southern Negro appeared 13 years after Sprigle's newspaper series. Griffin's 1961 book about his experiences, which was turned into a Hollywood movie and is still read widely by high school students, reads more like a novel than a work of serious journalism. It dwells primarily on Griffin's personal feelings, impressions, and inner thoughts as he encounters the legal and cultural racism of Jim Crow.

Later in his life Griffin said he had not been aware of Sprigle's journey when he began his.

The brief foreword to *In the Land of Jim Crow* was written by Margaret Halsey, a best-selling author known for both her Dorothy Parker–like wit and her social conscience. She was chosen for the job because of her 1946 book *Color Blind: A White Woman Looks at the Negro*, which her *New York Times* obituary said was called "straightforward, courageous and delightful" by Margaret Mead and was banned from schools in Georgia. She nicely summed up Sprigle's short book, saying it contained "the spontaneous, unstudied reactions of a self-respecting white man trying to live from one dawn to the next under the disabilities imposed on colored Americans." Halsey, who lived for a time in England, said "the reflective reader will be struck by the fact that *In the Land of Jim Crow* inadvertently shows us how we look to Europeans. . . . It is an unexpected glimpse into a mirror we had forgotten was there."

Epilogue

By Christmas of 1948 the intense debate over the future of Jim Crow seg-regation had burned out in the national media. Ray Sprigle, Walter White, Hodding Carter, and John Wesley Dobbs returned to what they had been doing before Sprigle's undercover mission brought them together. Sprigle quickly resumed his role as the *Post-Gazette*'s ace reporter, troublemaker, and trusted civic watchdog. In February he wrote another multi-part series about one of his favorite subjects—the awfulness of the Pennsylvania state mental hospital system.

The "evils, shortcomings, failures and inevitable neglect" of the forty-three thousand mentally ill patients in the state's twenty-two hospitals was an ongoing political scandal and human tragedy. The conditions Sprigle observed in 1949 were nothing like they were in 1931, when he had gone undercover as a mental patient in Pittsburgh. Nor were they as bad as in 1947, when he had assumed the name and phony resume of James Rayel Crawford and gotten himself hired as a ward attendant in Byberry, the notorious overcrowded state "madhouse" near Philadelphia.

After *Life* magazine had shocked the country in 1946 by exposing Byberry's inhumane, concentration camp–like conditions with a set of covertly taken photos, Sprigle had portrayed Byberry's hopelessness and squalor with words. His first-person, you-are-in-here-with-me account in 1947 included graphic descriptions of filthy wards and hallways, touching details of love and kindness among the six thousand inmates, and unfor-gettable character sketches of the sick and crazy souls he fed, showered, and cleaned up after for a week. For his 1949 series Sprigle didn't go undercover. Based on his fresh observations of conditions at Byberry and hospitals near Pittsburgh, he concluded that the state system had made progress. But he said it was still poorly run, understaffed, and ill-equipped in large part because the "penurious" taxpayers of a prosperous state didn't care enough about the mentally ill to properly fund their care.

Sprigle was sixty-two and had lost some weight, but his pace had hardly slowed. When the *Post-Gazette* started a Sunday edition in March, his "Newspaper Guy" feature was a major draw. Each week he wrote long articles about colorful crime figures he knew, famous murder cases he covered, and the time he got disgruntled KKK members in Alabama to give him the documents he needed to prove Hugo Black's Klan membership. On May 3 in New York the Pulitzer Prizes for 1948 were announced. Though the *Post-Gazette* had submitted "I Was a Negro in the South for 30 Days" and lobbied hard for it to win, it did not. The fact that Hodding Carter and his editor friend at the *Providence Journal* were among the sixteen members of the judging committee probably didn't help Sprigle's chances.

A week later the book *In the Land of Jim Crow* was published. By September the $2.50 volume would sell only 4,134 copies, which disappointed Sprigle and Simon and Schuster. But the *Los Angeles Daily News* loved it. So did the *Waxahachie Daily Light* in Texas. The *Dothan Eagle* in Alabama hated it. The *Chicago Defender*'s reviewer endorsed it. Walter White, admittedly not exactly a neutral observer, reviewed it for Norman Cousins's literary magazine the *Saturday Review*. In the process of praising Sprigle for his courage, White took potshots at Hodding Carter and his gang of so-called southern liberals for their claim that things were improving swimmingly for blacks in Dixie and no one north of Nashville needed to worry or interfere.

As for southern liberals, Ralph McGill of the *Atlanta Constitution* reviewed the book for the *New York Times*, which in 1948 had never printed a word about Sprigle's Jim Crow trip, his newspaper series, or the *Town Meeting* segregation debate held in their backyard. McGill credited Sprigle with writing a book that was honest and not sensationalistic. But singing from the official Hodding Carter Hymnbook, he said it ignored the steady progress blacks were making in the South, exaggerated the fears of blacks, and engaged in sweeping generalizations. For good measure, he quoted at length from the *Atlanta Daily World*, the conservative black paper that had editorialized that Sprigle's incendiary newspaper series was "No Help to Our Cause."

In June of 1949 Sprigle flew to Europe. For a month he toured the still-crowded displaced persons camps of Italy, Germany, and Austria.

Working with the International Refugee Organization, he interviewed nearly thirty survivors of Hitler's wars and concentration camps who were going to be relocated in the Pittsburgh area. He visited Dachau as well as Hitler's looted and crumbling *Berchtesgaden*, the mountaintop retreat where "the little mountebank turned madman and murderer sought relaxation from the rapine of peoples and nations and surcease from slaughter." Sprigle's freedom to mix straight reporting and his opinions in his news stories meant he had the pleasure of calling Hitler "the screaming screw-ball who wrecked Europe and sent more men and women to execution than Genghis Khan and all the other conquerors of history." His trip ended with a nine-day voyage to Boston on a transport filled with 841 displaced persons whose serious psychological issues, while perfectly understandable to him, had clearly gotten on his nerves.

When the *Post-Gazette*'s new Sunday edition proved unprofitable and was shut down, Sprigle returned to his old ways of exposing important public institutions that were broken or corrupt because of politics. He seldom just reported or complained about the problems he found; he usually provided solutions. In early 1950 he turned out "What's Wrong with Our Police?" Heavily promoted in advance, running on Page 1 for fourteen days, Sprigle's articles pounded away at the city's corrupt and incompetent police force.

Comparing Pittsburgh's failed police administration with cities that had good ones, he pointed out specific examples of bad policing, dirty cops, and poor training. He said the chief cause of the problem was politics, and he put the pressure to fix the police on the politician at the top—Mayor David Lawrence. Genuflecting to the authoritative wisdom of Ray Sprigle, Lawrence, who would someday be governor, quickly promised changes and ended up implementing some of the fixes Sprigle had suggested.

Later in 1950 Sprigle cranked out a twenty-four-part first-person series called "Inside the Rackets." The *Post-Gazette*'s promotional campaign, which included front-page banner headlines that read "Sprigle's Exposé Worrying Racketeers and Cops," promised he would tear "the cover off the local world of numbers, gambling and vice." Using his contacts in the underworld and law enforcement, Sprigle showed how the city's rackets were "controlled, franchised and ruthlessly milked by political overlords and top law enforcement officials." He and other reporters dropped in on numbers parlors, whorehouses, and gambling dens, described what they found, and put the establishments' addresses in the paper. Repeating another tactic he had used when he was the *P-G*'s city editor in the late 1920s, he named corrupt police inspectors who let crime thrive in their jurisdictions.

Into the mid-1950s Sprigle was a front-page troublemaker and celebrity watchdog. He was a respected reporter and investigator whose name still sold papers and whose concerns and opinions could affect crooks, cops, and politicians. He turned out a string of series that exposed the wide-open gambling operations and political corruption in adjacent counties and in Steubenville, Ohio. He covered gang murders, wrote about wrongly accused murderers, and did a series on the waste and stupidity of adult education classes that used taxpayer money to teach subjects like checkers and basket weaving.

In his column, "Sprigle Says," he took on smaller issues that bugged him, like the backlog of two hundred thousand unpaid parking tickets in City Traffic Court. Meanwhile, he was in constant demand as a local speaker. He gave dozens of speeches every year to women's clubs, business groups, and schools. In New Castle, a town north of Pittsburgh, eight hundred people showed up to hear him speak about his southern trip. He was interviewed regularly on radio and TV.

In 1954 Sprigle went up into the Lower Hill District to inspect the black and white slums that were soon to be leveled to make way for the "Pittsburgh Center," the city's proposed cultural center. The eight-part "Why Are There Slums?" was his last major series. It pinned the blame on greedy slumlords—many of whom he named—and a city government that for decades had not properly policed the entire Hill District, paved its streets, or provided basic services. As he concluded, "Nobody gives much of a damn about the Hill."

Little did Sprigle know how right he was. The Lower Hill was to be the first victim of a series of destructive redevelopment projects in poor neighborhoods later heralded as the "Pittsburgh Renaissance." It and the people who called it home were doomed. With the full support of the

Hill's black state representative, city hall planned to flatten seventy acres of the Lower Hill and replace it with a cross-town highway, a gleaming new cultural center, and a set of sterile apartment blocks only a Soviet architect could love. The "Pittsburgh Center" was a classic—and pioneering—example of how poor black Americans suffered when city halls and their planners targeted "blighted" neighborhoods for urban renewal—aka "Negro removal."

The project ultimately would flatten nearly one hundred acres of the Lower Hill and displace eight thousand humans—80 percent of them black. A bustling, diverse, funky, and admittedly rundown neighborhood alive with great jazz was replaced by the Civic Arena, the stainless steel home of the Civic Light Opera, and a sea of asphalt parking lots. The white newspapers didn't care about the Pittsburgh Center's steep social costs. They cheered it on from the start. To them, destroying the Lower Hill was progress at work. They didn't write editorials questioning the project or write sad feature stories about its victims. Not even Ray Sprigle, the great friend of the underdog, tried to stop the grand plan that would permanently tear out the commercial, cultural, and spiritual heart of Little Harlem.

In New York City on March 21, 1955, Walter White dropped dead of a heart attack at sixty-one. He was still the official head of the NAACP, the organization he had guided to such great influence. But his power had waned considerably because of his declining health and the internal trouble he caused at the NAACP in 1949 by divorcing his black wife and marrying a white woman, *Mademoiselle* celebrity food editor and cookbook writer Poppy Cannon. According to White's obituary in the *New York Times*, during his long career fighting for civil rights he traveled a million miles, made as many as ten thousand public speeches, and wrote a hundred articles for national magazines. He also had two syndicated weekly newspaper columns, one for white papers and one for black papers. His five books included two novels.

Called by one of his friends "the best lobbyist our race has ever produced," White was given a huge funeral in Harlem, lionized by his friends and enemies in the black press, and praised as "a vigorous champion of justice and equality for all our citizens" by President Eisenhower. Harry Truman and many other notables also telegrammed their sympathies.

George Schuyler had known White since 1922. White was his boss for ten years at the NAACP's national office in New York when Schuyler was the group's business manager. They also lived near each other in Harlem for decades—when they weren't traveling the country or the globe. They disagreed on many important political, practical, and philosophical topics. But on April 2 when the *Pittsburgh Courier* mourned White's passing on its front page with big headlines and photos of his funeral, Schuyler wrote a fine eulogy.

He said the light-skinned black man he called "Blondie" and often criticized in his columns was not only wise, courageous, principled, and influential, but also "gave Negroes the type of civil rights leadership needed to make the gains of the past quarter-century toward full citizenship. . . . A unique man, the creation of a particular period in history, we shall scarcely see his like again. But so well did he fight the good fight that the momentum he stirred and sustained will long be influential and his able associates will carry aloft the torch he held so high."

In Atlanta, Ray Sprigle's old road-mate John Wesley Dobbs was seventy-three and fighting to make his segregated city live up to the landmark *Brown v. Board of Education* decision. He was still "a race man" who used the weapons of reason and morality to fight for the equality and expanded voting rights of blacks. In 1955 he still had two cars, carried a fat roll of big bills in his left pocket, and had become known as the unofficial mayor of Sweet Auburn Avenue. The grand master of Georgia's Prince Hall Masons was still giving speeches to churches and colleges and Masonic gatherings from Boston to New Orleans. Still a faithful Republican and state party official, he met General Dwight Eisenhower twice during the presidential election of 1952 and would be invited to Ike's inaugural in 1956.

Dobbs had become a player to be reckoned with in Atlanta politics. A few years earlier he traded his ability to deliver a bloc of ten thousand black votes to the white mayor in exchange for three miles of new street-lights along Auburn Avenue's business district and a new city park for blacks with a gym and a swimming pool. In 1952 he stood up to the white city planning board's proposal to clear the slums in Dobbs's Fourth Ward and relocate the Auburn Avenue business district to the other side of town. He and other black leaders fought against the redevelopment idea, which was a cousin to the racist "Negro removal" plans being proposed—and implemented—in other major eastern cities, including Pittsburgh. Dobbs appeared before the planners at a public meeting, eloquently tell-ing them how much he loved Auburn Avenue and why he was opposed to their destructive and evil plan. It was a miracle, but somehow he and his allies persuaded the city to drop it.

In 1952 Dobbs and his wife, Irene, had sailed to Europe on the *Queen Elizabeth* so they could see Mattiwilda sing in the opera houses of Eng-land, Spain, and France. On the vacation trip, which was a gift from the Masons, it was not lost on Dobbs that his daughter had been able to climb to the highest heights in Europe without any impediments being placed on her because of her race. He saw half the countries of Western Europe with his wife and then flew on alone to Greece, Turkey, Jerusalem, and North Africa. When he came back he was more determined than ever to fight for human rights, civil rights, "and for every bed-rock prin-ciple laid down in the American Declaration of Independence and the United States Constitution."

Mattiwilda's growing fame overseas brought her attention from the black press back home. After *Ebony* did a story on her, Dobbs got into a spat with the magazine over a sensationalized headline that made it seem he had an issue with her marriage to a Spaniard, which he did not. In 1956 Mattiwilda came to the United States to make her debut at the Metropolitan Opera in New York. She was the first black singer to be given a principal role at the Met. Dobbs and his wife traveled to New York to see her perform, as did as many family members as possible. Not long afterward Dobbs sat in his living room at 540 Houston Street and watched his daughter "Geekie" sing on Ed Sullivan's TV show *Toast of the Town*. The *Atlanta Constitution* didn't bother to write up Mattiwilda's appearances at the Met or on the Sullivan show, but it did report the "news" that after her first white husband died she had married a second white man, a Swede.

By 1958, at age seventy-six, Dobbs's solid frame was finally showing signs of wear. His muscles and joints ached painfully and he had trouble negotiating stairs. Cortisone injections didn't always help. Martin Luther King Jr. had set up the headquarters of his Southern Christian Leadership Conference in Dobbs's Masonic Temple and office building on Auburn Avenue and was beginning his campaign against segregation. In 1960, after years of being opposed to the use of large demonstrations and boycotts in Atlanta to fight discrimination, Dobbs joined his first protest march. For a few hours he wore a large "Don't Buy Here" sign over his shoulders and walked along the sidewalk outside Rich's, Atlanta's big downtown department store, to protest against its discriminatory lunch

Best Wishes For 1960

— REFLECTIONS OVER A CENTURY OF PROGRESS —

"The Mills of God grind SLOWLY—but, SURELY!"

1857—Dred Scott Decision—Our Darkest Hour!
1858—Lincoln-Douglas Debate—Spelled out the ISSUE.
1859—John Brown's Tragic Death—Ignited The Flame.
1860—Lincoln's Election—Fixed the Course.
1863—Emancipation Proclamation—Opened the Door to Freedom.
1865—13th Amendment—Abolished a Diabolical Past.
1868—14th Amendment—Gave birth to the Doctrine of Equality.
1870—15th Amendment—Guaranteed a Free Ballot to all.
1876—Election of Pres. Hayes—A Political Set-Back.
1896—Plessy vs. Ferguson Decision—A Judicial Set-Back.
1954—U. S. Supreme Court—Corrects The Errors.
1959—U. S. Supreme Court—Continues to Follow Through.

"Therefore, ye Soft Pipes—play on!"

Mr. & Mrs. John Wesley Dobbs
540 Houston St., N. E., Atlanta 12, Ga.

counter policy. Soon afterward Dobbs felt so sick he flew to the Mayo Clinic in Minneapolis for a checkup, where he was told he had rheumatoid arthritis.

In the fall of 1960, when the *Pittsburgh Courier* picked what it said were the ten "most colorful" black personalities of the past fifty years, John Wesley Dobbs was one of them. To make the list the paper said the selectees had to project "personality, dynamism, fearlessness and unadulterated nerve." The brief biography of Dobbs summed up his big life well. It said he was nationally famous as a "spellbinding" orator who could "hold thousands entranced, as he rolls back the pages of history. He quotes eloquently from the more than 500 poems he has memorized, including 'Paradise Lost'... is seen at all Kentucky Derbies, World Series, championship fights ... and is revered by both races in Atlanta." The short item didn't point out that Dobbs—the son of a freed slave and the grandson of a slaveowner—had met two American presidents. But it noted that he had traveled with Pulitzer Prize–winner Ray Sprigle for his "memorable series 'I Was a Negro in the South for 30 Days.'" It was probably the only time his secret role was revealed to the public before 1998.

On August 21, 1961, Dobbs suffered a stroke and was hospitalized in the black wing of Grady Hospital. On August 30—the first day that Atlanta's public schools were integrated—he died. His obituary ran in the *Courier*, the *Chicago Defender*, and other black papers, and he was buried with full Masonic honors from Big Bethel AME Church. One of his honorary pallbearers was his friend Thurgood Marshall. His younger friend and former neighbor Martin Luther King Jr. delivered the opening prayer. Praising the beauty of Dobbs's family life, his "love for people and his unswerving devotion to the cause of freedom and human dignity," King gave thanks to God on behalf of those present "that a man like John Wesley Dobbs had lived among them, worked among them, had spread his love among them and done so much good to so many people."

The city of Atlanta eventually honored Dobbs's lifetime of contributions. In 1994, at the end of his grandson Mayor Maynard Jackson's third term, Houston Street was officially renamed John Wesley Dobbs Avenue. The house at 540 was later renovated and the top marble step leading from the sidewalk to the front porch is still carved with "J.W.

Dobbs." In 1996 Dobbs's remarkable life was documented in rich detail, and with great affection, by former Atlanta newspaperman Gary Pomerantz in *Where Peachtree Meets Sweet Auburn: The Saga of Two Families and the Making of Atlanta*. Described as "a multi-generational biography of Atlanta and its racial conscience," half of the book was devoted to the family history and accomplishments of Dobbs and Mayor Jackson. In 1996 a gigantic bronze "portrait mask" of Dobbs's head called "Through His Eyes" was installed on Auburn Avenue in a small corner plaza named Dobbs Plaza. Visitors can stand inside the head and look through the mask's eyes at downtown Atlanta, the city John Wesley Dobbs loved and worked so hard to change for the better.

At sixty-nine Ray Sprigle was slowing down, but he was hardly desk-bound. In late 1954 he had gone to Cleveland to join the national media circus covering the famous Dr. Sam Sheppard murder trial. In 1955 when the Buffalo, Rochester and Pittsburgh Railroad closed its "Honeymooner" passenger service to Niagara Falls, he gave it a send-off in the *Post-Gazette* by traveling most of the 292 miles from Pittsburgh to Buffalo in the cab of a locomotive. In addition to riding along on traffic patrols with state police officers, his feature stories included accompanying an "oil-well shooter" who dropped nitroglycerin into Pennsylvania's older oil and gas wells to stimulate their production—an early low-tech form of what someday would be called fracking.

In April of 1956 the *Pittsburgh Courier* enthusiastically reprinted "I Was a Negro in the South for 30 Days" in its entirety, complete with photos. The introduction explained that the "amazing document" was being reissued because it had been written by one of the few white reporters in the country who knew how blacks in the South think and feel because "he lived and suffered as a Negro instead of getting information second-hand."

By 1957 Sprigle's health was still pretty good and at seventy he was described by one of his colleagues as "rugged and vital, a well-preserved physical specimen." His "stentorian" voice could still be heard above the human and mechanical din of the *Post-Gazette*'s newsroom. When he left the office in the late morning to do his reporting or schmoozing, he always packed four loaded-and-ready corncob pipes in his coat pockets. Marking ten years since he had taken his undercover job as a ward attendant at Byberry Mental Hospital, in February he wrote yet another series on the state's mental hospitals. This time he didn't find inmates in shackles and cuffs or a ward filled with hundreds of naked men "wallowing in their own ordure." He declared that the hospitals were vastly better places and was especially impressed to see well-trained attendants reading the poems of great poets aloud to a room of cleaner, tidier, and less-hopeless-looking inmates.

Shortly after that series Sprigle suffered a sudden problem with his eyesight. After an unsuccessful operation for a detached retina, he went on sick leave for most of the rest of the year. He was left with minimal vision, which caused him to sell his little farmhouse in the woods and move into the city of Pittsburgh. As he told his wife, Agnes, "I can't stand to stand on the front porch and look out at the hills and not be able to see them." During the next decades his wooded redoubt was abandoned by its owners, slowly trashed and burned by party-going teenagers, and taken back by Nature. Hard to find, imprisoned by bushes, trees, and vines, by 2016 his house was little more than a collapsed concrete foundation, random piles of rubble, and a tall stone chimney.

Sprigle went back to work in December 1957. His chronic health problems—diabetes and chronic bronchial asthma—were reasonably well controlled. To his colleagues he looked much older, and tired. But they found he still had his old zest for newspapering. When they asked how he was feeling, the best he could come up with was "fair." But he added, "It's a funny thing. There's something about this place that makes me feel better when I'm in it. It makes me want to get to work."

His first story back was a Sprigle special. He had been attracted to a local political fight in the nearby town of New Castle. After doing some reporting that convinced him the defendant was being jobbed by his political enemies, he traveled fifty miles north by bus to cover the so-called "pink slips trial."

"The first week he stayed in New Castle," said his daughter, Rae, in 2016, "Mummy stayed with him. The second week he went up on his own. I drove him to the *Post-Gazette* Building and from there someone was going to take him over to the bus station. I can still see him walking away, tall and straight, dark blue overcoat and a black Homburg hat."

Sprigle covered the "pink slips trial" all week, including night sessions and a court session on Saturday. On Saturday evening he rode a bus back to Pittsburgh, grabbed a Peoples Cab at the Fort Pitt Hotel, and was headed for his home across the river. Seconds later, at 7:45 p.m., as his taxicab crossed the intersection of Penn Avenue and Tenth Street, a speeding car driven by Orlando Gigliotti ran a red light and hit the taxi broadside, spinning it around. Though he had been violently thrown around inside the cab, he appeared to have only a few minor scratches and a small cut on his hand when he was taken to the emergency room of Allegheny General Hospital. But Sprigle—who often predicted he'd die at his desk at the *Post-Gazette*—died Sunday morning at 4:15. An autopsy showed he had suffered a fractured skull, a concussion, a crushed chest, eight broken ribs, and other injuries.

COURTESY OF THE *PITTSBURGH POST-GAZETTE*

Each edition of Monday's paper broke the sad news to three hundred thousand readers in cold headlinese—"Ray Sprigle Dies After Car Crash." His iconic photo with his familiar hat and corncob pipe was larger than usual. "Sprig" was remembered somberly on the editorial page, not for his big awards but for the stories he wrote every day that "crackled and zipped and boomed with the zest that faithfully reflected the spirit of the man who wrote them."

> He was what biographies of this business call an old-time star reporter. His enterprise and courage as a reporter and as a city editor had become legendary in his own lifetime. Many of us here have private memories of Sprig which today are added cause for our grief at his death. For the record: Pittsburgh has lost one of the best newspapermen, and assuredly the most colorful, it will ever know.

The news of Ray Sprigle's death was spread by the wire services to hundreds of papers around the country. The governor of Pennsylvania, George M. Leader, issued a statement, paying tribute to Sprigle's "great sense of moral indignation" and expressing gratitude for his special series on the state's mental health system—"an exposé which helped to improve conditions in our mental hospitals."

Part of the *P-G*'s homage to their fallen star included an inside page that was nearly covered with seven large photos of Sprigle in action. A greatest-hits compilation, they showed him speaking into an NBC microphone about his Hugo Black exposé, boarding a plane for embattled Britain in 1940, carrying a basket of vegetables on his farm, signing his Jim Crow book in a department store, and being in full disguise as a coal miner, a black-market meat dealer, and a black man.

Introducing the photo spread, under the title "Ray Sprigle: Newspaperman's Hero," was an informal eulogy written by an anonymous *Post-Gazette* copy editor or editor. It captured Sprigle's character and explained what made him a great journalist better than anything that would be said in print or the next day at his simple funeral service.

No amount of words or pictures can adequately describe the amazing newspaper career of Ray Sprigle. In a period of more than 50 years as an editor and reporter—46 of them in Pittsburgh—he has written an indelible record. It may be found in the files of this newspaper, but most certainly of all it may be found in the grateful hearts of countless thousands he has befriended. For Ray Sprigle was a newspaperman with a heart—and that was, perhaps, the secret of his greatness. The oppressed and the abused found him a sympathetic champion; but to the rogues and racketeers, the vultures of humanity, he was an implacable foe.

Whoever wrote those words ended their little homage to Sprig with the lines, "The pictures on this page cannot begin to tell the story of Ray Sprigle. They can only suggest a few of the highlights." It was true. Pittsburgh's greatest newspaperman had turned out far too many highlights to fit on a single page. It would take a book.

Bibliography

INTERNET

This book would not have been possible without the Internet. It allowed me to find and read everything from Harry Truman's personal letters and 1950 US Census reports to *American Mercury* articles, postcards for old hotels, and the top speed of a 1947 Mercury. The website Newspapers.com allowed me to read and search virtually every copy of the *Pittsburgh Post-Gazette*, *Pittsburgh Courier*, and the *Delta Democrat-Times* from 1920 to 1960.

ARCHIVES

Amistad Research Center
—John Wesley Dobbs Family papers

Beinecke Rare Book & Manuscript Library
—Walter Francis White and Poppy Cannon Papers

Carnegie Museum of Art
—Teenie Harris Archive

Harry S. Truman Library & Museum
—Truman papers

John Heinz History Center
—Ray Sprigle papers

King Library & Archive
—Martin Luther King Jr. archives

Library of Congress
—NAACP papers

Mitchell Memorial Library, Mississippi State University
—Hodding Carter papers

New York Public Library
—*Town Hall Meeting of the Air* papers

Rita and Leo Greenland Library & Research Center
—Anti-Semitism in the United States, 1947

NEWSPAPERS AND MAGAZINES

American Mercury
Atlanta Daily World
Atlantic Monthly
Chicago Defender
Chicago Tribune
Commentary
Delta Democrat-Times
Ebony
Editor & Publisher
Fortune
Jet
Life
Nation
National Review
New York Herald Tribune
New York Times
New Yorker
Newsweek
Pitt Magazine
Pittsburgh Courier
Pittsburgh Post
Pittsburgh Post-Gazette
Pittsburgh Press
Portland Oregonian
Red Book Magazine
Seattle Daily Times
Smithsonian Magazine
St. Louis Dispatch
The Saturday Review
Time
Town Meeting Bulletin

Books

Bean, Jonathan, ed. *Race & Liberty in America*. Lexington: University of Kentucky Press, 2009.

Carter, Hodding. *Southern Legacy*. Baton Rouge: Louisiana State University Press, paperback, 1966.

Egerton, John. *Speak Now Against the Day: The Generation Before the Civil Rights Movement in the South*. Chapel Hill: University of North Carolina Press, 1995.

Ferguson, Jeffrey B. *The Sage of Sugar Hill: George S. Schuyler and the Harlem Renaissance*. New Haven: Yale University Press, 2005.

Ghiglione, Loren, *CBS's Don Hollenbeck: An Honest Reporter in the Age of McCarthyism*. New York: Columbia University Press, 2008.

Ghiglione, Loren, ed. *Radio's Revolution: Don Hollenbeck's CBS Views the Press*. Lincoln: University of Nebraska Press, 2008.

Griffin, John Howard. *Black Like Me*. New York: New American Library, 2003.

Gunther, John. *Inside U.S.A.* New York: Harper & Brothers, 1947.

Janken, Kenneth Robert. *White: The Biography of Walter White, Mr. NAACP*. New York: The New Press, 2003.

Myrdal, Gunnar. *An American Dilemma: The Negro Problem and Modern Democracy*. New York: McGraw Hill, paperback, 1964.

Pietrusza, David. *1948: Harry Truman's Improbable Victory and the Year That Transformed America*. New York: Union Square Press, 2011.

Pomerantz, Gary M. *Where Peachtree Meets Sweet Auburn: The Saga of Two Families and the Making of Atlanta*. New York: Scribner, 1996.

Roberts, Gene, and Hank Klibanoff. *The Race Beat: The Press, the Civil Rights Struggle, and the Awakening of a Nation*. New York: Vintage Books, 2007.

Savage, Barbara Dianne. *Broadcasting Freedom: Radio, War, and the Politics of Race, 1938–1948*. Chapel Hill: University of North Carolina Press, 1999.

Schuyler, George S. *Black and Conservative: The Autobiography of George S. Schuyler*. New Rochelle, NY: Arlington House Publishers, 1966.

Sheffer, Alan Guy. *Investigative Reporter: Ray Sprigle of Pittsburgh*. Dissertation, Pittsburgh: Carnegie-Mellon University, 1973.

Sprigle, Ray. *In the Land of Jim Crow*. New York: Simon and Schuster, 1949.

Thomas, Clarke M. *Front-Page Pittsburgh, Two Hundred Years of the* Post-Gazette. Pittsburgh: University of Pittsburgh Press, 2005.

Waldron, Ann. *Hodding Carter: The Reconstruction of a Racist*. Chapel Hill, NC: Algonquin Books of Chapel Hill, 1993.

White, Walter. *A Man Called White, The Autobiography of Walter White*. Athens: University of Georgia Press, 1995.

White, Walter. *How Far the Promised Land?* New York: Ams Pr Inc, 1955.

Williams, Juan. *Eyes on the Prize*. New York: Penguin Books, 2013.

Woodward, C. Vann. *The Strange Career of Jim Crow*. Oxford: Oxford University Press, 2002.

Interviews

Jordan Arline
Juliet Dobbs Blackburn-Beamon
John Brewer
June Dobbs Butts
Rod Doss
David Gillarm
Dorothy Haslerig
Willie Haslerig
David Jackson
Mattiwilda Dobbs Janzon
Robert "Bobby" Jordan
Rae Sprigle Kurland
Norman Wolken

Index

Mellon Bank, 34
Mencken, H. L., 6, 54
  on the South, 92
Mill, John Stuart, 269
Miller, Harris, 140
Milwaukee Journal, 197, 223
Mississippi
  black schools in, 148–50
  Delta Democrat-Times in, 13
  the Delta in, 145–46, 150,
    159–62, 237
  gambling in, 167–68
  Mound Bayou in, 162–64
  prohibition in, 166–67
  Sprigle in, 1–2
  in spring, 1948, 3
Montgomery, Isaiah T., 162
Moon, Henry Lee, 212
  and 1948 election, 253
Morse, Ralph, 185
Morse, Sen. Wayne, 58, 61
Mound Bayou (MS), 162–64
Murrow, Edward R., 213
  film about, 214
Musmanno, Michael, 84
Myrdal, Gunnar, 9–10, 61, 96, 280

Nanty-Glo Journal, 223
Nation, on 1948 election, 252
National Association for the
    Advancement of Colored
    People (NAACP), 2, 3, 98
  See also White, Walter, 224
National Football League,
    integration in, 7
National Negro Council, 189
Negroes. *See* African-Americans

Negro Motorist Green Book, The
    (Green), 114, 115
Newsweek magazine, 199
New York Herald Tribune, Sprigle's
    series in, 197, 211–13, 219, 223
New York Journal-American,
    213, 214
New York State, integrated guard
    units in, 250
New York Times, 213
  on Atlanta riot, 99–100
  on 1948 election, 252
  on Israel, 133
  and Monroe Massacre, 176
  and radio debate, 271
  review of Sprigle's book, 285
  on Sprigle's reporting, 17–18
  on Truman's speech, 60
  on White's autobiography, 247
New York World, 204
  and Atlanta riot, 102
  See also Swope, Herbert Bayard
Nixon, Isiah, 267
Nixon, Richard, 5
  and 1948 election, 253
"The Non-Existent Negro Vote"
    (Schuyler editorial), 250–51

Office of Price Administration
    (OPA), 28–29
Ottawa Journal, and Sprigle's
    story, 197
Owens, Jesse, 14

Paige, Satchel, 43
Palestine, war in, 133–34
Parker, Charlie, 5, 260
Parks, Rosa, 280

debate with Carter, 276–77
on difference between white and
    black men, 252
on Dobbs and gas stations,
    175–76
at Dobbs' house, 110, 111–12
"Down in a Mine Pit" series by,
    21–22
on Flint River Farms project, 118
in Georgia, 121–24, 125–28,
    169–71, 172
and Gilbert's murder, 142–43
at Haslerig's farm, 129–30,
    132–33, 135–36
home of, 17–18, 29–30
"Inside the Rackets" series,
    286–87
"I was a Negro" series of, 193–202
and Jordan, 179–80
later years of, 293–97
leaves the South, 180–82
legacy of, 278–81
Martin's help for, 68–70, 71
meeting with White, 63, 65,
    67, 68
meets Dobbs, 75, 76
memo book of trip, 184–85
in Mississippi, 11, 144, 147–50,
    158–60, 162–68
and Monroe Massacre, 176–78
motivation of, ix–x, 1–2, 64–65,
    123–24
"Newspaper Guy" feature, 285
opinion of Jim Crow, 120–21
and *Pittsburgh Daily Post*, 19–21
prepares for project, 72–73, 74
and reactions to debate, 273
school in Bluffton, 124–25

and Schroeder-Dague case,
    22–23
series on Hill District's numbers
    game, 41–42, 43–44
series on Pennsylvania mental
    hospitals, 284
on Silver Comet (train), 78–80
in *Town Meeting* debate, 246,
    254, 256, 257, 261, 262–63,
    267, 268, 270
use of restrooms, 174
visits Engrams, 117, 118
visit to dentist, 137–38
"Why Are There Slums" series,
    287, 288
in WWII displaced persons
    camps, 285–86
St. Louis Globe-Democrat, and
    Sprigle's series, 197, 215
St. Louis Post-Dispatch, on Truman's
    speech, 60
Stalin, Josef, 3
States' Rights Party, 191
Stevens, Samuel, 207
Swope, Herbert Bayard, 204–5

Taborian Hospital, 163
Taft, Robert, 185, 186, 187
Taft, William Howard, 77
*Take Your Choice: Separation or
    Mongrelization* (Bilbo), 155
Talmadge, Eugene, 174, 177
Taylor, Mrs. Ralph W., 273
Taylor, Zachary, 77
"The Other Side of Jim Crow"
    (Carter), 231, 233, 234–35,
    236–40
Thompson, Irene Ophelia, 81

About the Author

Bill Steigerwald spent thirty-five years as a newspaperman. The 1969 Villanova University history major started his career in 1973 as an associate editor of the *Mt. Washington Press* in suburban Cincinnati. Next stop was Hollywood, where he worked briefly for CBS-TV as a docudrama researcher before working for the *Los Angeles Times.* He was a copy editor, freelance writer, and letters editor in the *Times'* Sunday Calendar arts and entertainment section until 1989, when he returned to Pittsburgh. He worked as a reporter, Sunday feature writer, and weekly columnist at Ray Sprigle's old paper, the *Pittsburgh Post-Gazette,* until 2000. In 1998 he retraced part of the journey Sprigle and his companion, John Wesley Dobbs, made across the South fifty years earlier for an article in the *Post-Gazette.* In 2000 he moved across town to the *Pittsburgh Tribune-Review.* There he was an associate editor, weekly op-ed columnist, editorial writer, feature writer, letters editor, book-page editor, and weekly interviewer of important newsmakers, politicians, authors, and celebrities. After a million or two words under his byline, he retired from newspapers in 2009. His interviews and libertarian op-ed columns were nationally syndicated for about five years by CagleCartoons.com and TownHall.com. His freelance stories, interviews, and opinion pieces have appeared in dozens of major American papers and in magazines as disparate as *Reason, Family Circle,* and *Penthouse.* In 2013 he self-published *Dogging Steinbeck,* an investigation into John Steinbeck's iconic *Travels With Charley* road trip in 1960. Steigerwald has five kids — Michelle and John in San Francisco, Billie in Brooklyn, and Joe and Lucy in Pittsburgh. He and his wife, Trudi, live on a hilltop in the woods south of Pittsburgh.